The Life and Ideas of Shaheed Bhagat Singh

A Lesson for Today

Edited by
Dr. Vir Singh

Originals
(an imprint of Low Price Publications)
Delhi-110052

ISBN 13: 978-81-8454-100-7 (H.B.)
ISBN 10: 81-8454-100-7 (H.B.)
ISBN 13: 978-81-8454-101-4 (P.B.)
ISBN 10: 81-8454-101-5 (P.B.)

Published by
Originals
A-6, Nimri Commercial Centre,
Ashok Vihar Phase-IV, Delhi-110052
Phones: 27302453
e-mail: info@Lppindia.com
url: www.Lppindia.com

Printed at
D K Fine Art Press P Ltd.
Delhi-110052

PRINTED IN INDIA

समर्पण

जिनके प्रबुद्ध संरक्षण में सूरजमल स्मारक शिक्षा-संस्था के प्रांगण में महाराजा सूरजमल अनुसंधान एवं प्रकाशन केन्द्र की स्थापना एवं उसका विकास हुआ, उनके ही मार्गदर्शन में वहाँ उत्तर एवं पश्चिमोत्तर भारत के इतिहास पर राष्ट्रीय संगोष्ठियों का आयोजन आरंभ हुआ, मुझे मेरे शैक्षिक व्यक्तित्व के दूसरे चरण की ओर प्रेरित करके उक्त अनुसंधान केन्द्र के प्रथम निदेशक के चुनौतीपूर्ण पद का दायित्व सौंपने वाले, मेरे मार्गदर्शक एवं प्रेरणास्रोत स्वर्गीय श्री रामनिवास जी मिर्धा की पावन स्मृति में यह श्रद्धांजलि समर्पित है।

-- वीर सिंह

Contents

Foreword

Inspired by the ideals of Maharaja Surajmal, the 18th century ruler of the State of Bharatpur, Surajmal Memorial Education Society was established in the year 1972 with the aim and objective to provide educational facilities to the weaker sections of the society, especially those belonging to the rural areas. To fulfill its objectives, the Society established three Professional Institutes in its campus at C-4, Janakpuri, New Delhi and also two Public Schools - one each in U.P. and Rajasthan. It is in the process of establishing a new campus in Haryana also. The Society also established **Maharaja Surajmal Centre for Research & Publication** which has been undertaking the collection, preservation and publication of the material on rural heritage, especially relating to the life and role of peasantry in our national movements. So far, the Centre has published 19 books which include research work of scholars, translation of the prominent works in Hindi language, reprinting of the famous works of peasants of the North and North-West India and proceedings of the National Seminars organized by the Society from time-to-time.

Maharaja Surajmal Centre for Research & Publication has attained the status of a Premier Research Institution, primarily because of the untiring efforts made by its honorary Director - Dr. Vir Singh. It is a matter of great satisfaction that the Indian

Council of Historical Research, New Delhi has approved the Centre as a recognized Institution for research projects of history in the year 2006. The scholars can utilize the services of the Centre as Institution of Affiliation for their research projects submitted to ICHR. The Society has established a good library and also provides boarding and lodging facilities to the Research Scholars.

The Society has always strived for excellence and in that attempt, organized National Seminars on various occasions. As a matter of fact, these Seminars have become a regular feature of the activities of the Centre which are attended by eminent scholars from all over India. The broad theme of the National Seminar was - *"The Jats: Their Role and Contribution to the Socio-economic Life and Polity of North and North-West India"*.

On the occasion of the 150th anniversary of the First War of Independence, the Society organized National Seminars on the "Role of Common People in the Freedom struggle". The proceedings of these seminars have been published in book form: *"People's role in 1857 Uprising: Delhi and Neighbouring Region"*. Another National Seminar on *"The Life and Ideas of Shaheed Bhagat Singh - A Lesson for Today"* was organized in 2007 highlighting many, hitherto, unknown aspects of the life of this great patriot. The outcome of the Seminar was a fitting tribute to Shaheed Bhagat Singh who was an idealist and wanted to change the Society. He espoused revolutionary vision. The present volume is a modest attempt to delineate Bhagat Singh as a source of inspiration for the youth and to recount his ideology.

We dedicate this book to the memory of our late President Shri Ram Niwas Ji Mirdha for the inspiration, support and leadership he extended in organizing National Seminars. But for his constant guidance, the Society would not have attained the present status.

I take this opportunity to appreciate the efforts of the Office bearers and members of the Society who have helped us in various ways in organizing National Seminars.

I acknowledge the serious efforts put in by our Honorary Director, Dr. Vir Singh and Shri Surendra Kumar, Research Associate in compiling and editing the data to bring out this volume.

S.P. Singh
President
Surajmal Memorial Education Society

Editorial

Maharaja Surajmal Centre for Research and Publication of Surajmal Memorial Education Society on the occasion of the birth centenary year of Shaheed Bhagat Singh organised a National Seminar *'The Life and Ideas of Shaheed Bhagat Singh: A Lesson for Today'* at the premises of the Society at C-4 Janakpuri, New Delhi on 28 September 2007.The objective of this Seminar was to highlight the ideas and activities of the great martyr, Bhagat Singh who has continued to ignite the minds of our youths for generations as also to bring out the lesson that we can learn in today's world. It is the responsibility of scholars to take the glorious legacy of Bhagat Singh in a big way before the Indian people as a source of inspiration to rally them in their maximum numbers for combating the challenges of today. He stands out as a modern National leader and thinker, emphasizing the separation of religion from politics.

In this publication we are reminded of Bhagat Singh and his passionate involvement with the lives of workers and peasants. 21 Research papers presented in the National Seminar have found place here along with Inaugural and Keynote Addresses by the renowned historians. In this volume we have given English articles first and then Hindi articles follow. It has been done to facilitate the typing work.

I received full cooperation of the scholars who supplied to me the written and in some cases revised copies of their contributions. All of them are entitled to my very sincere thanks. Infact what we claim to have achieved is the real outcome of the contribution made by the participants in the National Seminar.

I extend my hearty thanks to Dr. S.S. Rana who has helped me in coordinating the sessions of the National Seminar, selecting the articles and giving this volume the final shape. I convey my heartful thanks to Shri S.P. Singh, President, Shri Ajit Singh, Secretary and Dr. R.P. Dahiya, Treasurer of the Society for their unsolicited help and cooperation rendered to me in accomplishing my endeavour.

I also acknowledge the hard work of my Research Associates Dr. Manjeet Tokas and Mr. Surendra Kumar in organizing the Seminar and in the work of Publication. I would not forget to thank Shri Pradeep Mittal for typing out the press copy of the manuscript and for printing it neatly and publishing this volume in an attractive shape.

Dr. Vir Singh
Director
Maharaja SurajmalCentre
for Research and Publication

1

Shaheed Bhagat Singh: An Immortal Revolutionary

(Address by Chief Guest)

Prof. A.K. Kapoor

I feel honoured for being invited in this National Seminar. When I was young child studying in 6 th class. Visual media movies cleared the ideology of Shaheed Bhagat Singh. impact was much more. some of the thoughts of Bhagat Singh and other personalities which I want to share you all.

From September 28, 2006, we began the celebration of the Birth Cenetary Year of Bhagat Singh, a powerful. symbol of the still ongoing struggle of the people of India against that is imperialism, capitalism, feudalism, communalism and certain pessimistics dispositions about (my) future career.

"*It is easy to kill individuals but you cannot kill. Great empires crumbled while the ides survived. I have been areested while waging a war. For me there can be no gallows. Put me into the month of canon and blow me off.*"

These were words of Bhagat Singh who is symbol of heroism of youth'a symbol of courage a symbol for patriotism, person who welcome death and spirit is an unfalling for the youth even today.

with a shy, nature, who had certain pessimistic dispositions about (my) future career.

Vice chancellor, Jiwaji University, Gwalior.

(3) While in prison he wrote:

"*The aim of life is not merely* to control the mind, but to develop it harmoniously; not to achieve salvation here after, but to make the best use of it and not realise truth, beauty and good only in contemplation, but also in the actual experience of daily life; social progress depends not upon the ennoblement of the few but on the enrichment of democracy; universal brotherhood can be achieved only when there is an equality of opportunity in the social, political and individual life." - Bhagat Singh's prison diary, p. 124.

(4) The distinctiveness of Bhagat Singh in the revolutionary firmament of the national movement has been well captured by *B. T. Ranadive in his Foreword to the Selected Writings of Shaheed Bhagat Singh edited by Shiv Verma. He writes:*

"The name of Bhagat Singh and his comrades has secured a permanent place in the minds of the Indian people. No other revolutionary of those days struck such a deep feeling of sympathy, solidarity and oneness among the people. Bhagat Singh and his comrades became part of the people's consiousness, the symbol of their aspiration and prestige, the symbol of the fight to put an end to enslavement...."

(5) A. G. Noorani concludes his book *"The Trial of Bhagat Singh- Politics of Justice with words:"* "What distinguished Bhagat Singh from all others, besides his courage, patriotism and commitment to moral values, was his intellectual strength. A voracious reader, he was also willing to rethink. He had the capacity to brood and to torment his soul over the past. That led him to renounce terrorism, and to advise the young to follow suit; indeed, to counsel moderation and readiness to compromise. He was only 23 when he was hanged. On his death, Indian leaders vied with one another in lavishing praise on him.

One wonders how many of them knew then they had lost a man who, had he lived, might have had an incalculable impact on the course of India's politics."

(6) Bhagat Singh was then just 12 years old was studying at the D A V School in Lahore. He was deeply enraged by the Jallianwala Bagh massacre. It has been recorded that he immediately went to Bagh, collected its soil in a bottle and kept it as a constant reminder of the hurt and humiliation that the Indian people had suffered.

(7) In 1924, Bhagat Singh had to give up his B. A. Studies and leave Lahore because his father and grandmother were forcing him to get married. He wrote to his father, " This is not the time for marriage. The country is calling me. I have taken oath to serve the country physically, mentally and monetarily." When his father continued to insist, Bhagat Singh again wrote back, "I am astonished to read the contents of your letter....You are caring for Dadi, but in how much trouble is our Mother of 33 crores, the Bharat Mata. We still have to sacrifice everything for her sake." Finally, when leaving home, he wrote, "I dedicate my life to the lofty goal of service to the motherland. Hence there is no attraction in me for home and fulfilment of worldly desires." He left Lahore for Kanpur.

(8) Secularism was, indeed, an article of faith with Bhagat Singh all his life. Bipan Chandra described it thus: "More than any other contemporary leader, with the exception of Gandhiji, he understood the danger that communalism posed to Indian society and Indian nationalism. He often warned his comrades and followers that communalism was as big an enemy as colonialism...Religion, said Bhagat Singh, was the private concern of a person, but it had to be fought as an enemy when it intruded that people must free themselves from the mental bondage of religion and superstition."

(9) In a sense, Bhagat Singh had himself forewarned that such developments were bound to occur if one form of exploitative rule was merely replaced by another. Referring to the workers and peasants, he had asked in his last testament, "What difference does it make to them whether Lord Reading is the head of the Indian government or Sir Purshotamdas Thakordas? What difference for a peasant if Sir Tej Bahadur Sapru replaces Lord Irwin!" That is precisely what happened at the time of the transfer of power.

Bhagat Singh is an extremely powerful symbol of the freedom struggle and of revolutionary change, The four remarkable strands in the life, work and thought of Bhagat Singh and his comrades are: a) uncompromising struggle against imperialism, b) unflinching resistance to communalism and caste oppression; c) unbending opposition to bourgeois-landlord rule, and d) unshakable faith in Marxism and socialism as the only alternative before society.

(10) These are precisely the strands being championed by all patriotic and progressive forces in India today. In Bhagat Singh's Birth Centenary Year, it is these strands that must be consciously taken to the people of India through a massive and well-organized campaign by the Left, democratic and secular forces. Bhagat Singh is a special source of inspiration to the students and youth of India, who are facing serious problems of education and employment. They must be rallied in this campaign in the maximum possible numbers.

There is also much to learn from the magnificent qualities of character that Bhagat Singh displayed through his short life of 23 years. His courage, sacrifice, integrity, determination, studiousness, humility and comradership have been described in the memoirs written by his comrade and by other contemporaries. These are traits that all true revolutionaries must constantly try to imbibe and develop, first within themselves and then among others.

I shall end with the inspiring words with which Bhagat Singh concluded his last testament:

If you start the work on these lines, you shall have to be very sober...It requires neither the emotion nor the death, but the life of constant struggle, suffering and sacrifice. Crush your individuality first. Shake off the dreams of personal comfort. Then start to work. Inch by inch you shall have to proceed. It needs courage, perseverance and very strong determination. No difficulties and hardships shall discourage you. No failure and betrayals shall dishearten you. No travails imposed upon you shall snuff out the revolutionary will in you. Through the ordeals of sufferings and sacrifice you shall come out victorious. And these individual victories shall be the valuable assets of the Revolution.

* *"The young boy who sacrificed his life for the nation...The one who gathered all youth to get freedom...I salute the great soul."*

We all have experienced that we all unite on the face of natural or man made calamities. When we integrate only then we can win the war against imperialism, capitalism, feudalism, communalism and casteism.

2

Inaugural Address

Prof. Suhash Chakrobarthy

Very significant celebration of the birth anniversary of Bhagat Singh. I thank you all but I feel very illimitated because I am very limited man with limited mind and perception and infact despite the eloquent description of Prof. Rana, I am inadequate to speak to you. I feel almost like a primitive before the joint scholars here. I am supposed to be speaking on a person who was simple formulation.

Bhagat Singh was anti-imperialist. He fought against the most powerful empire of the world. No one can deny this fact. And he died for that, he was executed for that, he was haunted for that. In 2007, there is imperialism in the world. The imperialism implified by one nation-which is a super power. Though Govt. of India- my Govt. of India does not say anything. We have struck to non-align movement completely. We are surrendering before the American pressure on everything. We did not say a word when the entire civilization of Missopatamia were disseminated by the Americans without any reason. We did not say a word when one of the friends of India-Saddam Hussain was hanged publically-international level, before the television cameras, our Prime Minister said nothing. The leader of the Congress Party said nothing. The

---

University of Delhi.

Foreign Minister said it is an unfortunate affair. There is a story. We are not conducting and concluding our oil pipeline understanding with Iran because we are scared of America and they are threatening. We are establishing American median moving around all over the place and we are participating under exercise fully known and the ship goes back to almost to bomb Iraq and preparing for the Iraq participating in American onslaught in Middle East. So where is Mr. Bhagat Singh. Mr. Bhagat Singh fought against the imperialism. He died for it. Our entire nation is succumbing to the American pressure. Where is Bhagat Singh. Where is his themes and life. This is why I am very pained when I think I am asked to speak about something which is just a ritualistic now. It is nothing more than ritualistic. I am sorry to say this stupid thing now. The fact in its that this anti-imperialist of India was born in 1907 in a small place in Punjab in a family of ordinary well-to-do family, who were themselves somewhat revolutionary. Father and grandfather had been to jail. They are great admirer of the famous Gadar Movement. They admirer of Gurjeet Singh, one of the young boys who was hanged in was the loss figure of Bhagat Singh and in fact when Ferozepur Cantonment was to be taken over by this Gadarist, here is a man who saw that there got a betrayal from the Indian side and whole movement pitted out. He was the man very young boy was crime. He can't belive the Indians will betray Indians. Now the point in justice is here the man of only about 12 years when this famous Jalian Walan Bagh was enacted. Interesting part of it people don't remember that nobody outside this military world knew about it. For 10 or 15 days nobody in India outside Jalian, Amritsar, the censoring was so sharp. And yet news reached Tagore through the Tribune family. There was a grand niece or somebody who was married there in the family and the latter went there. So it's voice of protest started somewhere in Shanti Niketan and there he became a part of the society and he became a protest movement unprecedented in the world that is called Jalianwalan Massacre anti protestant and in fact it let to the total transformation of Indian nationalism. It's a total transformation from begging, petitioning to a society that it is Stanestate. Gandhi said it's an Stanestate. It must be opposed. That's transformation from a bully Gandhi, loyal Gandhi, to enable Gandhi was brought down by this Jalianwala Bagh. Young boy of 12. He goes there and picks up a fistful of soil keep sits all his right with him. He wants to take avenge. He has to take total avenge of the retribution giving to the Indians by the British imperialism. He has to fight for it. That was a boy of 12. And the interesting part of it, if you look through the writings, speeches of Bhagat Singh, a new collection has come by the NBT, he has come out a new collection of his speeches, or his writings not complete selection, and its quite clear from this that man was not wholly a reader, a vicious reader but a creative reader. No one in those days in 1923-24, apart from few columnists, who had hardly organized, nobody managed to reach the things that he read about history, revolution, movements, society-not only of India but French, Italian, German and also of American history. Here is a man who studied history and I am a very very partial man, I am a very strong devotee of this discipline history and I know you don't like it but it was not ordinary person Mr. Manmohan Santhal didn't like it either. He reads a statement in Oxford that everything Britishers done were civilized by them.

So he can do anything if he is like. He cannot, I cant desist from them, I scared with them. But they have some figure to play with it. History...it gives you the understanding and social movement and process of our life and this is what Mr. Bhagat Singh did all his life in the library. When he was a student of DAV School, still a school student, he was a member of this library which was started by Lajpat Rai and then he became a member, thorough member, three seats were reserved for him. One for his books he is reading, the other table where he was writing the third where he was reading. There was so many books at any given point of time in the library – one man show – Bhagat Singh. He was reading, understanding, assimilating; trying to understand the processes of life. The static phenomena. What he learnt at the age of 23 could have been grown, could have been matured and could have been higher and higher level of perfection. But there is life first terminated. What did he get? I give you only a few-1 don't know much about life but the point is one slogan-*Inqalab Jindabad.* Who said this – Bhagat Singh. The Bengali scholar who was an editor of a modern review not edit. What is this bloody Inqalab. Where is this Inqalab? What you are talking about? He wrote a long editorial in modern review some projecnty is a grand father of Prof. Seal of Kemian University. Now this man not catching and Mr. Bhagat Singh at the age of 21 deprives back. You don't know what is revolution. You have to study. The beginning of revolution is the expansion of human freedom, the essendesia of common man and he started in French revolution which is not a complete revolution but it led to the expansion of human freedom and common man came to the existence. He took part in East India in region. It was the same thing which is expansional freedom, which part of the unification of Germany, it was the same nation, which you find in the mainly restoration in Japan as a fall of the Togo War fogonate. The same mission you find in the main force movement of China is all Mr. Bhagat Singh. I am not concocting it's a part of speech it's a lecturer and finally it lead to reculminating point in revolution was absolutism was destroyed, old impire was destroyed. Fuedalism was destroyed. Aristocracy was destroyed and a common man – that peasants, the worker, that brought to the forefront by one great man – known as Lenin. And this soviet revolution became his ideal and he started learning all about soviet revolution – Marxism study. In fact he became and without acknowledging what he is doing, he became a some sort of a procomarxists. India guys No. 1 important. He says Marx was a product of his own time. Had there been no industrial revolution, there have been no capitalism. There is no capitalism, there is no Marx to drawl. Now try to find out the laws and motion of capitalism. So Marx is a product of his time. In other words, this is breaking news and likely to give it or not. This is nothing but inversion of Marxism possession. A man is a product of the society, his idea is reflectible to the society, his vision is reflection of the society as a future. This is precisely how we dealts and in fact and in case this is how we talk about revolution. That revolution is still unfulfilled and that revolution has to be fulfilled. The role of the Indian youth he says is to be vowed that revolution in India. And its possible (a) by overthrowing imperialism which is loksum, exploitative word reconstruction of the society or the fashion in which peasants and the workers will have a due share in the deliberation and prospects of the future. He looked at the French revolution, he looked at the Italian revolution. He did not see masses anywhere. Because there is no masses. Even in Russian revolution in 1917, there were no masses. It was masses came only when the land was given to the tiller and when industrialization process started taking place. So he says, mass movement is necessary. Now here is a gradual change in Bhagat Singh's perception and understanding. A man who thought force is indispensable, is a part of midlife of the history etc. We have forced everything is funny etc., made fun of Gandhi and his withdrawal of the non-cooperation movement. Here is the man finally saying masses are important, mass movement is important, awareness of the masses is most important thing, which is the masses he is taking about. Not the French revolution and masses and even they are not from outside France out of place. Which masses he is taking about. The masses of Gauri Bawli and did not have any masses have at all in India. They have all masses from Bismark or Germany unification and manufacturing Russia they have no masses in medi-restoration. There was a sum in air force movement but that was also reflection of Russian revolution. What sort of movement he was talking about. He was talking about the masses which he himself projected in 1921 he is turn about Gandhi's mass movement. Mass movement is a movement which in 1921 he joined and he withdrew because of the Chauri Chaura. That's mass movement, where for the first in the history of the world – peasants, workers, urbans, rural, men, women, caste hindus, and low caste, and Hindus, Muslims, Parsis, Christians, and all the linguistic groups participated in Haryana as well as Chauri Chaura also in Nizam district in Orissa, also in Surat, also in Bombay and Maharastra, also in Kerala and Cochin, the whole of India was unified by the mass movement and this is what he talking about. In other words, towards the end of his life, towards the very short life, the man had matured already. He says, force if necessary, non-violent is not absolutely necessary, but booked non-violent, enforce is required diplomacy negotiation, compromise, concession unnecessary part in the phases of the history and cannot be linked rejected. Here tremendous synthesis. He has already brought about in 1923 there was a same time, in about the same time, when he was assassinated, he was killed by the Britishers. There was also another man killed by the Britishers whose name was Surya Sen. The Chittgaon armeryrade man. And he was as congress president who defied Gandhi and he took to this arm struggle. And he did this important, important action, as it militant to say action, and action was chatted long armery was raided and it was occupied by them. There was neniment also. P.C. Dutta while the young girl of sixteen who committed suicide when he was caught with taking protest with cyanide and she said also a congressman defecting to are it with military movement and violent action. All of them said and infact was important thing is Mr. Surya Sen on the canals when he been hanged. What do you want to say - he said Mahatma Gandhi ki Jai. What I am trying to say is that there was a synthesis coming as synthesis which is Gandhi is not the only thing, non-violent is not the only thing, we are also violent people who can reviolent, it is not terrorism. Mr. Bhagat Singh repeatedly said – We are not terrorist. We don't here to come to kill people. We are when we kill Souhnders on the face of the other police officer he was very young then. But he came out with a pamphlet which is posted all over the Lahore that is said – We are so sorry that man has been killed but can't help it, it happens in revolutionary situation. So where I am trying to say, don't call them terrorist, historians called them terrorist. I have seen terrorists being talked about the history books you see, terrorists done this etc. etc. He was not terrorist. They had a perception. That perception was stupefied and actualized and the ideas and the activities of Bhagat Singh who wanted a revolution, he wanted a free man, he wanted revolution and the constructive programme. Constructive programme must have actions not only of overthrowing a system but also reconstruction of a new system where peasants and workers will have a rightful place. It is universal. It is not nation oriented, it's a part of the historical process for the expansion of human freedom from French revolution to Italian revolution to unification Germany to Chinese revolution to Russian revolution and finally it was to be expected to be done when British empire is overthrown by BP Wichapapas not with. without any purpose, not for the power, for the sake of power by using power for the benefit of the mankind and the welfare of the people at large. Thank you very much.

3

Bhagat Singh:

Understanding a Unique Phenomenon

Prof. K.C. Yadav

Bhagat Singh is a household name today. He is very much a part of people's memory – almost everywhere. But, regrettably, two serious lapses scar this memory. One the memory is of fragmentary character, and two, it has been reduced more or less to a ritual. In other words, the way, Bhagat Singh is generally remembered is worse than forgetfulness!

Why, a question may arise here, things are like that? Why Bhagat Singh, his memory is treated this way? The reason is on 23 March 1931, proud like a plumed peacock, that slim, smart and what we call in the Punjabi folk manner of speaking, *ghabru jawan* (youthful young man) mounted the gallows with a smile on his face and *'Inquilab Zindabad'* (Long Live Revolution) on his lips and staring the death in her eyes as daringly as one could, he made supreme sacrifice that millions envied, but could not make. Even Gandhiji, standing with bent head, said :

> *In this country of suppression and timidity almost bordering on cowardice, we cannot have too much bravery, too much sacrifice, and in this one's head bends before Bhagat Singh's bravery and self-sacrifice.*[1]

85, Sector-23, Gurgaon, Haryana.

This grand spectacle dazzled people's mind's eye to such an extent that even today, after about 75 years, we can only see that short but spectacular act of great bravery and supreme sacrifice alone. But that is not Bhagat Singh - full Bhagat Singh, to be precise! That is only a small tip of a huge ice-berg. A part has obscured the whole!

I am tempted to quote here the words of Jaichandra Vidyalankar, an enlightened Professor of History at the National College, Lahore, who was in many ways instrumental in preparing Bhagat Singh[2] for doing what he later did.

> *The young man (Bhagat Singh) who was suspected to be the murderer of Saunders could have easily committed, had he wished, many such actions by remaining underground, beyond the reach of the authorities; and that could have caused a sort of terror in the hearts of the enemies of the country and given solace and strength to the sufferers at their hands. I don't know how far was it correct for such a young man to have got himself arrested for doing such a small job (throwing bomb in the Assembly), But as far as I am concerned, I wouldn't have been happy even seeing Bhagat Singh doing the former job-that is leading a band of some 10 to 20 guerrillas and doing daring deeds (to frighten the rulers and encouraging his countrymen) - for I have always visualized a different Bhagat Singh. He had infinite potential to be one who could, after receiving proper education in warfare, lead, at an appropriate moment, the armies for the liberation of India and be arbiter to decide the fate of battles fought for changing her history. That Bhagat Singh had capacity and capabilities to play such roles wouldn't be known to the persons who are full of him only after seeing a small part played by him.*[3]

Throwing of the bomb in the Assembly was a small step or a big action is not an issue at hand here. What I am concerned with is the blank in the story that the statement fills. I am in agreement with Prof. Jaichandra that Bhagat Singh had tremendous potential to be a general or a leader of his people, and an arbiter to decide the fate of his country. But even this does not supply the full desideratum and complete the story. A serious reading of the contemporary material, sometimes between the lines, Bhagat Singh's own writings[4] and more importantly, his 'Prison Notes'[5] will show that Bhagat Singh was much bigger than even what Jaichandra has portrayed. He was a superfine specimen of humankind and had capacity and capabilities to be a world leader - of the whole humanity, I mean!

It is no exaggeration. Look at the multi-directional infinite potentials that he had. And the incredible speed that he grew with. People may need, ordinarily, lives to achieve what he achieved in months, a few years. Ajay Ghosh, his close associate, and a former Secretary General of the Communitst Party of India had observed this phenomenon with great wonderment : Ghosh met him at Kanpur. Bhagat Singh was in his late teens then. "He was tall and thin", says Ghosh,

Shabbily dressed, very quiet, a typical village lad, lacking smartness and self-confidence. I did not think very highly of him and told (B.K.) Dutt so when he was gone.[6]

After about two years later, 1928, he met him again, and says :

I was surprised when a young man walked into my room and greeted me. It was Bhagat Singh, I had met two years before. Tall and magnificently proportioned, with a keen intelligent face and gleaming eyes, he looked a different man altogether. And as he talked, I realized that he had grown, not merely in years.[7]

It is not one man's opinion. Everybody whosoever saw Bhagat Singh about this time took him to be a wonderful phenomenon :

All those who have met Bhagat Singh, says Ghosh, then and afterwards, have testified to his remarkable intelligence and to the powerful impression he made on people.[8]

He was a fine specimen of humankind, I have said. It is well known that he was a highly intelligent man. He was to quote Prof. Bipan Chandra, "the finest brain."[9] He was a voracious reader,[10] An intrepid thinker. An intellectual par excellence![11] What is, however, not so well known is that he was a fine creation of nature. Perhaps a part-nature itself. And there lies the secret of his growth-colourful, impressive, stupendous growth, very natural growth.

He was full of life, brimming with colour and ambitions. He wished to enjoy it to the hilt. He was full of love, which in moral terms, he said, "was nothing but passion – not animal passion, but human passion, which always elevates a man".[12] He loved nice things in life[13]-good food, good clothes, good shoes, a lot of films, a lot of fun, pranks and pats.[14]

In what way was he different, then, from the other man in the street? He possessed what he, the other man in the street, doesn't – a superhuman peculiarity, which made him what he was – great Bhagat Singh. The peculiarity was : he could transport himself from the ordinary world of the ordinary people to the great world of the great. He told this secret to Sukhdev. "Brother", he said, "I can renounce everything at the time of need... These things should never be hindrance in the way of man, provided he is a man"[15]. He was the man!

About 1919, the need arose, which compelled Bhagat Singh to walk out of his world to play the roles, which were, to quote Raja Ram, his very close friend and the librarian of the Dwarkadas Library, Lahore, not essentially his. "He was forced by the circumstances", explains Ram "to play the roles of different persons."[16]

These circumstances were : Bhagat Singh's Punjab was (about 1919) in the worst political depression imaginable. Fiery Ajit Singh was gone. And so were the brave Babbars and good Ghadrites. Lajpat Rai was there minus his earlier luster. He was, in Bhagat Singh's words, the "Lost leader". The Punjab-peasant was in deep slumber. The worker was depressed. Punjab's poets had ceased to sing revolutionary songs – *Pugree Sambhal O Jatta!* was a thing of the dead past. Its young men in schools and colleges, concerned with their book and basta, had no taste for politics – nationalist politics, to be precise! And the imperial Dyers and demons were out destroying innocent humanity![17]

These were the circumstances that compelled Bhagat Singh and his friends to come to nationalist politics. Fortunately, Gandhiji came on the scene about this very time. He, especially his great words, "Swaraj in a year" had tremendous appeal for these young men. They joined him at once. Bhagat Singh was a Gandhian non-cooperator now![18]

But he was a non-cooperator with a difference. He did not become a part of a faceless crowd, did not offer *satyagraha* and passed some days in some jail. He went instead to the National College, Lahore, continued his studies, and trained himself to become an active instrument for the nation-building process![19]

When Gandhiji withdrew his movement, and dark forces of depression engulfed Punjab in particular and the entire country in general, again, Bhagat Singh, Sukhdev, and his friends burnt their candles and showed light to their countrymen![20]

Bhagat Singh, a voracious reader as he was, read a lot of books[21] and journals these days. He travelled far and near.[22] Met people of different ideas and views.[23] He organized groups and parties.[24] In the process, his ideas, ideology, persona changed at a stupendous speed. He acquired new baggages and left old ones-sometimes completely, sometimes in parts – these days. His metamorphosis from an Arya nationalist[25] to a Babbarite,[26] to a Gandhian non-cooperator,[27] to an anarchist of Irish, French, Russian hues,[28] to a socialist Marxist[29] is interesting. And so is the change in his perspective, vision and approach to his work – from local[30] to provincial,[31] national,[32] to global![33]

In 1931, his journey ended. He had done a lot to serve the cause in hand, but what he wanted to do but couldn't was still vaster. Even at 23, he had a well developed ideology. But it was yet to flower into something which could have helped him change the world. Given time, this miracle would have happened. In a short span of about two decades, he had evolved into a fine specimen of human kind. The process of his evolution was, however, nowhere nearer completion. The way he was going and growing, we can guess, he would have touched the zenith after some time in the spheres that he was operating in. He would have been a unique phenomenon the like of which the world sees but rarely.

Taking a serious stock of the two situations as to what Bhagat Singh was, and What he might have been if the soulless alien government had spared him, we should study him in detail with scientific method and multi-disciplinary tools. The first step in this direction may be deconstruction of the old discourse where he is mostly shown, indulging in violent activities, that is, throwing a bomb here and killing a policeman there to free his country from the foreign yoke. Let us have a full Bhagat Singh, for we need him now as an ideologue, as a leader, as a role-model, and as a rouser of spirits in the fight against evil, impeding the way leading to a better, happier, healthier and freer world.

References

1. See *The Tribune* (Lahore), 28 March 1931.
2. Chhabil Das, the principal of National College, Lahore says that it was Jaichandra Vidyalankar who inculcated the feeling of revolution in Bhagat Singh and Sukhdev. "He inspired these people to go for Irish type of activities. Jaichandra was Professor of Indian History in the National College. He was a graduate of Gurukula Kangri. He was a man of few words. He never talked to anybody-he was a silent man. He used to discuss revolutionary matters in his classes and maybe elsewhere too". See Bhagat Singh : *Making of a Revolutionary, Contemporaries'* Portrayals (hereafter Portrayals), eds. K.C. Yadav. Babar Singh (Gurgaon, 2006), p. 138.
3. *Abhyudaya* (Allahabad), 8 May 1931.
4. *Frangrance of Freedom : Writings of Bhagat Singh* (hereafter Writings), eds. K.C. Yadav, Babar Singh (Gurgaon, 2006); Shiv Verma, ed. *Selected Writings of Bhagat Singh* (Delhi, 1986); Bhagat Singh : *Selected Writings* (NBT, 2007). Most of his writings are available in Hindi and Punjabi as well.
5. See Bhagat Singh : *Ideas on Freedom, Liberty and Revolution : Jail Notes of a Revolutionary* (hereafter Jail Notes), eds K.C. Yadav, Babar Singh (Gurgaon, 2006).
6. Ajoy Ghosh, *Bhagat Singh* (Delhi, 1956), PP. 31, 32.
7. Ibid.
8. Ibid.
9. See Bipan Chandra, *'Introduction' in Bhagat Singh : Why I am an Atheist?* (hereafter Atheist) (Gurgaon, 2006), P. 9, 12.
10. Besides being a voracious reader himself, he "tried to inculcate the reading and thinking habit among his fellow revolutionaries and younger comrades". Ibid. "Always passionately fond of studying", he always carried some book or magazine with him. Ajoy Ghosh, *Portrayals*, P. 103.
11. "The Sword of revolution", he believed. "is sharpened at the whetstone of thought." *Atheist.* P. 12.
12. Bhagat Singh to Sukh Dev, Lahore, ? April 1923. In this highly emotional but philosophical letter, Bhagat Singh has opened his heart to Sukh Dev in this matter. "I say with all the emphasis at my command that I am overfilled with life brimming with colourful hues and ambitions of a full life...As regards the moral status of love, I may say

that it in itself is nothing but passion, not animal passion but a human one, and very sweet indeed. Love itself can never be animal passion. Love always elevates the character of a man". *Writings,* p. 301.

13. Bhagat Singh mostly wore white shirt with shakespearean collar and half sleeves. His shoes used to be of 'Victory' brand. Asking his friend Jaidev Gupta to send these things, he said : "You should not think that even in jail we have not been able to check our expensive mode of living. But these are, after all, necessities and not luxuries. Send two *'langots,* made of soft cloth for bathing and exercise, a few soap cakes for washing clothes, also some *badam* and one swan ink bottle." Bhagat Singh to Jaidev Gupta, Lahore, 30 June 1930, *Writings,* p. 304.

14. A very interesting account is furnished by Raja Ram in this regard in his memoirs, *Amar Shahidon Ke Sansmarana,* 1981, excerpted in *Portrayals,* pp. 183-90.

15. *Writings,* p. 301.

16. *Portrayals,* pp. 183-90. This aspect touched by some of his associates like Yashpal, etc. should be probed deeply.

17. K.C. Yadav, *Punjab : Colonial Challenge and Popular Response.* 1849-1947 (Gurgaon, 2003), pp. 60-131.

18. Jitendranath Sanyal, *Bhagat Singh : A Biography*, 1931, (Reprint, Gurgaon, 2006), p.30.

19. *Ibid.*, p. 23.

20. "After the failure of the non-cooperation movement in 1921, many impatient young men sought to resort to other methods than those advocated by Mahatama Gandhi for the realization of their ideals". *Ibid,* p. 23.

21. Says Sanyal, his associate, and biographer, in this regard : It was during the years 1925 and 1926 that Bhagat Singh built up an intellectual reservoir which supplied him material for the rest of his life. He joined the National College, founded and run by Lala Lajpat Rai, and devoted himself whole-heartedly to the study of history, politics and economics. Here he had with him two other devoted followers, namely Sukhdev and Bhagwati Charan, and the three with one or two others created a study-circle on the model of the Russian revolutionaries like Kropotkin. The Servants of the People Society generously helped them by indenting for the Dwarka Das Library all such books as were asked for by these ardent revolutionary students.

    We have the testimony of such eminent men as Professor Chhabil Das of the National College and Mr. Raja Ram, the librarian of the Dwarka

Das Library, as to the eagerness with which Bhagat Singh devoured books. At the National College Library also, under the guidance of Sardar Bhagat Singh, a unique collection grew up. As far as we are aware, we have nowhere seen such a collection of suitable literature. Most up-to-date publications on the history of the revolutionary period in Italy, Russia and Ireland were procured and many rare books on the early history of the revolutionary movement in Russia were collected". See *Ibid.*, pp. 33-34.

22. *Ibid.*, pp. 30-34.

23. *Ibid.*

24. *The Punjab Students Union, Naujawan Bharat Sabha, Hindustan Republican Association,* later *Hindustan Socialist Republican Association.*

25. See *Atheist,* pp. 21-22, 36; Sanyal, op. cit, pp. 23-25.

26. *Ibid.*

27. *Ibid.*

28. *Portrayals,* pp. 134-136.

29. Bhagat Singh's associate, Sohan Singh Josh says that he was a full blooded Marxist. Ajoy Ghosh, however, believes that he was not a Marxist. Prof. Bipan Chandra thinks that he was a Marxist in the making which is, I think, a historically correct position. What sort of 'Marxist' he would have ultimately become, only God that he did not believe in might know.

30. He started his activities from National College, Lahore.

31 After joining the *Naujawan Bharat Sabha,* his sphere of activities changed from local to provincial.

32. After joining the HRA, later HSRA, his sphere of activities got enlarged to the national level. Shiv Verma says that, "in the beginning of 1928, Bhagat Singh took initiative and floated the idea of forming an All-India Organisation". See *Portrayals,* pp. 46-48, 158-161.

33. See *Jail Notes*. Here his concern is not a country or a continent but the entire humanity. He is preparing to bring about a revolution to change the world.

4

Bhagat Singh and His Political Ideology

Dr. S.R. Bakshi

The Doab region comprising of Jallandhar, Hoshiarpur and Ludhiana produced a fairly rich crop of disciplined patriots whose sacrifices are well-remembered in the annals of our history. Greatly helped and supported by the youths of northern and eastern regions, they could guide the destiny of our nation with confidence and sincerity. The anti-raj struggle was a long drawn phenomenon in this context.[1]

If we browse through the pages of our history, we come across a small village, *khatkar kalan,* about 25 K.M. from Phagwar in the Doaba region. The ancestors of Bhagat Singh lived here since generations. But during the viceroyalty of Lord Curzon, the family, being given the basic facilities migrated to Layallpur, the canal irrigated area.[2] Sardar Arjun Singh, the grandfather and later on Sardar Kishan Singh could else out their livelihood having deep learing on Indian nationalism.[3]

As a student, Bhagat Singh was intelligent, active, smart and above all well-disciplined. He showed much respect to the teachers and they had immense love for him. His academic results were fairly satisfactory as he never shirked his studies. Besides he was a superb actor and a dramatist.[4] As a regular member of the local National Club, he often acted the historical roles of the Mauryas, Guptas and Maharana Pratap. He had a natural command in Punjabi, Urdu and English. Besides he knew Hindi and Sanskrit well. With his typical Punjabi youthful physique, he had gained much prominence amongst the students and teachers not only of his own college, but also of other local colleges.[5]

Principal Chhabil Das of National College reminsced besides them being my students, we had good personal relations too. In the evenings we could meet and talk informally on so many subjects. We spent several nights on the bank of the River Ravi and spent moonlit nights, boating and rowing there giving expression to our innermost feelings on any subject.[6]

'There were no books at hand. So it was for the teachers to select books from the libraries and give the relevant portions to the students...in our National College, we used to talk about Mazzini and Garibaldi. We used to talk about Ireland, about Sinn Fein movement of De Velera and other movements and about the Russian Revolution.

It is a remarkable phenomenon on the part of revolutionaries to start national institutions- the parallel educational centres in various parts of northern India. The teachers working in these institutions were men of ability, scholarship and missionary zeal. They functioned with a small pittance.[8] The national fervour and revolutionary excitement which they inculcated in the minds of the new generation with their principal examples, brought about a new model in the field of education. Undoubtedly, this kind of association of the youths with the dedicated band of teachers greatly awakened the mental faculties of the former and enabled them to take a broader view of human life. Besides the literature, a part of their curriculum, opened new vistas of knowledge for them which they made use of to achieve their cherished object in the spectrum of the anti-raj activities.[9]

In mid-twenties there was so much revolutionary fervour amongst the young men that it, indeed, became essential for them to work under the banner of an organized and well-disciplined forum. *The Naujawan Bharat Sabha* was formed in March 1926 at the suggestion of Dr. Satyapal to educate young men, especially the student community of the educational institutions located at Lahore.[10] The programme of the Sabha comprised debates on morality, literacy and social subjects: the popularisation of swadeshi goods, the inculation of a sense of brotherhood, simple living and physical fitness and the stimulation of interest in Indian languages and civilization. All these principles proved greatly effective for the youths during this period.[11]

Bhagat Singh's leanings towards Soviet Russia were so deep rooted that he not only studied, again and again, the model of revolution brought about in that country in 1917, but also greatly valued the doings of their leadership which were anti-Czar in character. So far so, he and his associates sent their greetings to the Soviet Union in 1930 on the occasion of the anniversary of the November Revolution. This kind of felicitations showed the working of mind of Bhagat Singh and other revolutionaries and the great change which they had been inspiring to bring about in India. Besides Bhagat Singh derived inspiration from Guru Gobind Singh because it was he who used to say;

Chidiyan noon baaz naal ladaoon tud Guru Gobind Singh Kahalaon. in a melodious voice, Bhagat Singh used to sing in the jail room;

Maan mera rang de basanti chola issi rang main rang ke shiva ne maan ka bandhan khola

Maan mera rang de basanti chola.

Majority of these youths were in their teens and at one stage or the other, they bade good bye to their institutions in order to do the political work in the villages and towns. The pamphlets and literature they distributed amongst the people and the arguments they had with numerous youths of various regions who joined the revolutionary struggle at a later stage, obviously shows how much knowledge they possessed about the outcome of the revolution. They were much impressed by their political dogmas of liberty, equality and fraternity. Indeed 'long live revolution' was the repeated slogan by each and every one of them during their speeches, private dialogue as well as at the time when they went to gallows.

It is, however, an important phase of Indian nationalism and part and parcel of the freedom struggle launched in Indian sub-continent. In fact this style had much contribution in its own way as it clearly brought about a sort of permanent nightmare in the British minds as well as in England. With the passage of time, it became difficult for the Raj to crush these elements once for all and they did prove as obstacles in the smooth functioning of the administrative machinery of the government. The glaring proof of this kind of nightmare in the form of an assessment of the work of these revolutionaries and their achievements in various regions of India is available in the private and official correspondence of British Viceroys in India with the Home Government.[12] The very fact that their exploits occupy a significant place in their private and official papers, gives a definite, concrete and significant colour to their anti-British activities in India. It also shows the degree and magnitude of apprehensiveness in the minds of the British bureaucracy in India.[13]

Jai Dev Gupta, an active worker of the *Naujawan Bharat Sabha* reminsced thus...the platform of Naujawan Bharat Sabha was utilized to create hatred or some sort of ill-feeling against the British and prepared the country for final assault in due course...the story of Kartar Singh Sarabha's life was also propagated from that platform. His photographs were exhibited with projected slides. So the Naujawan Bharat Sabha, on the one hand, wanted to preach non-existence of God and removal of mental slavery, on the other hand, they wanted to enthuse nationalism by highlighting the heroic deeds and sacrifices of such revolutionaries.[14]

Ganesh Shankar Vidyarthi's house was the centre of political activities of numerous young revolutionaries with whom Bhagat

Singh formed deep connection in the common cause of fighting the violent war for independence. He became a member of the *Hindustan Republican Association,* an organization run by the revolutionaries in North India, but mainly in the United Provinces. Already, some well-known and devoted young men like Batukeshwar Dutt, Chandrashekhar Azad, Jogesh Chandra Chatterjee, Bejoy Kumar Sinha, Dr. Gaya Prasad, Bhagwati Charan Vohra and others were the active members of this organization.

Bhagat Singh's political ideology revolves round a very pertinent point i.e. his faith in God. What were the reasons for adopting a particular kind of faith which had taken him far away from the belief in the supreme being. A true and sincere revolutionary in the best traditions of Marx, Engels and Lenin, he explains his belief with a comprehensive straight forwardness in his views and reasoning in an article, *Why I am an Atheist'*...'Let us see how I carry on, one friend asked me to pray...for selfish motives I am not going to pray. Readers and friends. "Is this vanity"? If it is, I stand for it.'

Jawaharlal Nehru gave a beftting tribute to his ideology, working of mind, patriotism and supreme sacrifice. 'Bhagat Singh did not become popular of his act of terrorism but because he seemed to vindicate the honour of Lala Lajpat Rai and through him, of the nation.[15] He became a symbol, the act was forgotten, the symbol remained, and within a few months, each town and village of Punjab and to a lesser extent the whole of northern India resounded with his name. Innumerable legends grew up about him and the popularity the man achieved was something amazing.[16]

The continuous work by these youth required first-rate organization of the whole scheme. It needed dedicated workers who could implement the political programme, big or small, in an efficient manner. They were meticulously trainee in the art of maintaining perfect secrecy taking care that they were not entrapped by a policeman or a government official. And to maintain it in the best possible way, they changed their guises when they sniffed any kind of danger from the police. Such type of behaviour was very tactfully, intelligently and successfully shown by Bhagat Singh at a number of occasions when the police were very much concerned about his arrest and conviction. There were occasions when he was face to face with a policeman in a *mela,* on railway station or in a railway train.

The most significant aspect of the Karachi Congress (1931) was the presence of Sardar Kishan Singh and his speech on the occassion which was in a mellowed tone.[17] It is significant to note that he expressed his sentiments in appreciation of Pandit Motilal Nehru and Pandit Madan Mohan Malaviya for their efforts to save the lives of Bhagat Singh and his comrades. He also advised youngmen to maintain self control which was the need of the hour. By doing so, he assured them that they would be able to free India from the shakles of slavery.[18] This kind of programme, of elaborated must be under the advice and support of the prominent leaders of the Congress.[19]

Prof. Bipin Chandra stated about the political ideology of the revolutionaries thus....these idealist youth could not see anything wrong with Chauri Chaura. Nor could they appreciate a conception of politics and morality which could fell a powerful popular movement with a single blow. Nor were they satisfied with the two substitutes that the national leadership offered them: parliamentary politics of the *Swarajists* or the so constructive programme of the no-change...Their rejection of Gandhism made them search for alternatives. This search led them to socialism on the one hand and revolutionary terrorism on the other. They embraced both, as had been done half a century earlier by the Revolutionary Russian Youth.[20]

A leader must live if he is to fulfill the definite political programme which he cherishes as sacred to his mind and heart.

In case of these patriotic revolutionaries, the tragedy as explained in this paper, was serious if judged from the results of their sacrifices. In fact most of them were cut off at the prime of their youth. Before their ideology could be followed in a proper perspective, they were no more visible on the scene. But weighed in the balance, Bhagat Singh was a remarkable brave young man who always dreamt of a free India. And for the attainment of his cherished objective, he was prepared to sacrifice anything dear to him. His sacrifice was, indeed, supreme and therefore he became an enviable symbol for the nation, viz. for India, South East Asia and emerging nations in Europe and elsewhere.

It is quite evident that Bhagat Singh willingly offered himself to the police soon after throwing the bomb in the Central Assembly. This kind of gesture was not advisable as it ultimately proved fatal for him, his comrades and the organization. Since then the police did not leave him for a day. Numerous cases were hatched up against him and his comrades. Unfortunately some of the youths became approvers and as a result there of, the police got full knowledge of them where abouts. The jail life and the arbitrary judicial proceedings adversely affected them.

References

1. For a detailed study see Virendra Sandhu, *Amar Shaheed Bhagat Singh,* Delhi, 1974.
2. Lord Curzon, *speeches,* 1898-1905, vol. II, pp. 94-105.
3. Virendra Sandhu, op. cit.
4. see *'Bhagat Singh and His Comrades'* an article by Ajoy Ghosh in *New Age,* 22 March 1931.
5. Ibid.
6. Transcript of interview with Chhabil Das in Nehru Memorial Museum and Library, NMML-Teen Murti New Delhi.
7. Ibid.
8. Ibid.
9. Ibid.

10. Home poll. File 173 I VIII, 1930.

11. Ibid.

12. Home poll. File 192,1929.

13. Ibid.

14. Transcript of interview with Jai Dev Gupta, NMML, Teen Murti New Delhi.

15. Jawaharlal Nehru, *An Autobiography*, Delhi, 1962, pp. 175-76.

16. Ibid.

17. See the proceedings of the Indian National Congress, the Karachi session 1931, presided over by Sardar Vallabhbhai Patel.

18. Ibid.

19. Ibid.

20. For a detailed study see the writings of Prof. Bipin Chandra, emphasis on *Nationalism and Colonialism in Modern India*, New Delhi 1979; Home Poll. File, 492, 1930; an article, 'Remembering Bhagat Singh by Prof. Bimal Prasad in the *Mainstream*, 28 March 1981 and Manmathnath Gupta, *They lived dangerously: Reminiscences of a Revolutionary*, Delhi, 1969, p. 92.

5

Shaheed Bhagat Singh

A Great Humanist and Revolutionary

Dr. Nirmal Kumar

In order to know the personality correctly, the environment covering the person, correctly, his family and contemporaries' along with tensions prevailing is to be traced. It is because man is product of social milieu, economic condition and political ideas and institutions. Therefore, the activities of various streams of work forces are to be discovered. Bhagat Singh's family had rich tradition of Indian Revolutionaries.

Here a perusal of character of British rule required attention. Penetration of British rule was made possible only with the help of elite classes of Indian society. This class was created by the British rulers. It became distinct from the masses. It fully helped in exploiting the lower sections of Indian society. So, English rulers ruled India with the help of Indian *zamindars* and princely classes. So, Indian revolution required complete social change for mass contact programme.

Now we see the Indian national movement had been working through many political ideologies like constitutionalism, moderation, extremism, terrorism, socialism, communism, and revolutionary. Every group had its impact on each other. As aim was one i.e. to liberate India from British rule so entire Indian tradition could influence each other. Indian culture,

NMML, Teen Murti House, New Delhi.

literature could mould each of them but extreme point of exploitation of man by man could create terror at everybody's mind.

No doubt, foreign landmark events like English Revolution (1688), French Revolution (1789) and Russian Revolution (1917) etc affected the course of the movement of Indian freedom struggle. But the identity of aim influenced the strategies of leaders of Indian freedom movement suited to Indian realities.

Under such prevailing conditions this paper seeks to situate Bhagat Singh at due position in the galaxy of freedom fighters on the basis of his speeches and writings and also contemporaries, writings about his life and works.

The confusion relating to adopting a single method for liberating the country was prevailing.

Indian national movement faced a lot of problems relating to use of violence or non- violence. Here strength of Indian tradition was not to be ignored. Indian tradition defining the essence of justice based on even on violence is human if cruelty passes the extreme point. This essence was described in the epic the *Mahabharata* through the speeches of Lord Krishna to warrior Arjuna. This approach was also used by Mahatma Gandhi during Quit India movement of 1942. Bhagat Singh had joined the congress but he left it.

Some Ideas and Strategies of Bhagat Singh

He wrote massively on exploitation of peasantry and mill-workers in our country by British rulers aided by *zamindars* and capitalists. In two of his letters, Bhagat Singh also affirmed the revolutionary terrorist faith in Socialism. He wrote, "The peasants have to liberate themselves not only from foreign yoke but also from the yoke of landlords and capitalist."[2] "Regarding the labour's rise to power he wrote a letter dated 3 March 1931. He declared that the struggle in India would continue so long as "a handful of exploiters go on exploiting the labour of the common people for their own endows. It matters little whether these exploiters are purely British capitalists, or British and Indian in alliance, or even purely Indian."[3]

Bhagat Singh was Indian terrorist in the eyes of British rulers, but he was a human being. Humanity was his prime object. The inner feelings of kindness imbued with humanity always influenced him but Indian tradition also gave scope to kill devils who had destroyed the humanity. Some illustrations are as follows: A dramatic manifestation of revolutionary terrorist activity was the assassination of a British police officer by Bhagat Singh, Azad and Rajguru, who had earlier ordered laathi charge on a demonstration led by Lala Lajpat Rai. This had resulted in a fatal injury to the great Punjabi leader. The assassination was justified by the revolutionary Youngman as follows, "The murder of a leader respected by millions of people at the unworthy hands of an ordinary police official was an insult to the nation. It was the bounden duty of youngmen of India to efface it. We regret to have had to kill a person but he was part and parcel of that inhuman and unjust order which has to be destroyed. In him, an agent of British rule has been done away with shedding of human blood grieves us but bloodshed at the alter of revolution is unavoidable. Our objectives is to work for a revolution which would end exploitation of man by man."[4]

Bhagat Singh and B.K. Dutt threw bomb in the Central Assembly on 8 April 1929. They wanted to protest against the passage of the Public Safety Bill, which would have reduced civil liberties. The bomb did not harm any one for it had been deliberately made harmless. The aim was not to kill but, as a terrorist leaflet put it, "to make the deaf hear."[5]

Bhagat Singh and B.K. Dutt could have easily escape after throwing the bomb but they deliberately choose to be arrested, for they wanted to make use of the court as a forum for revolutionary propaganda.

The Sikhs had old tradition to sacrifice their life for the welfare of India. Freedom was more precious than bonded human life. It was just like to defend humanism, to defend religion, to observe duty towards *Swadharma.* It was an answer to the exploitation of man by man. Defending humanity was a key to serve God, to protect religion, even paving the right way for martyrdom.[6]

Bhagat Singh had studied Communism and he had a dream to shape destination of India. He was humanist no doubt. What he had thought can be got in his following words, at the time of his trial, Bhagat Singh said, "revolution to him was not the cult of the bomb and pistol, but a total change of society culminating in the overthrow of both foreign and Indian Capitalism and establishment of the dictatorship of proletariat. Revolution is the inalienable right of mankind. Freedom is the imprescriptibly birth right of all. The labourer is the real sustainer of society. To the altar of the revolution, we have brought our youth has incense, for no sacrifice is too great for so a magnificent a cause. We are content. We await the advent of revolution."[7]

His life inspired our freedom fighters and leaders. It is irony that even during post independent India we could not be free from exploitation of man by man. Hence security of humanity must be fond out. The life and teachings of Bhagat Singh was fully centered at exploitation free Indian society. Exploiter should have no place in our society. Thinking on it seems better to begin with Bhagat Singh. No doubt, he is an ideal martyr. Bhagat Singh was a revolutionary and noted Sikh and was much influenced by experiment launched in Russia. He opined in September 1928 on behalf of H.S.R.A., "Apart from some individual converts to communism, and a few efforts at combining the old and the new in what came to be called 'Terro-Communism- the sheer weight of the established terrorists' tradition still prevented serious rethinking on matters like Hindu religiousity, individual terror and the cult of heroic self sacrifice by the few."[8]

The patriots, nationalist heroes of our motherland were very popular among the masses. The whole environment was full of sympathy. Nehru in his Autobiography mentioned in his following words," On the eve of the Congress session, a few element of resentment had crept in the execution of Bhagat Singh. The feeling was especially marked in North India and Karachi. Being itself in the North, had attracted large number of people from the Punjab."[9]

"It has increased our power for winning freedom for which Bhagat Singh and his comrades have tried", said Mahatma Gandhi.[10]

Our First Prime Minister, Pandit Jawaharlal Nehru also said, "Their magnificent courage and sacrifice has been an inspiration to the youth of India. They died so that India may live."[11]

Finally, it may be said, "their sacrifices accelerated the pace of Indian freedom movement. It was realized by the rulers and the leaders and to the large extent of the masses that solution of the Indian problem lies in the Indian independence at any costs. Their sacrifices exposed the barbarism and exploitation under the Raj. It also exposed the defects of the moderates' politics of Indian National Congress. It tried to save humanity at the extreme sacrifice of human life. So British right to rule over India was challenged by every country of the world."[12]

Lastly our respected valued the life of humanity through his last letter dated 22nd March 1931.

References

1. Sen, S.P.—*Dictionary of National Biography,* Vol.-1, p. 155.
2. Bipanchandra-*Modern India,* New Delhi, 197, p. 23.
3. Bipanchandra-*Ibid,* p. 23.
4. Bipanchandra-*Ibid,* p. 281.
5. Bipanchandra-*Ibid,* p. 282.
6. Kumar, Nirmal (Dr.)—*Sikhs in Indian National Movement—Their approaches, methods and Martyrdom,* PHC-2007 (to be published).
7. Sarkar Sumit—*Modern India,* New Delhi, 1975, p. 252.
8. Kumar, Nirmal (Dr.)—*Ibid* p. 3.
9. Nehru, J—*An Autobiography*—New Delhi.
10. Sen, S.P.–*op-cit,* p. 155.
11. Sen, S.P.—*op-cit,* p. 155.
12. Kumar, Nirmal—*op-cit*, p. 9.

6

Bhagat Singh's Ideology of Socialistic Communism

Dr. Ram Pande

Bhagat Singh 1907-1930 took political inspiration from Maharana Pratap, Chhatrapati Shivaji and Hari Singh Nalva while socio-economic philosophy's inspiration came from No Tax Movement of the Punjab i.e. to say *Pagri Sambhal Jatta*. In 1924, Bhagat Singh organized the Naujawan Bharat Sabha, with a view to mobilizing youth power against the British Government. The membership fee was Rs. one per annum. Soon 125 members had been enrolled. Addressing his young comrades at the first meeting, Bhagat Singh said, " Comrades, times has come for us to uproot the foundations of the foreign government. We have to put an end to the naked dance of hunger and unemployment in our land. You are the name-bearers of Rama and Krishna; you are the beloved (*piaras*) of Guru Gobind Singh. Adorn your heads with saffron turbans, as your brave Rajput ancestors did, and unshackle the chains of slavery of your motherland. As heroes like Maharana Pratap, Chhatrapati Shivaji, and Hari Singh Nalva had shed their blood in the past at the altar of the motherland, so does our motherland demand the sacrifice of the youth of today. Come forward, ye brave souls, to answer the agonizing call of your mother !" Hundreds of throats responded to his challenge with enthusiastic shouts of acclamation.[1]

B-424, Malviya Nagar. Jaipur.

Bhagat Singh came from a family of blue-blooded patriots. His father Kishan Singh and uncles Ajit Singh and Swaran Singh were great nationalists. In fact, Swaran Singh died in jail in 1908, soon after the birth of Bhagat Singh. Ajit Singh was deported to M'indalay (Burma) with Lala Lajpat Rai in the same year, when they mounted the 'No Tax movement' in the canal colonies of the Punjab. This movement gave birth to the famous revolutionary song: *Pagri sambhal jatta, pagri sambhal oye; Vairiyan nein lutt leya ajj tera mal oye, Khushali da daataa ho gaya haal behaal oye, pagri. ..* (Take care of your turban, oh! the tiller of the soil! enemies have looted your wealth; The giver of prosperity is today in a sad state of adversity. Take care.)

Thus Bhagat Singh was brought up in an atmosphere of intense national fervour.[2]

Naujawan Bharat Sabha was very active in carrying forward their message. In July 1928, at a meeting of some revolutionaries assembled in Jhansi, it was decided to summon a conference of representatives of all like-minded groups at Delhi, in September. This conference was held in the forest near Indraprastha, Delhi. It elected Chandra Shekhar Azad as its leader and accepted the proposal of Bhagat Singh to establish the *Hindostan Socialist Republic Association* and its action wing, *Hindostan Socialist Republican Army.*

The words 'socialist' and 'republican' may be noted, for they were to become the sheet anchors of the constitution of free India in time to come. The Army was to function under the Association, which had two categories of members: firstly, those who would devote themselves day and night to national tasks, and secondly, those who would help the Association by donations and supply of resources needed for active operations.

Terro-Communism

The Lahore and Kanpur groups of revolutionaries had started moving towards socialism in 1926-27. In Delhi meeting of

September 8, though socialism was accepted as the ideology and establishment of a socialist society as the ultimate aim of the party, in practice we stuck to our old individual style of actions. We talked of organizing the workers, peasants, youth and middle class intelligentsia; yet, except for the formation of Naujawan Bharat Sabha in Punjab, no serious effort was made in that direction anywhere else. In this regard, our understanding of scientific socialism, i.e. Marxism, was faulty. We failed to understand that Marxism does not permit the separation of theory from practice and that there is no place for individual actions in it. We hoped to combine violent activities, which included murder of tyrannical government officials and sporadic insurrections, with the building up of mass organizations of workers, peasants, youth, students. But, in practice, our main emphasis remained on preparations for violent activities and armed actions. This, we thought, was necessary for rousing the people from their slumber and also for retaliation against mass repression resorted to by the government. While talking to Comrade Sohan Singh Josh at Calcutta in December 1928, at the time of the Calcutta Session of the Congress, Bhagat Singh had said: "We entirely agree with the programme and activities of your party, but there are times when the blow of the enemy has to be immediately counteracted by armed actions to inspire confidence among the masses."[3] That is how our minds were working then. The inherent contradiction in our approach had its own logic. Our decision to organize the workers and peasants remained only a pious wish. The major part of our resources went in organizing retaliatory actions.

What kind of order would emerge after revolution? An answer to this question showed the extent of Bhagat Singh's understanding of the Marxist and socialist view of society and polity in the future. He envisaged a socialistic pattern of society for the liberated India. Injustice and exploitation would be replaced by liberty, equality and fraternity. *The Philosophy of the Bomb* delineated a bright picture of the future social order:

> '....it will usher in a new social order. The revolution will ring the death-knell of capitalism and class distinctions and privileges. It will bring joy and prosperity to the starving millions who are sweating today under the terrible yoke of both foreign and Indian exploitation. It will establish the dictatorship of the proletariat and will for ever banish social parasites from the seat of political power'.

Revolution would usher not only a new social order, but also establish a new co-relation of social, economic and political forces. In the future classless society, there would be sovereignty of the people and "establishment of dictatorship of the proletariat,"[5] which was considered as the ultimate goal of revolution. In order to realize their dream, Bhagat Singh and his friends made efforts to bring about a revolution which would end exploitation of man by man, as the leaflet, circulated after Saunders' 'murder' on 17 December 1928, proclaimed. Their commitment to socialism was reiterated in the pink leaflet, scattered after the Assembly Bomb Action. [6] 'The idea of a socialist society had been floated earlier by the Hindustan Republican Association in the *Revolutionary*, 1925. This pamphlet had suggested a few measures such as nationalization of railways, other means of transport and communication and of large scale industries such as steel and ship-building.[7] Such stray suggestions, however, don't prove that the leadership of the Hindustan Republican Association had grasped the principles of socialism. Later, Bejoy Kumar Sinha, an associate, of Bhagat Singh hailed him as a "crusader for the socialist causes."[8]

A great deal of intensive study of Socialism became an important factor in the development of Bhagat Singh's ideology. He made a serious study of books on the theories of socialism, economics and revolution. J.N. Sanyal, a close associate of

Bhagat Singh in the revolutionary struggle and the latter's first biographer, regarded him as "an extremely well-read man".[9]

Step by Step Towards Socialism

Bhagat Singh himself had explained this "we moved towards socialism step by step, and it was only after our arrests that we got enough time and material to read, discuss, ponder over our past and come to correct conclusions". This, however, does not mean that the period under review had nothing positive to its credit. There were weak points of course, but there were strong points as well. I have already explained the main defects in our understanding. To recount them in brief: firstly, our acceptance of communism was not based on a proper study of Marxism. Under the conditions prevailing in our country at the time, such a study of Marxism was not so easy either. Our second main weakness was our failure to realize the impracticability of reconciling counter-terrorism with the work of organizing the workers and peasants. With all these shortcomings and limitations, the short-lived phase under review had some very important positive achievements to its credit. The Manifesto of the *Naujawan Bharat Sabha*. Lahore (1928), the Statement made by Bhagat Singh and B.K. Dutt during the Assembly Bomb Case trial (1929), the Manifesto of the HSRA distributed at the time of Lahore Session of the Congress (December 1929), and *The Philosophy of the bomb* (January 1930) are the best representative documents of this period. On the basis of these documents, we can say that the first major step forward taken by the HSRA was the acceptance of Marxism as its ideology and socialism as the ultimate goal of the movement. In Bengal too, the direction of the movement was the same, though the march was comparatively slow. It may be noted that while HSRA had publicly declared socialism as its goal, in Bengal almost all the major parties and groups were still undecided on the subject.[10]

To Scientific Socialism

By the middle of 1929, a majority of the leading comrades of HSRA were arrested and put in jail, where they got full opportunity to read and discuss. In the light of their new understanding, they subjected their entire past to renewed scrutiny, especially the idea of individual actions and heroism, and finally decided to abandon it in favour of the idea of a socialist revolution. After intensive studies and prolonged discussions with other comrades in Borstal Jail, Bhagat Singh came to the conclusion that individual killings of informers and officers here and there would not lead to realization of the goal.[11]

Summing Up

It is a travesty of truth and a cruel joke on the people of India to say that the Indian Revolution was non-violent, and bloodless. True, that the British overlords were allowed to depart peacefully and even with honours and pensions *et al.* True, that we did not enact the *tragic fates* of Louis XVI, Czar Nicholas II. But come to calculate the price paid by Indian masses, common men and women, unsuspecting innocent children, old and young, the price was enormous, perhaps more than ever paid by any country seeking Independence. Not all the oceans of the Earth can wash the blood-stained hands of those who sought to emulate Halaku and Changez Khan (both heathens) to kill the disbelievers, and brought about a virtual civil war in India.

While the unprotected masses suffered, the instigators sat smug in their high and palatial towers, watching the satanic and cruel drama and the death dance being enacted by their credulous followers and subjects in the heat and frenzy of the moment. The diabolic deeds committed by them under the influence of self-seeking politicians were a disgrace to humanity and not sanctioned by any religion.[12]

The *Vedas* enjoin upon mankind to look upon all living beings with a friendly eye as one's own self. The *Quran* commands the followers of Islam not to deviate from the path of righteousness and to safe-guard the culture and rights of the non-Muslims living amongst them. The *Granth Sahib* says' all are descended from the same Divine Light. Who then is good or bad?' In the erstwhile Christian colonial state of India, differences between communities grew or were created and encouraged according to a set policy. The legacy left by the colonial state still haunts this benighted land, this *madare-watan* (motherland) of ours, on both sides of the Radcliffe Line, even in the post-colonial era, as self-centred Brown Sahibs educated in the Macaulay tradition and men with a myopic vision have hijacked the Indian Revolution and have come to hold the reins of power, while the lot of the masses below the poverty line remains unchanged, though theoretically they are the sovereign authority.

Did Bhagat Singh and his comrades of the *Hindostan Socialist Republican Association* mount the gallows for this? Did Ashfaqullah and Hari Kishan court martyrdom for this?

There is a Vedic mantra which says: 'Do not grieve over the death of the hero fallen in the battle-field. Pick up his bow and complete his unfinished task'. How can we rest so long as Bhagat Singh's task remains unfulfilled? The grinding poverty and dismal lives of a sizeable majority of the children of lesser gods pose a challenge to the youth of our two nations.

Bhagat Singh had nicknamed his sweeper and scavenger in the jail as his *baybay* because he used to do the same dirty work as his mother (*baybay*) used to do when Bhagat was a baby, viz, remove his excreta. When the jailor asked Bhagat Singh what his last wish was, Bhagat Singh desired to eat a *roti* made by his jail *baybay*. The *bhangi baybay* was astounded. 'How can this be, *huzoor*? I am an untouchable. I do the dirty work.' Bhagat Singh smiled and said: 'My mother also used to do the same dirty work. She did not become an untouchable for that reason. I ate *rotis* made by her.' The *bhangi* made the *roti* and Bhagat Singh ate it with his usual relish and playfulness.

This was Bhagat Singh's last Will and Testament, his *Wasiyatnama*.

This is the *Shahadat-nama* written in the blood of a long caravan of martyrs in the course of their glorious struggle for the attainment of:

1. Justice, social and economic and political,
2. Liberty of thought and expression, belief and faith,
3. Equality of status and opportunity, and to promote among all and,

Fraternity, assuring the dignity of the Individual and the unity of the Nation, (*as enshrined in our Constitution*)

References

1. Bhupendra Hooja (ed.), *A Martyr's Note Book*, Jaipur 1994, p.VIII, XII.
2. *Ibid.*
3. Punjab Conspiracy case papers (NAI) Rules and Regulations of the Hindustan Socialist Republic Association.
4. Ibid.
5. Delhi Court Papers- Assembly Bomb case Trial No. 9 of 1929 Vol. 2nd p. 145.
6. Kamlesh Mohan, *Bhagat Singh- The Man and his* Ideology, Chandigarh, p. 16.
7. Manmath Nath Gupta, *Bhartiya Krantikari Andolan Ka Itihas*, Delhi, 1960, p. 44.
8. Shiv Verma, *From Chapekars to Bhagat Singh*, Delhi, 1986, p. 26.
9. L.P. Mathur, *Indian Revolutionary Movement in United States of America*, New Delhi, 1970, p. 126, also *Shodhak*, Vol., 1, Pt. B, of 1972.
10. Bhupendra Hooja, No.1.
11. Shiv Verma, No.8.
12. G.B. Kumar Hooja, *Shahadatnama-A Saga of Martyrs*, Jaipur, 2001, p. 154-155.

7

Bhagat Singh's Ideas as Reflected in Contemporary Records

Zakir Husain, Archivist (OR)

Interestingly enough much has been said and written about Bhagat Singh, the well known freedom fighter, who is also credited for launching *Risala Kirti* in 1925 to give vent to pent up national feelings as its August 1928 issue published a poem by Rajindranath Lahiri saying that.

'we are ready to hang from the gallows for the nation. We give our blood to water the plant of liberty so that it may remain fresh and ever green.[1]

Bhagat Singh became the member of the Central Committee of the *Hindustan Socialist Republican Army* wherein he served as the link between the Provinces. *"Bhagat Singh was also asked to abandon his home and have his heir and beard and moustaches cut"* and he was known by him pseudonyms to its members as Ranjit.[2] Although Bhagat Singh's name came into prominence when Lala Lajpat Rai the famous leader of the Indian National Congress, received slight injuries (It is British version in Their reports-ed.) yet the agitation arising due to Lala's death from heart failure British version in the seports at Lahore on November,17th (1928) had largely overshadowed other events.[3] As a sequel to this incident the telegram from the Punjab Government dated 17th December,

---

National Archives, New Delhi-1.

1928 to Home Department at New Delhi reported that "Saunders, Assistant Superintendent Police was shot down and killed by two youths.[4] In this connection it was also reported that Bhagat Singh's house in Lahore was also searched and his 12 year younger brother was arrested.[5]

Consequent upon the murder of J.P. Saunders on 17th December, 1928 the posters clearly *stipulated that a revenge for Lala Lajpat Rai was taken.*[6] The posters lamented that the *respected leader of 30 crore people was attacked by J.P. Saunders, an ordinary police officer and his ignoble hands caused (Lalaji's) death. Now the world has seen that the Indian people are not dead. Their blood is not cold. They can sacrifice themselves for the pride of the country. The young have proved this....*

The police FIR contained Bhagat Singh's name as a leading convict. Furthermore the tall man who fired at Saunders "seems to have considerably improved...suspicion hardening that Bhagat Singh arrested in the Assembly was a party to Saunders murder".[7] In view of Bhagat Singh's ideas the two men (Bhagat Singh and Batukeshvar Dutta) made no attempt whatsoever to escape or offer resistance.... Bhagat Singh claimed that they were responsible.[8] It was but natural that they did not appear disturbed together with the bombs, leaflets, pamphlets to the 'notices' by the Hindustan Socialist Republican Party.[9] It was alleged that Bhagat Singh and Dutta were in touch with the group that run the *Hindustan Times* very shortly before the date of outrage.[10]

The ideas of Bhagat Singh can be gauged from the poster which clearly stipulated that there is need of a loud voice for the deaf. Through the Indian public we want to stress on this historically oft repeated lesson that it is easy to kill anyone but you can not eradicate his ideas. History is a witness (to the fact) that great empires perished while thought and ideas survived...The sacrifice of people is must on the altar of the great revolution so as to give freedom to everyone and make the human exploitation impossible.

When the proceedings started in the Session Court, then Bhagat Singh argued that he did not want to kill anyone. He further said that we are not lagging behind anyone in loving the humanity. Not to speak of personal vengeance we consider human life so pious which can not be narrated in words. He also clarified his purpose of throwing the bomb that we have dropped the bomb to register our protest on behalf of those who had no other means left to give expression to their heart-rending agony. Bhagat Singh also said the whole edifice of this civilization not saved in time shall crumble. A radical change is necessary and it is the duty of those who realize this to reorganize the Society on the Socialist basis. Our purpose was to listen to the deaf and awaken the careless before time. This statement praised the revolution and violence saying that, we are offering our youth-hood as objects of worship at the altar of the revolution because no sacrifice is great for such a great idea.[11] The English were cunning enough that they even tried to make sense of the remarks made by Kishan Singh to his son Bhagat Singh.[12] One can easily imagine the revolutionary ideas which Bhagat Singh had in mind that when he entered the court of the Additional District Magistrate, Delhi he shouted *'Long Live Revolution'* and *'Down with Imperialism.*[13] Although reports on the continuing threats to officials and non-officials by the Hindustan Socialist Republican Army began, saying *"that from the 1st June (1929) throughout India a war to avenge 1857 would begin, and after that there would be no more British rule"*, [14] yet it seems to be an echo of Bhagat Singh's ideas.

Bhagat Singh's boldness was such that both he and Dutt remained smiling and laughing throughout the Proceedings.[15] It was probably because of the manifesto by the Hindustan Socialist Republican Association saying that violence is physical force applied for committing injustice, that is certainly not what the revolution stand for...We shall have our revenge....people's righteous revenge on the Tyrant...Ours is war to the end to victory or death.[16] Bhagat Singh everyday from 4th to 7th and 9th June, 1929 shouted 'Long Live the Revolution.[17] However, the judge took lenient view on 12th June 1929 saying that "the accused are young men... Their youth must not be allowed to lead to an inadequate punishment". They were sentenced to transportation for life.[18] However, Bhagat Singh was conscious enough about his political rights, he sent an application dated 17th June, 1929 from Mianwali Jail to the Inspector General, Punjab, Lahore, saying, I must get special treatment as a political prisoner. Moreover he also demanded among others literature of all kind (History, Economics, Political Science, Poetry, Drama or Fiction, Newspapers). Bhagat Singh also indulged in hunger strike and claimed the same rights as is allowed for the political prisoners.

Interestingly, along with the common man those leaders of the Indian National Congress who were in total disagreement with Bhagat Singh's ideas began to support him. When there was discussion in the Central Assembly on 29th September, 1929 then Pandit Moti Lal Nehru praised him by designating him as a respectable great soul.[19] Pandit Madan Mohan Malviya said that 'he is such a person who has utmost patriotism and the desire of the independence of the country. He is a man of high ideas. However, Mohammad Ali Jinnah emerged on top as side by side declaring the hunger strike as legal he said that the hunger striker is a spiritual one. He is not a cruel and ignoble ordinary criminal. Jinnah criticizing the Governments's carelessness remarked that, I am sorry that either right or wrong today's youth is vigorous, you may condemn them as much or you may blame them that they have become strayed. It is due to the system. I am unable to understand the expeditiousness of the Government to settle the case. This person is imposing maximum possible punishment upon himself.[20]

'*Tribune*' on July 12th, 1929 reported in full the letter by Bhagat Singh and Dutt for better facilities in jail as these were the most reasonable demands,[21] Bhagat Singh refused to give up strike.[22] The 'public sympathy with the strikers was increasing and was manifest in quarters where it was not expected, This sympathy is not confined to the Punjab...The Lahore situation is arousing great public interests all over India.[23] It is reported in the *Times of India* that the Youth Movement continue to be a source of danger.[24] Congress true to its reputation of having double speaking policy in its Lahore Congress Session condemned the Delhi 'Bomb Outrage...(and) young revolutionaries who opposed the resolution. *Times of India* further remarked on 28th December 1929 that "if the cult of the Bomb was not praised little or no attempt was made to condemn it".[25] Bhagat Singh in such trying circumstances not only maintained his mental equilibrium but also enjoyed the luxuries of life *viz*., he solicited a tin of *ghee*, oranges and *rasgullas*[26]. Bhagat Singh maintained a diary in Jail extracts of which included his favourite readings from Tagore. Wordsworth, Tennyson, Victor-Hugo, Karl Marx, Lenin etc.[27]

Despite a letter found with Sukhdev Singh which spoke of the motivations behind the acts of revolutionaries.[28] Bhagat Singh together with his two colleagues was sentenced to death. However, quite contrary to Government expectations a fortnightly intelligence report for Punjab for the period ending 15th October, 1930 said that 'What appears to arouse the popular indignation to the greatest extent is sentence of death passed on Bhagat Singh whose 'sacrifice' for the national cause has been publicly extolled as an example to be followed by the patriotic youth of India".[29] The processions "expressing approval or sympathy with the convicts sentenced to death....." were to be banned.[30] In view of Bhagat Singh's appreciation for his ideas even numerous Hindu and Muslim residents of Punjab thus began praying (to the Viceroy) that the death sentence passed upon Sardar Bhagat Singh... may be commuted.[31] Even Bhagat Singh's mother's appeal to the Governor General to commute her son's death sentence proved futile[32] like her request to meet her son'[33] Similar effort were made by Bhagat Singh Appeal Committees and all regarded Bhagat Singh as a national hero.[34]

Since Bhagat Singh's ideas and his sacrifice had a deep impact the *Daily Worker,* New York, in a news items, London, dated March 24th, reported that the three Lahore prisoners—Bhagat Singh, Raj Guru and Sukhdev, fighters for the independence of India have been executed...in the interest of British imperialism.[35] That is why the general belief that Bhagat Singh was innocent in the British perception might 'do great harm if it gained wide currency in England and America and simultaneously suggested that the Commissioner to get in personal touch, with the American Correspondent present in Karachi (for the Congress Section).[36] Subsequent to agitation. processions and appeals Bhagat Singh's letter addressed to the Government was published saying that, "We are political prisoners. We should be given the same treatment as prisoners of war. Soldiers of the nation are not hanged. Government can sent army sepoys to the jail to shoot us down.[37] A fortnightly intelligence report for Punjab says that *Baisakhi Day,* April 13, was utilized by *the Naujawan Bharat Sabha* for organized glorification of Bhagat Singh.[38] Subhash Chandra Bose remarked today he (Bhagat Singh) is known to be a brave Sikh hero throughout the world.[39] Sikh community has to produce hundred thousand of Bhagat Singh for the cause of the country. Today Bhagat Singh is not a man but he has become a symbol of revolutionary spirit which is spread throughout the country. Sukhdev's letter to Gandhiji published in the '*Young India*' clearly says that by his repeated advice to the revolutionaries to stop their activities he is strengthening the hands of the Government in suppressing them. He (Gandhiji) should know that even the hearts of the revolutionaries there is a desire for the freedom of their country such ideas are clearly influenced from Bhagat Singh's thoughts.[40]

An officer of the secret agency frankly called the sacrifices of Bhagat Singh for the patriots to serve as a means of inspiration to the Home Department of the Government of India.[41] Even Bhagat Singh stressed that till the establishment of socialist society this struggle shall be continued more vigorously.[42] Bhagat Singh even imagined the shape of things to come and he visualized the facts more confidently than was excepted which would ultimately bring him to gallows.[43] Bhagat Singh was such a visionary who thought that he was going to be sacrificed for the country which was the heightest reward for him. He said that the British could kill him but they could not crush his spirit. He thought that the British Government shall be compelled to leave India due to his ideas and that the dead Bhagat Singh shall be more dangerous than the living Bhagat Singh as his death shall spread the fragrance of his revolutionary ideas which shall inspire the youth for freedom and revolution.[44] The tragedy was however forgotten the symbol remained. Although much inspiration has been drawn by the poets from his sacrifice yet Bhagat Singh himself drew inspiration from Allama Sir Mohammad Iqbal's poetry as he has specifically quoted his couplet in his letter which proved correct for him.

Koi din ka mehman hun ai ahle mehfil,
Chirag-I sahar hun bujha chahta hun.[45]

Josh Malihabadi poetically referred to his sacrifice thus :

Woh Bhagat Singh jis ke gham mein dil nashad hai
Uski garden mein jo dala tha who phanda yad hai

Perhaps the soil collected by Smt. Ralla Thapa, Mother of Sukhdev from the cremation site of Bhagat Singh, Raj Guru and Sukhdev available at the National Archives, New Delhi is still an enigma[46] because they had been secretly hanged in Central Jail. Bhagat Singh was such a popular figure that even his latter years have been described by Maulana Mohammad Ishaq Bhatti on the strength of the information derived by him from those who were contemporaneous to these events.[47] A book based on proscribed literature regarding Bhagat Singh also contains a poem of Akhtar Sherani, because as more than 100 poems were banned by the British Government in various Indian languages 63 of which were in Urdu and Hindi.[48]

Notes & References

1. *Risala Kirti,* August 1928 (included in Punjab Conspiracy Papers, donated by Mr. D.R. Handa to the National Archives of India.
2. *Proceedings of the Lahore Conspiracy case,* 1930, Crown V/s Bhagat Singh and others, Part-I.
3. *Home Poll.* F.No. 1/1928, October 1928.
4. *Home Poll.* F.No. 4/7-1930.
5. *Abhyudaya,* 4 April, 1929.
6. See Malvinderjit Singh Vadich and Gurdev Singh Siddhu (eds), The *Hanging of Bhagat Singh.* See page 199 for the contents of the poster.
7. *Home Poll.* F.NO. 4/7-1930.
8. *Home Poll.* F.No. 192/1929.
9. *Jayakar Papers,* Vol. 77.
10. *Home Poll.* F.NO. 192/1929. It is not however, surprising that Bhagat Singh was such a revolutionary who very well knew the importance of the press as he himself had started a weekly magazine to spread these ideas through his *Risala Kirti.* The *Hindustan Times* sided with the freedom fighters in their bid to free the country from the British yoke. However, side by side, Maulana Azad's *Al-hilal* and Muhammad Ali Jahar's *Comrade* spearheaded this national movement through their Urdu and English weekly magazines.
11. A.G. Noorani, *The Trial of Bhagat Singh.* p. 34.
12. *Home* Poll. F. No. 192/1929. Assembly Bomb Case No. 9, 1929, Crown V/s Bhagat Singh, Dutta Vol. II/VII, Acc No. NAI-306 P.A.
13. *Abhyudaya,* 11th May, 1929.
14. *Abhyudaya,* 18th May, 1929.
15. *Ibid.*
16. *History of Freedom Movement,* Unit Papers's R III 6/3 Ent No.p/
17. *Home Poll.* F.No. 192/1929.
18. *Assembly Bomb Case* No. 9 of 1929, Crown V/s Bhagat Singh.

19. *Central Assembly Debate Part* 4 No. 9 page-1.
20. *Natinal Archieves 'Home Poll.* F.No. 4/36/1931.
21. Home Poll. F.No. K.W. to 244/1930.
22. Abhyudaya 3rd August 1929.
23. *Home Poll.* F.No. 242/1929.
24. *Home Poll.* F.No. 17 of October, 1929.
25. *Jaykar Papers,* (Press Clippings), Vol. 63.
26. Photocopy of the letter received from Shri Kulbir Singh younger brother of Bhagat Singh.
27. NAI-7422 photocopy of the extracts of the diary of Bhagat Singh.
28. *Home Poll.* F.No. 139 October, 1931.
29. *Home Poll.* F.No. 18/XI October, 1930.
30. *Home Poll.* F.No. 4/21/1931.
31. *Home Judicial* F.No. 152/1/1931-KW.
32. *Ibid.*
33. *Ibid.*
34. *Home Poll.* F.No. 4/20/1931.
35. *Home Poll.* F.No. 9/XI/1931 K.W.
36. *Home Poll.* F.No. 4/21/1931.
37. *Abhyudaya,* 25 March, 1931.
38. *Home Poll.* F.No. 18/IV/April 1931.
39. *Home Poll.* F.No. 143/1931.
40. *Abhyudaya* 20th April, 1931.
41. Home Poll. F.No. 18/3 Weekly Report, No. 2 dated 24.3.1931.
42. Widech & Siddhu; op cit, p. 237.
43. Shiv Verma *"Documents of Bhagat Singh and his Colleagues"* eds. Jagmohan Singh, Chaman Lal, p. 48.
44. *Phansi Lahore Ki,* ed. Gurudev Singh Siddhu, NBT New Delhi, 2007.
45. Bhagat Singh's affectionate letter to his younger brother.
46. *Yadon Ki Barat*, 1972.
47. *Abhyudaya,* 25th March 1931. If we believe in the story that a Jail servant secreteries brought the mother of Sukhdev inside the jail for collecting the same then this riddle can be solved.
48. *Phansi Lahore Ki,* ed. Gurudev Singh Siddhu.

8

History of Naujawan Bharat Sabha : Some Misconceptions

Dr. Chander Pal Singh

Being one of the most loved sons India has produced, Bhagat Singh is a much written about figure. A close look at the available literature reveals that his short life of 23 years has not been fully explored. There are many gaps in the available chronology of Bhagat Singh's life. His biographers ascribe at least eight different dates to his birth. Dictionary of National Biography concludes that exact date of his birth is not known. Similarly, there is no consensus on chronology of some of important events in Bhagat Singh's life such as his departure to Kanpur; his work as a journalist in newspapers such as 'Pratap', 'Akali', and 'Arjun'; his coming back to Lahore; reception of Akali Jattha in his village; his stint as headmaster in a national school etc.

Similar lacunae are present in the current history writing on Naujawan Bharat Sabha which occupies an important place in Bhagat Singh's career. He was its founder Secretary and remained in that position till September - October 1928. Here certain misconceptions have been wrongly accepted as facts and have gone uncontested so far in the literature on Bhagat Singh:

1. Naujawan Bharat Sabha was established in March 1926.
2. Ramkrishna was the first President of Naujawan Bharat Sabha.
3. Kirti group had a smooth relationship with the Bhagat Singh group in the Sabha.

All the recent works on Bhagat Singh have taken up the position that Naujawan Bharat Sabha (hereafter NBS) was founded in March 1926. Source of this flawed information can be traced of two reports from the Punjab Government to Home Department dated 21st March 1929 and 2nd August 1929, respectively. These reports have another flow as well. They do not give the credit of establishing NBS to Bhagat Singh and others of National College Lahore but to Dr. Satya Pal. Absurdity of this fact was pointed out by R.B. Bhagwan Das, a senior intelligence officer. D. Petrie, Director of Intelligence Bureau upheld the opinion of Bhagwan Das.

March 1926 as the date of formation of NBS is not acceptable to Bhagat Singh's colleagues in NBS. Comrade Ramchandra (1903-1997), who was the founder member of NBS as well as its second President, has dealt with the problem of date of foundation of NBS in the following words:

"Some uniformed people have made many wrong statements about this. There is no record of the Sabha available too. From my memory and connected events of that time I say that it was formed towards the end of 1924. Chhabil Dass too agrees with this timing. I have come across a file in the...... National Archives ..... It is Home Political File No. 27/5 of 1931".

"This is a file in which the English translation of the speeches of political workers prosecuted under Section 124-A is given ...This is the speech I delivered on May 17, 1931 at Ganj Mandi, Rawalpindi, on return from Peshawar, I earned prosecution for it".

"In my speech I had said that Naujawan Bharat Sabha was established seven years back. This comes to 1924".

At another place Ram Chandra wrote that NBS was founded in 1924-25. Principal Chhabil Dass (1900-1988), who himself was one of the founder members of NBS as well as Principal of National College, was also of the opinion that NBS was formed around 1924. Though these statements do create some ambiguity but they definitely take the date of formation of NBS to well before 1926. It is more plausible to accept early 1925 as time when NBS was created because Bhagat Singh in the last part of 1924 was in Delhi, working with 'Arjun' and on 1st January 1925 he helped to distribute the pamphlet Revolutionary. 1925 as the year of formation of NBS is also attested by Ajay Ghosh, Gopal Thakur and Dictionary of National Biography.

Second misconception is about the first President of the Sabha. Guru Dev Singh Deol , Virendra Sindhu and Manmath Nath Gupta have named Ramakrishna as the first President of the sabha. But Punjab Government's letter to Home Department, dated 21 May 1929, very plainly gives the name of first President of NBS as Gurudutt Singh. Gurudutt at that time was headmaster in National School in Lahore. During the Non-Cooperation Movement he was expelled from Government College where he was a demonstrator in chemistry. Gurudutt has written about his tenure as the first President of NBS in his own memoirs. Comrade Ramchandra has also discussed him in detail. He continued as the President till 1926. Gurudutt's place was taken by comrade Ramchandra . Ramchandra was arrested on 1 August 1927 . Thereafter Ramkrishna was elected as the President of NBS, Lahore . Turning to Provincial NBS, Kedar Nath Sehgal was the first President (since April 1928) Sohan Singh Josh was elected as President of the Provincial NBS on 24 February 1929 . But he could work in that position for hardly a month when he was arrested on 20 March 1929 in

Meerut Conspiracy Case . It was then that Ram Krishna was elected as the president of the provincial NBS in place of Josh. on 30th March 1929.

An important event in the history of NBS was its association with Kirti group. The conflict between the two groups has not yet been explored. Kirti group had its origins in the defunct Gadar Party in USA. Russian Revolution (1917) had revived the hopes of its surviving leaders. With the active help of communist International, Santokh Singh, Bhag Singh Canadian, Karan Singh Cheema and Rattan Singh found Kirti Kisan party. Santokh Singh started 'Kirti' as party's mouth piece in Punjabi in February 1926. To begin with, Kirti group wanted to take part in the youth movement. But they did not have the requisite programme, cadre and experience.

On the other hand NBS had definite aims, objection and political experience. It had an experienced and committed leadership. Thus NBS presented a readymade platform of youth movement. Association with the Kirtis suited the Sabha too, NBS was short of funds and also it lacked a mouth piece. Kirtis were flush with funds from Communist International and Gadar party.

As a result, both NBS and Kirtis came together to work under a single organisation. They held their first Provincial NBS Conference in Jallianwala Bagh on April 13 and 14, 1928. As a compromise Kirti group adopted the name, Naujawan Bharat Sabha. Original NBS faction (Bhagat Singh group) agreed to slightly modify their objective from 'achievement of complete independence by all possible means' to achievement of a completely independent sovereign socialist republic of peasants and workers by all possible means.

But the relationship between the two factions was not smooth and there was continuous internal struggle for control of the organization. According to a Punjab Government report "the Kirti group showed some reluctance at first to finance or trust the Sabha unless the Kirti group could assume complete control of it, and these differences took expression in the successive moves of the head quarters from Amritsar to Lahore and back to Amritsar. This phase ended with the election of the new executive of the Sabha on the 24th February 1929 when the Kirti group came to the top with predominance on the executive. S.S. Josh becoming President, M.A. Mazid Vice-President and Hari Singh Chakwalia, Secretary".

Bhagat Singh group maintained a separate identity. Sohan Singh Josh has elaborated on the ideological differences between the Bhagat Singh group (which he calls as minority trend) and the Kirti group (majority Marxist trend). Main difference between the two groups as pointed out by Josh was that Kirti group lay emphasis on organization of peasants and workers, while "Bhagat Singh wanted to do something very quick, through the use of bombs and pistols, in order to politically awaken the slumbering youth". Josh went on to point out the limitations of Bhagat Singh and his group's ideology:

"Such thoughts and line of action immensely appealed to the immature youth. But these are bookish revolutionary knowledge ....Transplanting of revolutionary conditions of one country to another with different situation generally results in disaster."

Government kept a close watch on working of both groups in Naujawan Bharat Sabha. Fortnightly report of February 1929 noted that "weakness of this combination lies in the reluctance of the workers and peasants party to finance the youth movement".

Inherent differences between the Kirti group and Naujawan Bharat Sabha took a turn for worse during the Karachi session of Congress in March 1931. Karachi session of Congress was being held six days after the hanging of Bhagat Singh, Sukhdev and Rajguru. Gandhiji was under fire from youth leaders for not being able to save the lives of Bhagat Singh, Sukhdev and Rajguru. NBS also held its conference at the same venue at the same time and Subhash Bose was invited to preside it. Kirti group used this occasion to create disturbances during the proceedings and to denounce the national leadership. This was against Sabha's policy. Real reason behind Kirti group's irresponsible behaviour was the instruction from the Communist International. Sixth Congress of the Communist International had made a decision that there should be no joint front with any bourgeoisie party in the liberation struggles, as it held the possibility of betrayal at a crucial Stage. Guided by these resolutions of Communist International, Indian Communists declared Indian National Congress to be a class party of the bourgeoisie and broke all connections from it. Kirti group persuaded a number of Sabha workers at Karachi to present black flowers to Gandhiji. They were also able to circulate a manifesto on behalf of the Sabha, by clandestine methods, which used intemperate language against National leaders. Kirti elements also did not permit Madan Mohan Malviya to speak who was invited on behalf of the Naujawan Bharat Sabha. This unruly behaviour of Kirtis' was condemned by the Presiding chair, Subhas Bose, that foreign unruly elements had disrupted the meeting.

References

1. Home Political File, 130&K.W., 1930.
2. Ibid.
3. Comrade Ram Chandra, Naujawan Bharat Sabha and HSRA, published by the author, New Delhi, 2003, pp. 18-19.
4. Comrade Ramchandra, Ideology and Battle Cries of Indian Revolutionaries, Published by the author, New Delhi, 1989, p. i, 228.
5. Transcript of Chhabil Dass's interview, Nehru Memorial Museum and Library, New Delhi, p. 21.
6. Satya Ketu Vidyalankar (ed.), Arya Samaj Ka Itihas, Vol. VI, 1987, pp. 56-57; the pamphlet 'Revolutionary' dated 1 January, 1925 was

distributed all over India on I January 1925. (H.W.Hale, Political Trouble in India (1917-37), Chugh Publications, Allahabad, p. 196.

7. Gopal Thakur, Bhagat Singh: Man and His Ideas, People's Publishing House, New Delhi, 1953, p.4; Dictionary of National Biography, p. 155.

8. G.S.Deol, Shaheed Bhagat Singh a Biography, Publication Bureau, Punjabi University, Patiala, 1985, p. 25.

9. Virender Sindhu, Yugdrista Bhagat Singh Aur Unke Mritunjayayee Purkhe, Rajpal, New Delhi, 2004, p. 151.

10. Manmathnath Gupta, Bhagat Singh and His Times, Lipi Prakashan, Delhi, 1977, p. 103.

11. Born in 1901, in District Jhang (now in Pakistan), graduated from National College, Lahore. He became a Communist later. He died in early 1930s in central Asia.

12. Home Political File, 130&K.W., 1930.

13. Gurudutt, Bhav Aur Bhavana, Sashwat Vani, New Delhi, 2000, p. 81.

14. Comrade Ram Chandra, Naujawan Bharat Sabha and HSRA, Published by the author, New Delhi, 2003, p. 20.

15. According to Gurudutt, he resigned from Presidentship a little before the closure of national school. National School closed in 1926.

16. Comrade Ram Chandra, Naujawan Bharat Sabha and HSRA, Published by the author, New Delhi, 2003, p.20; Home Political File, 130&K.W., 1930.

17. Comrade Ram Chandra, Naujawan Bharat Sabha and HSRA, Published by the author, New Delhi, 2003, p. 37.

18. Ibid, p. 186.

19. Home Political File, 130&K.W., 1930.

20. Challenge: A Saga of India's Struggle For Freedom, PPH, New Delhi,1984, p. 337.

21. Home Political File, 130&K.W., 1930.

22. "Kirti asserted an urgent need to have some kind of militant organization based on mass movement. But what should be the nature of the organization, what kind of programmes should it put forward and towards What (which) social classes should it orientate its political activities? Not to speak of any attempt to answer such questions, they were not even being posed during that period (1926-27). The new vision was more like a dream rather than a concrete perspective suggesting ways and means to launch anti-imperialist

Struggles."(Bhagwan Josh, communist Movement in Punjab, Anupama Publication, 1979, p. 42.

23. Comrade Ram Chandra, Naujawan Bharat Sabha and HSRA, p. 40.

24. Home Political File, 130&K.W., 1930.

25. Sohan Singh Josh, My Tryst With Secularism, Patriot, New Delhi, 1991, p. 133.

26. Ibid.

27. Comrade Ram Chandra, Naujawan Bharat Sabha and HSRA, p. 77.

28. Bipan Chandra, India's Struggle for Independence, Penguin, Delhi, 1989, p. 302.

29. Comrade Ram Chandra, Naujawan Bharat Sabha and HSRA, pp. 171-72.

30. Ibid, p. 172.

9

Call to the youth

Dr. Shyamala Bhatia

When twenty three years old Bhagat singh sacrificed his life for the country, he became immortal, earning for himself the euphemism 'shaheed'. He became the symbol of determination of Indians to 'do and die' for the independence of the motherland. He himself understood the significance of his action and wrote "my name has become the symbol of Hindustani revolution and ideals". Other freedom fighters also agreed. Paying his tribute to him at a meeting of the Central Sikh League at Amritsar on 8 April 1931, Subhash Chandra Bose said, "Bhagat Singh who set an example of character and patriotism by sacrificing himself for the sake of the country's freedom, was from the Sikh community". Today, he is known to be a brave Sikh hero throughout the world. The Sikh community has to produce thousands of Bhagat Singh's for the cause of the country".

Bhagat Singh had been charged with the crime of killing a British officer who had been shot dead by the revolutionaries in retaliation of brutal lathi charge on Lala Lajpat Rai that had led to the old freedom fighter's death. While the people were still admiring the daring deed, Bhagat Singh and his comrades enacted another bold drama. A bomb was thrown in the assembly, which was in session to discuss important bills, and

Associate Professor, Dept. of History Bharti College, University Of Delhi, Delhi.

when the smoke cleared the young men, Bhagat Singh, along with his comrade brother stood fearless, openly challenging the imperialists to arrest and punish them. They gave a notice to the colonial government, "It takes a loud voice to make the deaf hear, with these immortal words uttered on a similar occasion by Valiant, a French anarchist martyr, and do we strongly justify this action of ours." They also threw down leaflets challenging the Imperialists and urging the Indian leaders, "Let the representatives of the people return to their constituencies and prepare the masses for the coming revolution, and let the Government know that while protesting against the Public Safety and Trade Disputes Bills and the callous murder of Lala Lajpat Rai, on behalf of the helpless Indian masses, we want to emphasize the lesson often repeated by history, that it is easy to kill individuals but you cannot kill the ideas Great empires crumbled while the ideas survived. Bourbons and Czars fell. While the revolution marched ahead triumphantly."

They were awarded capital punishment for daring to challenge an exploitative, repressive colonial government. The British got panicky, gave up the charade of "law and justice", and hurriedly convicting Bhagat Singh for Saundars murder, pronounced death sentence for him with his comrades' brothers. Bhagat Singh, Rajguru and Sukhdev were hanged on 23rd march 1931 in Lahore Central jail. Bhagat singh died, but he left indelible footprints in the pages of history of Indian freedom struggle. By his writings, daring acts and inspiring martyrdom he gave notice to the mighty British rulers that the Indian Youth was ready to go to any length for the sake of motherland. He announced to the world "This (hanging) is the highest reward for patriotism and I feel proud that I am going to be awarded this prize. They think that by killing my mortal body they can live safely in this country. This is their misconception. They can kill me, not my ideas. They can destroy my body, not my feelings. My ideas will keep hanging like a curse on British rule till the day they are forced to flee"

At the young age of 23, Bhagat Singh on the cusp of martyrdom, read and wrote extensively on the contemporary political conditions. In these insightful letters, essays and articles he educated the Indians about the power games that the British were playing with the Indians. At the same time he also tried to show to the general mass of the people that the real motives of the educated middle class that had been spearheading the freedom movement was to gain power and that the leaders were not really interested in real revolution which would ameliorate the condition of the masses.

By his writings, action and sacrifice Bhagat Singh aimed to awaken the people till then lethargic and indifferent Punjabi youth to fight for freedom. In the second decade of 20th century the Indian struggle against imperialist forces under the leadership of Mahatma Gandhi had strengthened and comparatively speaking broadened its base. But the movement had wide regional variation. In Punjab non cooperation movement begun by Congress under the leadership of Gandhi was not very strong. But when the colonial government interfered in the religious affairs of the Sikhs, the agitation was widespread, strong and satyagrah effective. The government surrendered, management of Gurudwaras was given to the Sikhs and the movement ended. Punjab was once again peaceful. Politics again took a backseat in the lives of the Punjabis. The valiant Punjabis who had in the past rebelled against the British government and had been killed by the rulers were all forgotten by their countrymen. Their sacrifices were lost in the pages of the British records. The people continued to suffer silently the unjust and oppressive rule of a foreign government. This political apathy saddened a patriot like Bhagat singh. He compared the sacrifices of Punjabis to that of men of other provinces and felt that Punjab had also produced valiant heroes but they had died unsung. Punjabis had forgotten these brave hearts and thus were found to be lacking in venerating their own heroes. He took upon himself the responsibility of acquainting and reminding and writing about the heroic deeds of Punjabis who had sacrificed their all for the sake of mother land. He lamented that the Punjabis did not remember the revolutionaries like Ram Singh kuka 153, Sarabha ,Madan lal Dhingra who all had fought and died for the national independence. Bhagat singh in his write up on Dhingra said "Great was that brave, great is his memory and writing about and remembering another unsung hero, Dr Mathura Singh, Bhagat singh wrote that "he was a man for whom even angels would have had admiration". Highlighting the stories of these patriots Bhagat Singh reminded the Punjabis that "Those who cannot remember their martyrs cannot achieve independence". He advocated that the only lesson required in India at present was to learn to how to die.

Bhagat singh was of the view that the Indian National Congress led by Mahatma Gandhi believed in politics of compromise and so signed deals with the British. In this way the congress party, he argued, was sacrificing hopes, vision, dreams and future of ordinary Indians. He was critical of the policy of compromise and surrender that the Indian National Congress under the leadership of Gandhi had been following since 1920. He said "No, they (Congressmen) will not run the risk. There they lack. That is why I say they never meant a complete revolution. Through economic and administrative pressure they hoped to get a few more reforms, a few more concessions for the Indian capitalists. That is why I say that this movement is doomed to die, may be after some sort of compromise or even without. The young workers, who in all sincerity raise the cry "Long Live Revolution", are not well organized and strong enough to carry the movement themselves. As a matter of fact, even our great leaders, with the exception of perhaps Pt. Motilal Nehru, do not dare to take any responsibility on their shoulders that is why every now and then they surrender unconditionally before Gandhi. In spite of their differences, they never oppose him seriously and the resolutions have to be carried for the Mahatma. In these circumstances, let me warn the sincere young workers who seriously mean a revolution that harder times are coming. Let them beware lest they should get confused or disheartened. After the experience made through two struggles of the Great Gandhi, we are in a better position to form a clear idea of our present position and the future programme."

He was extremely critical of the leaders who were spearheading the national movement "These arm-chair politicians have their eyes set on the handful of bones that may be thrown to them, as they hope, by the mighty rulers. That is extremely humiliating. Those who come forth to fight the battle of liberty cannot sit and decide first that after so much sacrifices, so much achievement must be sure and so much share to be divided. Such people never make any sort of sacrifice. We want people who may be prepared to fight without hope, without fear and without hesitation, and who may be willing to die unhonoured, unwept and unsung. Without that spirit we will not be able to fight the great two-fold battle that lies before us - two-fold because of the internal foe, on the one hand, and a foreign enemy, on the other. Our real battle is against our own disabilities which are exploited by the enemy and some of our own people for their selfish motives.

Again, writing about the direction ongoing national movement he wrote "This is a struggle dependent upon the middle class shopkeepers and a few capitalists. Both these, and particularly the latter, can never dare to risk its property or possessions in any struggle. The real revolutionary armies are in the villages and in factories, the peasantry and the labourers. But our bourgeois leaders do not and cannot dare to tackle them. The sleeping lion once awakened from its slumber shall become irresistible even after the achievement of what our leaders aim at." Disillusionment with the educated middle class that had been providing leadership to the freedom movement since the beginning of the struggle, he was extremely critical of their policies and method. He had no respect for comfort loving political leaders. He argued that congress leaders of his time were far away from reality because they were not in touch with the common man. He wrote "congress leader limits his journey only to places where he can easily reach by train". While Gandhi ji, Bhagat Singh said, had broadened the scope of his travels to places which were easily accessible(could be reached by dak gaari) he only stayed with rich people during his travels, spending most of his time in meetings, while the common uneducated men sometimes could only have a glimpse of him." "No man can understand the dreams and hopes and ideas of the general public by merely giving lectures and showing himself to the public from a platform", he thundered. Hence Bhagat singh believed that to achieve the goal of independence of India the gap between masses and leaders had to be bridged only then the real revolution could take place. And to bring about real, fundamental change new leaders had to come forward and the leadership could be provided only by the youth.

Bhagat singh was young and he recognised the potential of youth. He wrote "young men of today are countrymen of tomorrow, holding in their hands the destinies of land. They are the seeds that spring and bear fruit . But realising the helpless and directionless life the students were leading, he took upon his young shoulders the task of acquainting the young men of Punjab with their latent power, capabilities and responsibilities. Reposing great faith in the power of the youth. He said that the Young age appears to be peaceful and beautiful like earth, but like the earth it also has in it the power of the volcano. He urged the youth of India to continue the fight against imperialist as well as exploitative forces, "No matter, if your Government tries and succeeds in winning over the leaders of the upper strata of the Indian society through petty concessions and compromises and thereby causes a temporary demoralization in the main body of the forces, the war shall continue. It may assume different shapes at different times. It may become open, hidden, purely agitational, or fierce life and death struggle. The choice of the course, whether bloody or comparatively peaceful, rests with you. Choose whichever you like. But that war shall be incessantly waged with new vigour, greater audacity and unflinching determination till the Socialist Republic is established."

To motivate the young to come forward and take up political work, Bhagat singh said "Does it require any revelation now to make us realise that we are enslaved and must be free? Shall we wait for an uncertain sage to make us feel that we are an oppressed people? Shall we expectantly wait for divine help or some miracle to deliver us from bondage? Do we not know the fundamental principles of liberty? Those who want to be free must themselves strike the blow." Thus he urged the young to shake off apathy and indifference and come forward to begin active work in political field. He was impressed by what Rousseau had said, that "the aim of life is not to control the heart but to develop it" and felt that one can achieve anything when one begins to feel strongly about it.

He believed that the appeal to the young students would bear fruit because young are brave, energetic, and fear nothing. 301. Through the manifesto of Naujawan Bharat Sabha, Punjab, Bhagat singh and his compatriots appealed to the students."

We have appealed to the young only. Because the young bear the most inhuman tortures smilingly and face death without hesitation. Because the whole history of human progress is written with the blood of young men and young women. And because the reforms are ever made by the vigour, courage, self-sacrifice and emotional conviction of the young men who do not know fear and who feel much more than they think.

Manifesto of Naujawan Bharat Sabha, He exhorted the young to awaken from the sleep of uselessness, to awake and to rise "Young men, awake, arise; we have slept too long! The world history is full of sacrifices and blood shed by the young men". He warned that the struggle for freedom extracts heavy price but quoting a scholar, he said "life is dearer outside the prison walls but it is immeasurably dearer within the prison cells, where it is the price paid for freedom's fight."

Bhagat singh exhorted the youth of Punjab to take up politics but not adopt the path of violence. Though he himself had made use of bomb to send a strong message to the foreign rulers, yet he did not ask the young to take up arms. He urged that "at this time we cannot advise the youth to pick up bombs and pistols…there is even more important work to be done. In the coming Lahore session (1929), Congress is going to start a movement. This increases the responsibility of the young men. You carry the message of revolution to all corners of the country, to peasants and factory workers and awaken them."

Bhagat singh was saddened by the indifference of the Punjabis towards political work. By citing the work being done in other parts of India, Bhagat Singh tried to motivate the people of his own region, "Young Punjabis, the youth of other provinces are working tremendously in their respective spheres. The organisation and awakening displayed by young Bengal on February 3, should serve as an example to us.

Our Punjab, despite the greatest amount of sacrifice and suffering to its credit, is described as a politically backward province. Why? Because, although we belong to the martial race, we are lacking in organisation and discipline; we who are proud of the ancient University of Texila, today stand badly in need of culture. And a culture requires fine literature which cannot be prepared without a common and well developed language. Alas, we have got none".

The young students were not coming forward to do political work because they lacked direction and motivation. Faulty education policy was according to him, the cause of their political apathy and backwardness. He reiterated that the English education was introduced by the imperialist rulers to man the government offices with the English speaking Indians. . It is a historical fact that people learn a language which they believe would bring them monetary benefits and provide them with means of livelihood. Knowledge of English language was important in colonial times as it was a channel for communicating with the ruling elite. The knowledge of the language of the rulers was also important as it helped Indians get into government service as well as opened other service sectors like judiciary to earn a livelihood. It also ensured a higher social status because the Indian mindset was such that an English speaking Indian was at once admired and put on a pedestal. So the Indians soon took advantage of the opportunity offered and began to get western education in English medium because it got them jobs as well as respect in society.

Bhagat singh was dissatisfied with the existing education system. He believed that the educational institutions, both government as well as those started by various Indian trusts were not disseminating useful and meaningful education. The Indian organisations, like the Arya Samaj, the Singh Sabha, Brahmo Samaj and others, when they took upon themselves the responsibility of spreading education also followed the same pattern which was followed by the government. The schools and colleges started by these social and religious organisations for Indians were laudable, but they also fell short of imparting useful and real education and these institutions were also preparing boys to become clerks and lawyers. Moreover these organisations had also opened schools and colleges in the urban areas only, neglecting the villages where the benefits to the society and the nation would have been greater and that also at a much lower cost. So the existing education system was not making the life of the educated Indians meaningful. Bhagat Singh reiterated that to get education only to become clerks is useless and needless. Another draw back of the education system was that desire of getting western education through English medium with the aim of getting employment made Indians, including Punjabis, neglect their own languages. As a result, the educated class began to admire and depend upon western literature. This took the educated class away from the masses and created a gulf between the two. Political activity also became a victim of this language barrier because the educated elite could no longer relate to the problems of the people and the people could not understand the language of the elite. Consequently very few Punjabis became committed political workers. Thus, politically speaking Punjab had become a backward region in 1920's and the reason Punjab was lagging behind other provinces was that it had neglected its own language.

Bhagat Singh realised the potential of written word and took upon his young shoulders the task of giving real, meaningful education to the Punjabis.

Written word is a powerful weapon. It has great potential to infuse new life in the society. It can mould the minds and prepare men for struggle. Writers help create new intellectual environment and they sow the seeds of new ideas, show the way, arouse and guide the thought process of the people. Emphasizing the value of literary works Bhagat Singh gave the example of Italian leader who had spearheaded the movement for Italian unification. He argued that "Perhaps Garibaldi could not have succeeded in mobilising the army with such ease if Mazzini had not invested his thirty years in his mission of cultural and literary renaissance" .. But the writers are also a part of the society. So they respond to the existing conditions as well as to altered situations and this is reflected in their works. Thus while on one hand the writers are a product of the socio-cultural milieu on the other hand they are also creators of new ideological environment. He recognized that the language is not merely an instrument through which man transmits ideas and communicates with other human beings it also enables one to express ones thought and feelings. But writers can achieve very little if they write in a language which is foreign to the people and which the masses cannot understand. A man thinks, writes, responds and relates to a written or spoken word which is in his own language. But a language also has to adapt to new conditions and move with the times. Citing the example of the ceaseless sacrifices and sufferings of the Gurus, Bhagat Singh wrote that while we find devotion and self-oblivion in the preaching of the first Guru, We find a sense of fellow-feeling and helpfulness for the oppressed in the preaching of the next Guru, Guru Shri Teg Bahadur ji. After his sacrifice, suddenly, we sense a warrior spirit in the preaching of next Guru, Guru Gobind Singhji. When the Guru realised that along with spiritual devotion action was also needed to fight oppression and evil, he started Chandi worship and turned the Sikh community into a community of worshippers and warriors. He combined spiritualism with fighting spirit thus moulding the Sikh community into strong devotees and fierce fighters. So with the changing times the flow of literature and language also changes. But In the twentieth century Punjubi language failed to do so and consequently not only the language and literature but also the community suffered. No country or community can progress unless it has its own literature. While other regions like Bengal, which had well developed language continued to produce literary works and through that kept alive the stories of sacrifices of their great men, Punjab, which had also produced men of comparable greatness forgot its own heroes.

By 1920's political conditions in India began to change. The movements initiated to reform religion and society and the national movement, begun with the aim of demanding constitutional reforms, also made some Indians aware of the importance and richness of their own languages. Thus the period of freedom struggle in India was a period of awakening for small nationalities and ethnic groups. The dynamics that set the forces of Indian nationalism into motion were also responsible for the beginning of the movements of self assertion by various religious communities. While accepting language diversity as a distinctive feature of India, some politically conscious Indians also began to articulate desire for recognition and development of regional languages. So language consciousness in political terms also developed and grew.

By the second decade of twentieth century, the language issue had begun to stir the minds of Punjabis. The question of language had taken a religious connotation. Bhagat Singh realised the repercussions of this divide linking religion to politics. He had witnessed the spate of communal riots that had taken place in the aftermath of withdrawal of non cooperation movement by Gandhi. Bhagat singh was worried that these heightened communal feelings would deflect attention from goal so he warned against these increasing communal tension and said, "What are we Indians doing? Breaking of one branch of peepal tree hurts the religious sentiments of Hindus, Muslims who are supposed to be opposed to idol worship evoke the wrath of Allah on the heads of infidels even if a corner of Tazia, which is made of peepal is torn and then the Muslims are satisfied only if they shed the blood of the infidel Hindus." The victim of this heightened religious awareness and divide was the Punjabi language. The Punjabis came to identify language with religion. There was no consensus among Punjab's different religious communities about the language. The Muslims began to favour Urdu while the Sikhs began to propagate the idea of Punjabi language in Gurumukhi script. The Hindus in Punjab advocated use of Hindi. Bhagat Singh successfully pointed out in his essay on language and script of Punjab that Urdu language script could not do justice to our thinking and literature as it was based on Persian and Arabic. For unifying the country, he forcefully advocated one language-Hindi so that people of different regions could interact with each other, understand and exchange ideas. But before any national consciousness is formed he argued, men should be awakened to the value and richness of their region. And regional consciousness can be created by knowledge and awareness of the importance of the literature of their own region. And for literary activity language and script is needed, which unfortunately Punjab of this time lacked. For this the knowledge of their own language i.e. Punjabi, is required. Bhagat Singh thus highlighted the importance of ones own mother tongue as well as the literary heritage of the region in its own language. The deepest feelings can only be expressed best in ones own mother tongue. Punjab the land of warriors was lagging behind in the political arena because it had forgotten its cultural heritage. Punjabis had failed to produce literature of high standard because their language had not developed in recent past. He was saddened by the lack of literary activity in Punjabi language. He bemoaned the fact that because Punjab at this time lacked any one particular language, its progress in the literary field was stunted.

Bhagat Singh wrote, "An acquaintance with the literature of society or a country is of prime importance for the understanding of that society or country, because the consciousness of the soul of a society gets reflected in its literature also." History is witness to the authenticity of the above statement. Countries have followed the direction determined by the flow of their literature. Every nation needs literature of high quality for its own upliftment. As literature of a country attains new heights, the country also develops. Nationalists, both who work for social reform and others who make politics their field of work have recognised the importance of l literary activity. If new literature is not produced to meet the requirements of the changed times and contemporary issues and situations are not addressed in writings, then efforts to inform, educate and reform would not bear fruit and work of intellectuals and writers would prove transitory.

Emphasizing the value of literary works he gave the example of Italian leader who had spearheaded the movement for Italian unification, "Perhaps Garibaldi could not have succeeded in mobilising the army with such ease if Mazzini had not invested thirty years in his mission of cultural and literary renaissance". To some extent credit for the creation of a Punjabi speaking state in independent India can be given to Bhagat Singh who, as early as 1924 when he was still in his teens., recognised the importance of a people learning their own language Bhagat Singh qualifies to be called a real leader who was as disturbed about foreign rule as he was about Punjabis being indifferent to their culture and language So he tried to make the Punjabis adopt their own mother tongue and called upon the youth to be educated and learn the script of their mother tongue.

Bhagat Singh admitted that the task before the youth was difficult. "It requires a life of constant struggle and suffering and strife. Crush your individuality first. Shake off dreams of personal comfort. Then start to work. Inch by inch you shall have to proceed. It needs courage, perseverance and determination."

Obstacles in the way of struggle for freedom were also great while means were insufficient. But he believed that if the young are determined then success is assured. He also warned that they must be brave and not be disheartened by difficulties because, "success is only incidental while sacrifice is the norm". He encouraged the young not to lose heart if they find themselves alone in this big fight. He urged them to have faith in themselves. He asked them to remember the words of Italian leader Garibaldi when he sent his poor, poverty stricken, resource-less helpless, son out into the world to try his luck. "Nine out of ten times, the good thing that can happen to a young man is that he is thrown from the ship into the sea so that he swims and finds his own way." He said that he was appealing to the youth because it is only the young who are hardworking, ready for any sacrifice, brave and determined, they fear nothing, they think less and feel more, only they can bring about change. According to him old men, being wise and clever were not the apt medium to bring about any fundamental change. Gandhian wave, which had begun to sweep across the nation, left Bhagat Singh unimpressed. He analysed that congressmen were not really interested in freedom- they were merely interested in getting a share in power. But he was hopeful of a bright future. If the young men would shoulder the responsibility of bringing about reform and revolution then they can achieve anything. "The mind of youth today seems to be in thrall. It is also under narrow religious influence. But in the ferment and effort to be free of such mental constraints I see seeds of revolution".

Bhagat Singh's call to the youth did not go unheeded. In his death he achieved what he strove for in life. His death was mourned throughout Punjab. He became more popular than Gandhi. "The result was that when Gandhi was on his way to Karachi for the Congress session (March 29-31), he was greeted with black flags at all the major railway stations from Lahore to Karachi --- by the same masses who did not tire of calling him Mahatma ji.

The execution also evoked a series of violent protests in several parts of the country, and between 1931 and 1939 obscure youth shot at British officials at more than a dozen places in the name of avenging Bhagat Singh's execution. In one such incident at Betia (Bihar), Vaikuntha Shukla and Chandrama Singh---in no way related to Bhagat Singh---shot dead Phanindra Nath Ghosh who was the main approver in the second Lahore Conspiracy Case and did the maximum damage because he was a member of the HSRA Central Committee and was in the know of all its plans. Yet another act of such revenge took place at London in 1939." (Harikishan Surjit article)

His name, as he had written in his last letter, soon became "a symbol of Hindustani revolution". By sacrificing his life, Bhagat singh showed to the world what one individual can achieve. He showed the Indians the way to serve the nation and gave them an aim in life. By acquainting them with the past glory and heritage of Punjab region and sacrifices made by the Punjabis for the cause of religion and motherland, he gave to the Punjabis reasons and cause to be proud of their race, language and heritage. His message was clear., learn your language, respect your cultural heritage, venerate your countrymen who sacrificed their all for the sake of nation, love your country and be ready to for sacrifices. He tried to give an identity to the youth who were groping in the dark. He tried to give a purpose to the youth. He tried to shake them awake, rouse them from apathy and indifference and galvanise them into action. By his sacrifice, he achieved what he aimed; he roused the nationalist, patriotic and heroic feelings among the youth. He made the Punjabis proud of their heritage and he continues to inspire the youth even today. Legacy of Bhagat singh can be summed up in a few words: icon of nationalism, idol of, freedom fighters, fierce patriotism, and symbol of courage and ideal son of the soil.

The voice of the young man who combined in himself the lethal combination of a visionary as well as an activist was silenced by the rulers. He, by his writings and by his acts had become too dangerous for the imperialists to be allowed to live. So he was hanged. But Bhagat singh, by sacrificing his life achieved much more than what he could have hoped for. He became an iconic figure and continues to remain so even after eight decades of his martyrdom. Even today, his name is synonymous with patriotism and courage.

References

1. *Bhagat singh aur uske sathioyn ke sampuran uplabdh dastavez*, edited by Satyam, p. 433. (last letter of Bhagat singh).
2. The Hindustan Socialist Republican Army (Notice).
3. *Bhagat singh aur uske sathioyn ke sampuran uplabdh dastavez*, edited by Satyam op.cit. p. 65.
4. Ibid, p. 134.
5. Ibid., p. 153.
6. Ibid., pp. 143,139.
7. Ibid., p. 165.
8. Ibid., p. 121.
9. Ibid., p. 168.
10. Letter to young Political Workers, Agenda of Revolutionary work, *Bhagat singh ke Dastavez*, ed. Nilima Sharma and Surendra Manan, p. 73.
11. Socialist party manifesto *Bhagat singh aur uske sathioyn ke sampuran uplabdh dastavez*, edited by Satyam, p. 485.
12. To The Young Political Workers, *Bhagat singh ke Dastavez*, op.cit., p. 73.
13. *Bhagat singh aur uske sathioyn ke sampuran uplabdh dastavez*, edited by Satyam, p. 447.
14. Ibid., p. 97.
15. Ibid., p. 96.
16. Ibid.
17. Ibid., 635, jail diary, p. 124.
18. Ibid., p. 301.
19. *Bhagat singh aur uske sathioyn ke sampuran uplabdh dastavez*, edited by Satyam, p. 97.
20. Ibid., p. 359.
21. Manifesto Naujwan Bharat Sabha, 1928, p. 39 slim.
22. *Bhagat singh aur uske sathioyn ke sampuran uplabdh dastavez*, edited by Satyam, p. 271.
23. Ibid., p. 670.
24. Ibid., p. 534.
25. Ibid., p. 272.

26. Ibid., pp. 187-88.
27. Ibid., p. 81.
28. Ibid., p. 301.
29. Ibid., p. 86.
30. Ibid., p. 303.
31. Ibid., p. 81.
32. Dastavez, p. 80.
33. Bhagat singh aur uske sathioyn ke sapuran uplabdh dastavez, edited by Satyam, p. 304.
34. Ibid., p. 304.
35. Ibid., pp. 194-95.
36. Dastavez, p. 81.
37. Hindustan Republican socialist party's announcement, p. 422, dastavaze.
38. Harikishan Surjit article internet.

10

The Making of Bhagat Singh: Analysing the Psyche of a Revolutionary and Impact of his Ideas during the Freedom Struggle and Afterwards

Dr. M. Waseem Raja

Bhagat Singh: Biographical Profile

Shaheed Bhagat Singh as he is popularly known was the great revolutionary who had left indelible mark on the history of the India's freedom struggle. He had inspired the greater section of the Indian society and especially the youth of his time and afterwards found him a great hero to imbibe his ideals.

He represented a radical group of leaders who had adopted different recourse in achieving freedom, and differed from those who were not averse to violence as a means to achieve the freedom. The political leadership of conventional type did hardly suit him and that is why he disliked the ideas of those leaders who wrongly took up the ideas of non violence, compromise, conciliation and old method of prayer and petition. Those conventional ideas had angered a larger section of the youths who had by 1930's been almost unhappy with the plight of the country.

Asst. Professor in History, Dept. of History, AMU, Aligarh.

With colonialism at its peak in the face of emerging communist block against the imperialism and capitalist ideology, the radical youth of Bhagat Singh's fold were definitely inspired by the prevailing political thoughts and undercurrent. In the prevailing situation of India in those days the youth were angered with the plight of such a vast country like India. India which was carrying the burden of colonialism and continue to remain subservient to a small nation from overseas had caused consternation in hearts and minds of the youth. The youths were seething with anger, as they were no longer to tolerate as they were to see their country free. That led to the emergence of arrays of revolutionaries like Chandra Sekhar Azad, Ramprasad Bismil, Rajguru, Sukhdev, Subhas Chandra Bose and scores of others, who had left indelible impact on the Indian scenario. The age of Bhagat Singh represents the world of confronting the colonialist with all might possible, sending strong feelers that they no longer were to tolerate the foreign rule in the country which belonged to them. The revolutionary trend started with anti-Bengal partition or organizations like Anushilan Samiti were carried forward to 30's by the new youths along with the Congress extremist ideology of the famous Bal. Pal and Lal. The movements by the youths had revolutionary zeal but they were mostly youths who were aware of the happenings at the international level. After the World War I we find some new trends developing and countries were being reorganized and freedoms were being accorded, which was quite inspiring for them as well as they were well read in the literatures of the period, available to them at that time.

It is not difficult to understand how Bhagat Singh as a revolutionary was molded and how he became such an astonishingly popular and a symbol of fight against the British colonialism during 1930's. When we analyze the documents scattered all over the archives, libraries in the form of government records, private papers and other such documents we come across fascinating details about Bhagat Singh. The generation of Bhagat Singh was to witness active politics when the country was passing through the phase of active political participation of masses. It was well into 1930's when all section of the society had become quite active and was participating in the national movement and the trend had begun at the outset of 1920's.

Early Life--- Born as Bhaganwala on the 26th September, 1907, Bhagat Singh grew up in a petty-bourgeois Agricultural family in a rural backdrop of Sandhu Jats settled in the Jullunder Doab district of Punjab. Right from the beginning he showed remarkable quality of an emerging revolutionary.

Education-------Bhagat Singh began his primary education at the District Board Primary School in Banga. In 1916-17, his father moved to Lahore to be able to organize relief work for the victims of a severe earthquake in Kangra. Bhagat Singh was now shifted to the D.A.V. High School, Lahore. Writing about these years, Bhagat Singh said, 'It was through his (father's) teachings that I aspired to devote my life to the cause of freedom'.[1] In his first letter, written to his grandfather at the age of 12, Bhagat Singh reassures him that he has passed his school examination comfortably and the latter need not worry on that count. Two years later he wrote again to tell his grandfather that 'railway men are planning to go on strike. Hopefully they will start by the next week'. This letter is dated 12th of November 1921 and shows that he was aware of the Non-Co-operation Movement that Gandhi had launched. Both letters are in fluent Urdu. In 1923, Bhagat Singh joined the National College, Lahore. It was affiliated to the Punjab Quami Vidya Peeth and was founded and managed by Lala Lajpat Rai and Bhai Parmanand. The College was set up as an alternative to the institutions run by the Government, bringing to the field of education the idea of Swadeshi. The philosophy behind the establishment of such a College was to produce 'self reliant, aggressive (in order to be progressive) men and women that new India wants'.[2] Bhagat Singh seems to have had an impressive academic record in College. The Principal of the College, Chhabil Das wrote in his memoirs, 'There were no books at hand. So it was for the teachers to select books from the libraries and give the relevant portions to the students... in our National College, we used to talk about Mazzini and Garibaldi. We used to talk about Ireland, about Sinn Fein movement of De Valera and other movements and about the Russian revolution'.[3] Bhagat Singh was also a member of the College dramatics society and seemed to have 'gained much prominence amongst the students and teachers, not only of his own college but other local colleges'.[4] 'He was particularly impressive because of his youthful physique and commanding voice', one of his biographers, S.R. Bakshi tells us. Bhagat Singh was fluent in Urdu, Hindi, Gurmukhi, English and Sanskrit. In the pamphlet, 'Why I am an Atheist' Bhagat Singh writes about his days in college. 'Though a favourite with some professors and disliked by certain others, I was never an industrious or studious boy. I could not get any chance of indulging in such feelings as vanity. I was rather a boy with a shy nature, who had certain pessimistic dispositions about (my) future career'.

Marriage Issue----By the age of 16, Bhagat Singh was completely dedicated to the cause of national liberation. Nothing illustrates this better than his attitude to marriage. In 1924, Bhagat Singh was pressurised to get married. Unable to convince his parents of his determination not to marry, Bhagat Singh had left his house in Lahore and reached Kanpur, armed with an introduction by Jai Chandra Vidyalankar for Ganesh Shankar Vidyarthi. The reason for his leaving home is explained not in running away from responsibility but he wanted to join revolutionary.[5] In the note left behind for his father Bhagat Singh said, 'my life has been dedicated to the noblest cause, that of the freedom of the country. Therefore there is no rest or worldly desire that can lure me now. If you remember, when I was small, Bapuji (Arjun Singh) declared at my thread ceremony that I had been dedicated to the service of my country. I am, thus waiting to fulfill that commitment. I hope you will forgive me'. On being asked why he did not want to get married, Bhagat Singh told Jaidev Gupta, his classmate and friend, that he had chosen a path which was full of many possibilities. His two uncles had gone that way and they had left two widows. Should he also leave another widow?[6] Chhabil Das has left us an account of how when he was to get married, Bhagat Singh came and reproached him on getting married. 'Besides them being my students we had good personal relations too... when Bhagat Singh heard that I was going to be married... he insisted that I should not marry. I said, if I could get a really good life companion who, instead of retarding my activities, would invigorate them, what would be your view? In the same breadth I quoted three concrete examples of Mrs. Sun Yat Sen,... wife of Lenin and... companion of Karl Marx. (At this) Bhagat Singh replied "Guruji who can vanquish you in any argument". So he had then yielded.'

Early grooming----He belonged to a phase of Indian freedom struggle which was to see the emergence of two decisive streams of political ideologies in The 'Extremism' of Lal-Bal-Pal kind and the Gandhian ideology of non-violent mass action. Apart from such trend also found in Punjab Bhagat's family members Sardar Ajit Singh and Sardar Kishen Singh, Bhagat Singh's paternal uncle and father had already opposed non -violent method of Congress. Both brothers were consistently radical in attempting to mobilize the masses to oppose the British at every opportunity that arose. Groomed in such atmosphere of radical ideas Bhagat Singh took it from inception and imbibed such ideas with his peers.[7] As naturally Bhagat tilted towards the radical leaders of his youth time as his peers were greatly inspired by the boldness and steadfastness of leaders like Bal Gangadhar Tilak and others. 'Having seen their enthusiasm at the 1906 Congress Convention in Calcutta, Lokmaniya was pleased and in bidding them adieu, gave them the responsibility of strengthening the movement in the Punjab.' With a Paper called Bharat Mata and a society of the same name his parents brought into their fold Lala Lalchand 'Phalak', the 'national poet' of the Punjab, Lala Pindidas, Dr. Ishwari Prasad and Sufi Amba Prasad, Mahant Nandkishore. Definitely those political humdrum around him and in his family Bhagat's receptive mind easily caught those radical and strongly undercurrent ideas against primarily the unjustified rule of the British in India.

His Political Activeness---- Bhagat started his political activism with serving as the volunteer to the Non-cooperation movement, but with sheer disillusionment after its suspension by Gandhiji. He swinged to the cult of revolutionary. It was through the Newspaper called Pratap that from 1923-24, Bhagat Singh worked under the alias, Balwant. With Ganesh Shankar Vidyarthi in Kanpur he came into contact with other radical youth of his time like B.K. Dutt, Shiv Verma, B.K. Sinha with whom he founded the commonality of ideas and purposes. He developed close camaraderie. Though, initially the youths did not take him seriously as they found him to be typical Punjabi village boy, as is reflected from the writings of Ajoy Ghosh. '*I believe it was sometime in 1923 when I met Bhagat Singh... he was introduced to me by B.K. Dutt in Cawnpore. Tall and thin, rather shabbily dressed, very quiet, he seemed a typical village lad lacking smartness and self confidence. I did not think very highly of him and told Dutt so when he was one'.* [8] By that time Bhagat Singh was away from home free with his apparent agenda in his mind. At that time he was greatly helped by Ganesh Shankar Vidyarthi who secured him a job as a headmaster of a National school near Aligarh. It was perhaps the most important year in Bhagat Singh's life. It was in 1925 at Kanpur that he joined as a member of the Hindustan Republican Association, started by Sachindranath Sanyal. That brought him closer to another revolutionary of his time Chandra Shekhar Azad who might have greatly shaped his mind for future course of action. The philosophy of Violence it appears was the main instrument of HRA'S ideology and it was that ideology which led him towards the philosophy of the Bomb. Like the **Putchist or Carbonari's** or Marxist ideology, Bhagat did not find any harm in using violence or sudden revolution as a "means to drive the British from the country". He was alo influenced by the French anarchist Valliant whom he quoted while throwing the bomb in assembly as "it takes loud voice to make a deaf hear".[9] Then he plunges into serious water of 'fighting the imperialists' and starts the recruitment drive for his group. He went from village to village recruiting people and to activate the villagers in the United Provinces. His propagation of ideology took the government by surprise and attracted police activeness against him but he managed to avoid them and continued to work for his group. After his return to Lahore in 1925 Bhagat Singh started a militant youth organization called the **Naujawan Bharat Sabha**. In April 1926, Bhagat Singh established contact with Sohan Singh Josh and through him the '**Workers and Peasants Party**' which brought out the monthly magazine **Kirti** in Punjabi. For the next year Bhagat Singh worked with Josh and joined the editorial board of *Kirti*. In 1927, he was first arrested on charges of association with the **Kakori Case** accused for an article written under the pseudonym *Vidrohi* (Rebel). He was also accused of being responsible for a bomb explosion at Lahore during the Dussehra fair. He was let off for good behavior against a heavy security of Rs. 60,000. In 1928, Bhagat Singh and Chandra Shekhar Azad were the sole absconders of the Kakori case and the other leaders being put behind bars meant that they were the leaders of the Hindustan Republican Association.

The 169 days between the judgment and the execution were most politically intense days in the history of India. Everywhere there was talk of Revolution and most of the prominent leaders including Mahatma Gandhi pleaded for his life from Lord Irwin. There were Meetings, editorials were full about him agitations were going on, but to no avail. The revolutionary was hanged on 7.15 PM Monday, on March 23, 1931.[10]

Influences

Rural Punjab-----The young Bhagat must have been inspired by the relentless efforts of his village community to fight the injustices by the British Government. The issue like anti-farmer's regulations, the Canal colony issue dominated the topics of their discussion and were always in the minds of the most of the people. It must have affected the young mind of Bhagat when his people were involved in such situation as Rural Punjab suffered the British colonialism.[11]

Parents and Peers----- The family of Bhagat Singh was family of great freedom fighters. The generation of Sandhu family i.e;Arjun Singh, his sons-Kishan Singh, Ajit Singh, and Swran Singh had set an example of sacrifices for the nation and the lesson for young Bhagat to imbibe those ideas.[12] The atmosphere in the family in which Bhagat grew was extremely inspiring for him as both his father and uncle were greatly politically active. They took part in local issues and managed to collect people whenever there was urgency. We come across that as a result of their political activism Ajit Singh and Syed Haider Raja established a society known as Bharat Dẹsh Bhagat Society. Later on they managed to found a society know as *Muhhiban-I Watan* or *Bharat Mata* and paper of the same name which must have been greatly inspiring for the young Bhagat as these activities were closely associated with his family members.[13] (The revolutionaries like khudiram Bose, Madanlal Dhingra, Kartar Singh Sarabha, Ashfaqullah Khan and Ramparsad Bismil as pre-Bhagat revolutionaries had all left impression on and inspiration for the young Bhagat and their martyrdom must have emboldened him to take up fight against the British might not fearing even death.

Friends------The friends like Chandra Shekhar Azad Batukeshwar Dutt, Rajguru, Sukhdev all had inspired him.

Books------From the early life he devoted considerable time in studying literature relating to the exploits of several patriots.

He was supposedly a voracious reader of books on Politics and International happenings, Biographies of the revolutionaries, communist writings and many more. It appears that from his interest of reading those books that he was thoroughly emboldened and such ideas emerged. It is easier said than done----how could you challenge a mighty British empire unless and until one is aware of strength and weaknesses of the Raj. It was his passion since his childhood. In his childhood he had read few books from the collection of his uncle Ajit Singh. In the school along with regular studies he used to devote considerable time in studying books relating to patriots and nationalist of India and other countries. While studying in the National College, Lahore Bhagat Singh read several books which were selected by Chabil Das and Jai Chandra Vidya Alankar. Most of these books related to the Sinn Fein movement of De Valera in Ireland, the Russian movement and a few other revolutionary movements.[14] During his brief sojourn in Kanpur and Shadipur, he had sufficient time to study Karl Marx and his socialism. Even afterwards he continued his habit of reading books. Therefore, in order to overcome the solitude of the dingy jails Bhagat Singh decided to read as much as he could. He wanted to equip himself with strong please-----refuting the arguments advanced by the opposition and defend the 'cult of revolution' which was so dear to his hearts. Besides, he wanted to study methods to change the existing system in India. However, there were obstacles in the way of acquiring the books of his choice. It was sure that the government would not allow him to study literature on Marxism, communism and revolutionary philosophy as this type of books were banned by the government. Bhagat Singh overcame the obstacle in getting books of his choice. Warden of the jail Charat Singh was kind enough to allow Kultar Singh, the brother of Bhagat Singh, to smuggle all the books which he wanted to read. He used to borrow these books from the Dwarka Das Library of Lahore where such publications were available. These books were- 'Militarism' by Karl Liebknecht, 'Left Wing Communism', 'Why Men Fight' by Bertrand Russell, 'Land Revolution in Russia' and 'Spy' by Upton Sinclair. In addition to these books he read several other books. Among them were 'Second International', Left Wing Communism', 'Mutual Aid', 'Field, Factories and Workshops' 'Civil War in France', "Theory of Historical Materialism and Peasant, Prosperity and Debt". Bhagat Singh also kept a diary, he wrote whatever struck him while reading a book. In this diary there are passages mostly in English by thinkers such as Aristotle, Plato, Descartes, Hobbs, Locke, Rousseau, Trotsky, Bertrand Russell, Karl Marx and Engles. Extracts from the books of Rabindra Nath Tagore and Lajpat Rai are also available in it. He was fond of poetry. He could recite or quote poems or their portions from Wordsworth, Byron and Omar Khayyam. But his favorite poet was Ghalib whom he quoted frequently." He was also fond of patriotic poems composed by Ram Prasad 'Bismil'. He also wrote books 'The History of the Revolutionary Movement in India', 'The Ideals of Socialism'. 'Autobiography' and 'Door to Death' though now it is untraceable. On January 15, 1931 he wrote a lengthy foreword to a poem entitled 'Dream Land' written by Ram Saran Das. On February 2, 1931 he wrote a message to the nation. In this message he discussed the trends of the struggle for freedom. Shortly afterwards he wrote two letters in which he disapproved the way in which the defending counsel of Han Krishna, who had fired six shots on Sir Geoffrey Montmorency, the Governor of Punjab, at the time of his coming from the hall of the Punjab University, Lahore just after delivering the convocation address. The first letter is not traceable but the second one is available as it was published in 'People', as English weekly, in June, 1931.' He also wrote an article on 'the first outburst of Punjab in the freedom struggle.' Some of their portions were published in the successive columns of an Urdu weekly named Bande Matram. Bhagat Singh also wrote a paper on the exact meaning of the slogan 'Long Live Revolution'. This paper was written in reply to an article by Ramanand Chatterjee published in his journal Modern Review in 1924 ridiculing the above slogan. Two hours before his hanging Bhagat Singh asked his lawyer whether he had brought the book 'Revolutionary Lenin'. He has requested Mehta to bring this book and was very pleased to get it.

October Revolution-----Bhagat Singh was greatly inspired by the October Revolution as he finds this victory a victory over the Capitalism and Imperialism. The success of the October Revolution, the victory of the common man in that revolution was a great source of inspiration to the young revolutionaries who were coming in contact with Communists in India and abroad. According to Manmathnath Gupt Bhagat Singh had become symbol of the fight for socialism more than any person or party has.[15] A manifesto of the Hindustan Republican Association, an organization of revolutionaries, talked in 1925 about a Federal Republic of the United States of India based on universal suffrage. It also talked about nationalization of all public utility services, steel, shipping and mines, a clear evidence of the influence of the Russian revolution. This was a break with the past and the first step of the national revolutionaries towards the socialist ideology, towards the revolutionary masses. He wished the same to happen to India.

Contemporary International Scenario-------The 20's was a decisive decade and surge in the fight against the British Imperialism. Apart from that the period also saw the emergence of scores of revolutionary, anti-imperialist leaders, pan-Islamism and others who were bent upon changing the fortune of their people, their land and strive to achieve the independence for their people if they remained under colonial rule. The Turkish dismemberment saw the emergence of various revolutionaries like Mustafa Kemal Pasha, in Turkey, Amir Amanullah in Afghanistan, emergence of Lenin and Stalin. Thus in this backdrop of charged international happenings the emergence of Bhagat Singh in India is not an isolated phenomenon but his emergence in India should also be seen from the perspective of international development. He was well aware of such development in and undoubtedly he was thoroughly inspired by those leaders and affected by the happenings at international level. Apart from that his awareness about Gadar party and its overseas activities against British Imperialism had greatly inspired him as it was Ajit Singh who also directly associated with such revolutionary activities.[16]

Impression

A. If one goes through the writings of Ajoy Ghosh we find the impression of different kind in the beginning but later on he found him a revolutionary. 'One day in 1928 I was surprised when a young man walked into my room' **Ajoy Ghosh** remembers, 'and greeted me. It was Bhagat Singh but not the Bhagat Singh that I had met... before. Tall and magnificently proportioned, with a keen, intelligent face and gleaming eyes, he looked a different man altogether. And as he talked I realized that he had grown not merely in years.... All those who met Bhagat Singh then and afterwards have testified to his remarkable intelligence and to the powerful impression he made when talking. Not that he was a brilliant speaker. But he spoke with such force, passion and earnestness that one could not help being impressed. We talked the whole night and as we went out for a stroll... it seemed to me that a new era was dawning for our party. We knew what we wanted and we knew how to reach our goal'.

B. Pattabhi Sitaramayya, a close follower of Gandhiji and the writer of the history of the Congress, has said, "... *both Gandhiji and Bhagat Singh were equally popular, the first because of his experiments with truth and the second because of his essays in bravery.*" Undoubtedly, it was a great tribute to Bhagat Singh who represented the revolutionaries who adopted violent methods against a foreign government for shaking its yoke and aiming at the establishment of a society in which exploitation of any kind was to be eliminated altogether. It may also be mentioned here that for some time the popularity of Bhagat Singh seems to have outshone that of Gandhiji. The Intelligence Bureau in its special report on Terrorism (1927- 1936) has written *"For a short time Bhagat Singh had surpassed the popularity of Gandhiji as a foremost politician."* In the Congress session of Karachi the slogans 'Gandhi go back' and 'Down with Gandhiji' were raised, Bhagat Singh was regarded as a true symbol of Indian revolution. In session Subhash Chandra Bose said, *"He symbolizes the spirit of revolt that had taken possession of the country...* Before he passed away he had become the cynosure of millions of eyes and the symbol of the spirit and aspirations of a new India, dauntless in the face of death, determined to smash imperialist rule and raise on its ruins the edifice of a free people's state in this great land of ours."

D. Writing about the phenomenon of Bhagat Singh sudden and amazing popularity Jawahar Lal Nehru wrote," .. He did not become popular because of an act of violence, an act of terrorism. Terrorists have flourished in India, off and on, for nearly thirty years, and at no time, except in the early days of Bengal, did any of them attain a fraction of that popularity which came to Bhagat Singh". In the opinion of Nehru, Bhagat Singh became popular because he seemed to vindicate the honour of Lajpat Rai and through him of the nation. Subsequently, his stand during the Delhi Assembly Bomb Case and the Lahore Conspiracy Case and the manner in which he faced death made him amazingly popular.

F. Lord Irwin, the Viceroy of India, has expressed his great concern about the political developments of India in 1930's These developments were mainly linked with the mass participation of the people in the Civil Disobedience Movement launched by Gandhi and both secret and open activities of the revolutionaries under the leadership of Chandra Shekhar Azad, Bhagat Singh and others. The nightmare of these developments on the mind of the Viceroy was continuous and consistent. He tried his best to resolve it by a solution which should have a wide support in various circles of India as well as the Home Government. But he was not prepared to commute the death sentence of Bhagat Singh because he considered it his duty to work under the limitations of law and also to avoid giving an impression to the people to think that chances of remission of the sentence of death of Bhagat Singh, Rajguru and Sukhdev still existed. The activities of Bhagat Singh and his comrades posed a serious challenge to the government. With the passage of time, it became difficult for the British to crush these elements once for all. Their actions were regarded as obstacles in the smooth working of the machinery of the government. The glaring proof of this nightmare in the form of an assessment of the work of these revolutionaries is available in the private and official correspondence of Viceroy's of India with the Home Government. The very fact that their exploits occupy a significant place in their private and official papers give a definite, concrete and significant color to the anti-British activities of the revolutionaries in the country. It also shows the degree and magnitude of apprehensiveness in the minds of the British bureaucracy.

Impact of his Ideas

Impacted the Whole of 30's--- Comrade Shiv Verma has dealt with this latter aspect very nicely and has given ample facts to show how under the volatile conditions of the 1930s, young revolutionaries were breaking new ground, developing new ideology and seeking to establish rapport with the Indian masses. Their hatred for the foreign rule, their unrelenting hostility to the British regime was being reinforced by the more correct understanding. Because by the start of the third decade of the century a new generation of young anti-imperialist Indians had sprung up which was demanding complete national independence and which was not yet accepted by the leaders of the National Congress. They were impatient with such a situation and wanted substantial change. The process of ideological maturing, however, did not abate the desire for immediate militant action, the desire for self- immolation in the cause of the Indian freedom. It is this latter aspect of the activities of Bhagat Singh and his comrades that come prominently before the Indian people rather than the development of their maturing thoughts.

Sense of Solidarity and Oneness----The name of Bhagat Singh and his comrades has secured a permanent place in the minds of the Indian people. No other revolutionary of those days struck such a deep feeling of sympathy, solidarity and oneness among the people as Bhagat Singh did. Bhagat Singh and his comrades became part of people's consciousness, the symbol of their aspirations and prestige, the symbol of the fight to put an end to enslavement. During the critical days of Bhagat Singh's trial in Lahore in 1929 people from all walks of life- from upper circles of society to the working class and peasants, from the politically active to the politically dominant-all followed the heroic behavior of these revolutionaries before the British court and warmly applauded their resistance, seeing in it the assertion of the country's prestige.

Impact on Common People----No other revolutionary struck such deep rapport with the awakening people, no other became so endeared to the common people and youth as Bhagat Singh did. He symbolized his struggle in the slogan he raised after he threw a bomb in the Legislative Assembly of Delhi "Long Live Revolution", a slogan totally unfamiliar at that time' to the Indian people. No doubt, the Communist leadership had already started raising it a little earlier, but it had not yet reached the people.

Courage-----This restless revolutionary was not contented with slogans only. He embodied the indomitable courage, the death-defying spirit, the capacity to sacrifice everything and unflinching courage in the face of torture, without which all talk of revolution, just remains an empty talk.

Sufferings------Bhagat Singh's suffering for the sake of the freedom of the motherland can be termed as supreme. He suffered as he had chose to fight for the injustices to his motherland by the British government. No revolution, no revolutionary ideology can succeed without individual heroism and suffering; without outstanding individuals rousing the people by their courage and sacrifices, by their readiness to face the gallows and the executioner's axe. No revolutionary ideology can succeed without intense hatred for the enemy to be overthrown, without an all-sided war on the enemy, his institutions and instruments. Bhagat Singh combined the hatred for the British rule with immense personal heroism, and became the symbol of the struggling Nation, the embodiment of its hatred for the foreign rule. With Bhagat Singh and his comrades were in action, we find the masses were on the move, when every anti-British action drew their approbation. Their ultimate sacrifice, therefore, put a permanent impress on the consciousness of the Indian people. The conduct of Bhagat Singh and his comrades during their trial at Lahore created new precedents of revolutionary behavior. He and his comrades accused during the trials were making use of the British courts as a forum to address the people, to broadcast their revolutionary *views* and ideology different from the nationalist tradition set by Mahatma Gandhi. They refused to enter into any legal defence which hurt the British prestige... They were beaten and handcuffed in the court; they were assaulted with *lathis* till they bled profusely and fell unconscious. Inside the jail, too, they demanded better treatment, refused to obey humiliating rules, demanded writing material, newspapers and right to correspond outside. They were again and again brutally beaten, fettered, locked and denied food. They retaliated by going on indefinite hunger strikes. When attempts were being made to save Bhagat from going top gallows he courageously choose to say in the following passage:--- "*As things are, my weaknesses are not evident to the people. If I am saved from the gallows, these weaknesses would become obvious and the* *revolutionary tide would begin to ebb, perhaps even sink to stillness. But if I go to the gallows fearless and smiling, India's mothers will give the example of Bhagat Singh and urge their children to be like him. The number of people ready to sacrifice themselves for the country's freedom would increase and their number would continue to enlarge so much that the devilish power of the imperialists would not be able to hold down the progress of revolution." "But there does come to my mind one thought what I had set out to do for the country and the humanity has not been accomplished even to a thousandth of my wish. If I had been able to stay am I might have utilized the opportunity to do all I wished to accomplish." But for this one reason, I have never had any other desire to save myself from the gallows. Who can count himself more fortunate than I: I have these days much pride in myself? Now I am impatient to meet the test. I wish it would come soon".* The above letter shows the state of mind of Bhagat Singh. He was fully ready to face death and to face it cheerfully. He earnestly hoped that his example would inspire others to devote their life for the freedom to the country.

Exposing the Anti-India and Arbitary Character of British Justice in India----- The actions and instances of Bhagat Singh were always aimed to expose the arbitrary nature of the British justices in India. A number of instances are there where the Indians accused of something were not penalized at par with the British who committed the same crime. They had always tried to prove that the British had unjustified inhuman and arbitrary standard of justices in India. Jatin Das comrade of Bhagat Singh and co-accused, died in the course of a hunger strike. His death at the young age of 23 shook the Indian people. All these heroic developments could not be concealed from the people. Neither the nationalist press nor the official organs could black them out. Every day the incidents, clashes and beatings were reported in press. Bhagat Singh and his comrades succeeded in completely exposing the anti-Indian and arbitrary character of British justice in India and the barbarities of the

British Indian jails. This was the aim of their fight for which they were prepared to undergo all the tortures. They turned their trial into a trial of the British government before the people. They refused to defend themselves and they put the government on the defensive. Never before in India during the phase the freedom struggle had any revolutionary succeeded in turning the repressive machinery of the British government people's hatred against the British rule. The Government had to retreat. It was forced to announce better treatment of Political prisoners.

A New Modern Generation of National Revolutionaries -----Bhagat Singh represented a new modern generation of national revolutionaries whose outlook was different from his predecessors. The earlier generations from the beginning of the twentieth century to the second decade, did not have clear ideas about the real content of the national struggle and how to shape a new, liberated India. At least for two decades in the 20th century we find that the nationalist leaders found it hard to give any meaningful direction to the ongoing freedom movement. Apart from that happening like Rawllat Act and General Michael O'Dwyer's highhandedness at Jallianwala Bagh in the form of wholesome, massacre greatly anguished the youth of Punjab and the entire country in general. That was also followed by the inhuman treatment of the people in the form of martial laws. Those happenings caused consternation among the radical youths and thus emerged the second phase of national revolutionaries in India.

Radicalization of Mass movement----- Though the entry of Gandhiji in the Indian politics had started a new era of mass movements but that was not sufficient as it was basically peaceful movements with symbolic protest against British rule. Thus within Congress leadership too we find discontent and fissures and apparent division on the issue of agenda for the future and the methods to fight with the British Colonialism. This was natural because the national movement itself was in a formative stage and was as yet unable to define its objectives in modern democratic terms. Self-government, representative government, these were the initial slogans, and no political leader dared to say that a free India should break with the empire. By the time Bhagat Singh started his revolutionary activities things had changed very much. The first non-cooperation movement had already come and gone, and the masses had registered their entry into Indian politics. Democratic aspiration of the people had risen and the radical wing of the Congress was raising the demand for complete independence.

Marxian Thought, Communism as source of Inspiration--------With Bhagat Singh at the helm of affairs we find the revolutionary mainly took the example of Russian Revolution as that made it evident and apparent model to be tried in India. It was only through revolution of that magnitude that India could be saved and freed from the Imperialist clutches of the British. The success of the October Revolution, the victory of the common man in that revolution was a great source of inspiration to the young revolutionaries who were coming in contact with Communists in India and abroad. A manifesto of the Hindustan Republican Association, an organization of revolutionaries, talked in 1925 about a Federal Republic of the United States of India based on universal suffrage. It also talked about nationalization of all public utility services, steel, shipping and mines, a clear evidence of the influence of the Russian revolution. This was a break with the past and the first step of the national revolutionaries towards the socialist ideology, towards the revolutionary masses. This was probably two or three years before Bhagat Singh started his activities. The new trend was just shaping itself. Between 1925 and 1928 further developments took place. The prestige of October Revolution further increased.

Common Masses' causes------- Coming from rural agricultural family of Punjab Bhagat was never away with his thought for the suffering peasant, mill workers, labourers and combined with his moorings in the communist ideas the proletariat idea was never away from him. In India itself large sections of workers were waging strike struggles under Communist leadership and were raising radical political demands. The Congress was getting ready for the second Non-Cooperation Movement. The Congress leaders were being pressurized to accept complete independence as their objective. Bhagat Singh's entry into open public life announced that a young revolutionary was there to change the situation. That became evident from the joint statement of Bhagat Singh and Batukeswar Dutt during their trial in the Assembly Bomb Case.. After throwing *the* bombs they also threw red leaflets which ended with the slogan "Long Live Revolution" "Long Live the Dictatorship of the proletariat". In their statement before the court, they explained why they threw the bombs. They said 'their purpose was not to harm anyone but to expose the dependent character of the Legislative Assembly which was being paraded by the British as a Parliament to create the belief that India was being democratically modified'. Their statement condemned the Assembly which created Montford Act of 1919 "as a menacing monument of the strangling of the exploiters". The statement said that the bomb was thrown as a protest against the wholesale arrest of the leaders of the labour movement this was a reference to the communists and others arrested in the Meerut Conspiracy Case.

Workers' Plight------ There was general outcry against the arbitrary nature of bills like Trade Disputes Bill and Trade safety bill as it hurt the cause of the Mill workers. There was lot of agitation against the 'Trade Disputes Bill which sought to illegalize a general strike of the industrial workers. The British Government got frightened by the general strike by the British workers in 1926 which reached a revolutionary situation in Great Britain. The government sought to prevent such a strike in support of independence or for workers' demands. The entire Trade union movement protested against the bill. The national Leaders in the Assembly opposed it and Bhagat Singh joined in the protest, realizing that the government was striking at a vital section of the people whose strike could totally paralyze the administration. The statement asked "Can ordinances and Safety Bills snuff the flames of freedom in India? Conspiracy cases, trumped up or discovered and the incarceration of all young men who cherish the vision of a great ideal cannot check the march of revolution". And then follows the advocacy of socialism which brings the thinking of the young revolutionaries nearer the science of revolution-the Marxist outlook. After describing the imperialist exploitation and enslavement of the Indian people, the statement further says: *"A radical change, therefore, is necessary and it is the duty of those who realize this to reorganize society on a socialistic basis. Unless this thing is done and exploitation of man by man and of nations by nations is brought to an end, sufferings and carnage with which humanity is threatened cannot be prevented. All talk of ending war and ushering in an era of universal peace is undisguised hypocrisy. "By "Revolution" we mean the ultimate establishment of an order of society which may not be threatened by such breakdown and in which the sovereignty of the proletariat should be recognized and a world federation should redeem humanity from the bondage of capitalism and the misery of imperial wars".* Bhagat Singh went on churning his thoughts and proceeded more and more towards a better understanding of the Marxist stand on the issues facing the country. It may be stated without contradiction that his opinion on many national issues, his estimation of national leadership and its weaknesses, were more or less in conformity with the views and opinions of the leaders of the Communist movement who were building their strength among the workers. His writings on various topics and his letters to his colleagues reveal his growing reliance on the Marxist outlook.

An Atheist-------In a country like India which had suffered greatly in the hands of colonialism, it is no surprise that he declared himself an atheist and poured ridicule on the concept of a world created by a Supreme Being where there was so much suffering. As it may appear to us when injustices are perennially perpetrated by any aggressor one turns towards supreme but finding no clue, one can take recourse in denying the existence of god. That also inspires the individual or group of people to take up the fight for the cause on one's own. Apart from the Marxist ideology in order to bring suffering masses of different denomination together against the exploiters and treat them on equality basis they also decry the religion and find it a stumbling block in the way of progress. Thus it was but naturally suited to the person of Bhagat that he turned towards atheism as he and his comrades were permeated with an unfathomable sense of dedication to the cause of independence and freedom, to the cause of socialism. His study of Communist literature, of Lenin, led him to understand that India's struggle for freedom was part of the international working class struggle for socialism. On January 21, 1930, Lenin's death anniversary, the accused in the Lahore conspiracy case appeared in the Court wearing scarves and raised the slogans: *Long Live the Socialist Revolution, Long Live the Communist International. Lenin's Will Never Die, and Down with Imperialism.* The Manifesto of the Communist International which was read out by Bhagat Singh, said: *"On Lenin day we send hearty greetings to those who are doing something to carry forward the ideas of the revolution. We wish success to the great experiment which he is carrying out. We join our voice to that of the International working class movement. The proletariat will win, Capitalism will be defeated, Death to imperialism."*

Not A Terrorist------To the charges of many critics Bhagat had to come out with the statement that he was not a terrorist but rather working for the cause of revolution. The idea of Bhagat Singh was to show that what he was doing was to show the people how they could be able to fight the might of the British as the British authorities in India was hardly listening to the meek voice of the organization like Indian National Congress.

He was against the idea of individuals acting like terrorist hitting here and there causing panic etc but he was in favor of turning the youth of the country into revolutionaries like the Russians who overthrew Czarist regime. Bhagat Singh in a letter Written to the political workers on February 2, 1931, formally and renounces individual terrorism. He writes: *"Apparently I have acted like a terrorist. But I am not a terrorist I am a revolutionary who has got such definite ideas of a lengthy Planning as is being discussed here."* *His stand was being understood by all. He writes in the letter: "My comrades in arms might not like me, like Ram Prasad Bismil, for having been subjected to such severe torture ------ sort of reaction in the condemned cell, which is not true. They have the same ideas, same convictions, same zeal and same as I used to have outside perhaps, may definitely better I warn my readers to be careful while reading my words should not try to read anything between the lines. Let me declare with all the strength at my Command, that I am not a terrorist and I never was, except perhaps in the beginning of my revolutionary career. And I am convinced that we cannot get anything through these methods. . . . I do not mean that guns and pistols are useless, rather the contrary. But I mean to state that mere bomb throwing is not only useless but sometimes harmful to the cause.*

Hindu-Muslim Unity-----Bhagat Singh had greatly resented and regretted the stand taken by the leaders like Lala Lajpat Rai of Hindu chauvinism and division of country on the religious lines ----he wanted to save the people from blood bath that shows how much he stood for the Hindu Muslim unity and even reacted against the leaders of Lala 's stature to whom he still admired for his services to the country.[17] On his visit to Calcutta he had found that Bengal revolutionaries had also done away with the religious motifs and symbols when it come to fighting the British and he was very happy by that.

Slogan------ The slogans of 'Inquilab Zindabad', coined by Bhagat Singh, still echoes in the minds of freedom loving people of the country. Two of his favorite songs *Sarfaroshi ki tamanna ab hamare dil me hai'* and *'Mai, rang de mera basanti chola'* still inspires the youth of India. In the annals of the history of freedom Movement in India Bhagat Singh occupies a prominent place. He represents an embodiment of the defiant spirit against an oppressive government. He still reminds us that without sacrifices it is rather impossible to achieve one's objective. One should always be prepared to sacrifice his all for the freedom of his country.

In present scenario, when we are free nation of a billion and engrossed with various internal and external problems, Bhagat Singh's writings should inspire us in choosing the way to fight the injustices, corruption, exploitation prevailing in the country and also we must identify the enemy from abroad in the name of neo-colonialsim and cultural chavunism and and any such imperialistic conspiracies and fight them out. The writing of Bhagat Singh show how much the motherland was dear to him and how he was even ready to be called an atheist for the sake of preserving the unity, integrity and oneness of Indians..

In the end there is a sample of his poetic fervor which is full of call of sacrifices, dedication, and devotion to ones' motherland.

In the end Bhagat Singh wrote the following verse :

"उसे यह फिक्र है कि हर दम नया तर्जे जफा क्या है,
हमें यह शौक है देखें सितम की इन्तहा क्या है,
दहर से क्यों खफा रहें, चर्ख को क्यों गिला करें,
सारा जहाँ अदू सही, आओ मुकाबला करें।
कोई दम का मेहमा हूँ, ए एहले महफिल,
चरागे सहर हूँ, बुझा चाहता हूँ।
मेरी हवा में रहेगी खयाल की बिजली,
यह मुश्ते-खाक है फानी, रहे रहे न रहे।"

While bidding farewell he wrote "खुश रहो अहले-वतन हम तो सफर करते हैं।"

References and Other Sources

1. Bhagat Singh, *'Why I Am an Atheist'*, 5th-6th, October, 1930.
2. Lala Lajpat Rai, *'The Problem of the Education in India'*, New York, 1920.
3. S.R. Bakshi, *'Bhagat Singh and His Ideology'*, New Delhi, 1981. The Russian Narodniks seem to have been discussed with the history professor, Jai Chandra Vidyalankar.
4. S.R. Bakshi, *'Bhagat Singh and His Ideology'*, New Delhi, 1981.
5. Manmath Nath Gupt ; *Bhagat Singh aur unka Yug*, Delhi, 1977, pp. 97-98.
6. S.R. Bakshi, *'Bhagat Singh and His Ideology'*, New Delhi, 1981.
7. In an article called *'Emergence of the Punjab in the freedom movement'*, Bhagat Singh *'Emergence of the Punjab in the Freedom Movement'*, written in Urdu. Published in the 1931, weekly *Bandematram*. Reprinted in Jagmohan Singh and Chaman Lal eds. *'Bhagat Singh Aur Unke Sathion Ke Dastavez'*, Ludhiana, 1987.
8. Ajoy Ghosh, *'Bhagat Singh and His Comrades'*, Bombay, 1945, p. 14.
9. Mathur L.P, *Bhagat Singh, the Prince of Martyrs*, Avishkar Publisher, Jaipur, 2002, p. 86.
10. K.K. Khullar, *Shaheed Bhagt Singh*, Hem Publishers Pvt Ltd, Gk New Delhi, 1981, pp. 57-58.
11. Mathur L.P, *Bhagat Singh, the Prince of Martyrs*, Avishkar Publisher, Jaipur, 2002, pp. 5-6.
12. Mathur L.P, *Bhagat Singh, the Prince of Martyrs*, Avishkar Publisher, Jaipur, 2002, p.10, and also K.K. Khullar, *Shaheed Bhagt Singh*, Hem Publishers Pvt. Ltd. Gk., New Delhi,1981, pp.15, 94, 97, 149.
13. Sir Denizen Ibbetson's *Report on Political Situation in Punjab, 1907*, in K.K. Khullar, *Shaheed Bhagt Singh*, Hem Publishers Pvt Ltd Gk New Delhi,1981, p. 99.
14. Mathur L.P, *Bhagat Singh, the Prince of Martyrs*, Avishkar Publisher, Jaipur, 2002, pp.23.
15. Chapter on *Communist Evaluation of Bhagat Singh*, Gupt Manmath Nath : *Bhagat Singh and His Times*, Delhi, 1977.
16. *Overseas activites of Indian revolutionaries*, K.K. Khullar; *Shaheed Bhagat Singh*, Hem Publishers Pvt Ltd Gk New Delhi,1981, pp.18-19.
17. Mathur L.P, *Bhagat Singh, the Prince of Martyrs*, Avishkar Publisher, Jaipur, 2002, pp. 52.

Archival Materials

I. Records of the Government of India preserved in the National Archives of India

(1) Home, Political Branch-1921-1931 (From July, 1907 the Government of India established a separate confidential branch in the Home Department to deal with Political matters(2) Home, Judicial Branch, 1929-1931. Home, Political, File number 139/1931.

II. Proceedings of the Lahore Conspiracy Case, 1929.

(a) The proceedings at S No. (iii) were brought from Punjab State Archives (Pakistan), Lahore and are available in National Archives of India in its private collection as well as Microfilm Acc. No 418 (110/40).

(b) According to Kuldip Nayar the records in the Archives of Pakistan are not accessible to Indians and the India Office, Library London has practically nothing on the subject.

III. Government Reports

(i) Rowlatt (Sedition) Committee Report Government of India, New Delhi, 1918.

(ii) Punjab Jail Enquiry Committee Report, Lahore, 1930

IV. Original Letters and Documents of Bhagat Singh and his Associations

1. Verma, Shiv, Selected Writings Sardar Bhagat Singh, New Delhi, 1983.

2. Diary of Bhagat Singh available in Nehru Museum, Delhi.

III. Transcript Interviews of the contemporaries of Bhagat Singh available in Nehru Museum, New Delhi

(i) Chabil Das--Principal National College, Lahore, where Bhagat Singh studied for some time.

(ii) Jaidev Gupta-A close friend of Bhagat SingH from the childhood.

(iii) Durga Das Khanna; An active political leader of Lahore.

(iv) Manmath Nath Gupt-A revolutionary and a close associate of Bhagat Singh.

(v) Feroze Chand-A prominent leader of Purijab during the second decade of twentieth century.

(vi) Mathura Das Thapar---Brother of Sukhdev.

IV. Original Writings of Ajit Singh, uncle of Bhagat Singh and other political leaders

(i) Pardaman Singh and J.S Dhanki (Editors) Buried Alive- Autobiography of Ajit Singh.

(ii) Josh, Sohan Singh : Bhagat Singh Nal Men Mulaka ten At Char Mudhiey Inquilabi (Punjabi), Delhi, 1972.

(iii) Nehru, Jawahar Lal An Autobiography, Delhi, 1962.

(iv) Collected Works of Mahatma Gandhi, Volumes covering the period from 1926 to 1931.

(v) Joshi, V,C. (Editor) Lajpat Rai Writings and Speeches.

(vi) Earl of Halifax Fullness of Days, London, 1957.

(vii) Gopal, S. (Lord Irwin) Selected Works of Jawahar Lal Nehru, New Delhi.

V. Contemporary Newspapers and Journals

(a) Newspapers in English

1. Tribune
2. Hindustan Times
3. Hindu
4. Leader
5. Bombay Chronicle.

(b) Journals

1. Bengal - Past and Present (English)
2. Link (English)
3. Young India (English)
4. Vande Matram (Urdu)
5. Vikranz (Hindi)
6. Sandesh (Hirdi)

The books required by Bhagat Singh from Dwarka Das Library were as follows

Why Men Fight

Soviets at Work

Collapse of Second International

Left Wing Communism

Mutual Aid ,Karl Libk iie Khat Fields, Factories and Workshops

Civil War in France Marx

For Further Studies

1. Ajoy Kumar Ghosh, Bhagat Singh and His Comrades, op. cit., p. 15.
2. Shiv Verma (ED) Selected writings of Shaheed Bhagat Singh, National Book Centre, New Delhi.
3. Noorani, AG, *The Trial Bhagat Singh politcs of Justice,* Konark Publishers Pvt Ltd, Delhi, 1996.

4. K.K. Khullar, *Shaheed Bhagat Singh,* Hem Publishers Pvt Ltd Gk New Delhi, 1981.
5. *Jawahar Lal Nehru-An Autobiography*, pp. 174-176.
6. Young India, April 2, 1931, Speech by Gandhi at Karachi Congress.
7. Bipan Chandra, *Nationalism and Colonialism in Modern India*, p. 23.
8. Bardhan, A.S., Bhagat Singh, Pages from the Life of the Martyr.
9. Bakshi, S.R., *The Struggle for Independence: Bhagat Singh*, New Delhi, 1989.
10. Chandra, Bipin, *Nationalism and Colonialism in Modern India*, New Delhi, 1971.
11. Charidra, Bipari and Others, *India 's Struggle for Independence*, New Delhi, 20th Impression, 1998.
12. Deol, Gurudev Singh, *Shaheed Bhagat Singh : A Biography*, Patiala, 1969.
13. Ghosh, Ajoy Kurnar, *Bhagat Singh and His Comrades*, Bombay, 1945.
14. Gupt Marmath Nath, *Bhagnt Singh and His Times*, Delhi, 1977.
15. Karr, James Campbell, *Political Trouble in India, 1907-1917*, Delhi, Reprint, 1973.
16. Nayar, Kuldip, *The Martyr : Bhagat Singh Experiments in Revolution*, New Delhi, 2000.
17. Rahbar, Hans Raj, *Bhagat Singh and His Thoughts*, New Delhi, 1990.
18. Sandhu, Virendra, *Shaheed Bhagat Singh*, Delhi, 1974.
19. Sharma, Sri Ram, *Punjab in Ferment in the Beginning of the Twentieth Century*, Patiala, 1965.
20. Sanyal, Jitendra Nath, *Sardar Bhagat Singh*, Allahabad, 1931.
21. Singh, Swarn, *Path of Revolution : A Biography of Shaheed Bhagat Singh*, Delhi, 1998.
22. Thakur, Gopal, *Bhagat Singh: The Man and His Ideas*, New Delhi, 1961.
23. Earl of Halifax--Fullness of Days, pp. 149-150. (In his later life Lord Irwin was designated as Earl of Halifax).
24. Transcript of an interview with Manmath Nath Gupt. Transcript of an interview with Druga Das Khanna. S.R. Bakshi, pp. 184-185.

11

To Make the Deaf Hear

(Trials, Congress and Revolutionaries)

Dr. Syed Irfan Habib

'To make the Deaf Hear' is the book which I have just written and which was released two days ago on Shaheed Bhagat Singh on his ideology and programme and so I can just summarized what I have tried to say here today is nothing more to say a moment. So the book actually tries t to locate Bhagat Singh and his comrades in the national freedom struggle because most of us see the revolutionary trends or revolutionary moment as something contrary to the main stream congress movement for freedom struggle which I feel is not really the truth because congress party, the cadre the national leadership, state level leadership even the Taluka Tehsil level leadership all of them had very close links with most of the revolutionaries who were outside the purview of the congress party who did not agree with Gandhian non-violence, congress main stream, political ideology and programme but despite that there is very strong close linkages between the revolutionaries and the congress party. Most of the linkages were revealed very clearly in several resolutions which were put forward before the AICC at different sessions. You can go back to Gopinath Saha when he was killed and C.R. Das resolution. Gandhi and the whole congress tried to vote on that resolution whether it should be passed or not. The resolution could be passed by 78 in favor and 70 against.[1] Gandhi declared himself defeated and humbled despite the victory.[2] So these were the examples we have. We can take example from that session to the Lahore session 1929, to the Karachi Session 1931, so the movement, the congress leadership party, the cadre was equally with Gandhi as well as with the revolutionaries. There was a minor difference which reveals the general impression that Bhagat Singh and his comrades were actually fighting someverser lone battle there were bunch of individuals who were trying to do something for the country for the freedom. That the very questions they were really fighting for the freedom. But it was actually Gandhi and the congress that did the main job for us who really brought freedom for us. We have to see there are many instances because there are no times just give you few instances for example 1930-31 civil disobedience movement. Civil disobedience movement which was Gandhian movement of course nobody can denied that in North India UP, Punjab Sindh and Western UP etc. when mobilization began for civil disobedience movement in Punjab and Sindh especially the congress party had to enlist support of Naujawan Bharat Sabha. I could have talk in much more detail about that because that was the main organization which Bhagat Singh founded. NBS was the organization which was so popular in these years from 1926-27- 28-29 onwards that congress saw depletion in its ranks and they had to really need support of NBS most of the meetings for the mobilization of civil disobedience movement which was Gandhian movement of course, was done in collaboration with the NBS so this was the extent of their joint sort of programme which was not of course the disagreement but this speaks the both, the revolutionaries themselves despite their disagreements came forward to support the freedom struggle movement of Mahatama Gandhi.

Congress Party itself did not really keep away than they needed this support so they were actually together on so many counts when it came to the question of freedom struggle. There are fundamental differences and there is a full chapter in this when I have tried to deal with the congress and the revolutionaries, especially Gandhi and is not only violence there were so many other issues with which Bhagat Singh and his comrades disagreed. Nehru wants a sympathy with revolutionaries despite his Gandhian like his spell of Gandhism on him he was of course totally Gandhian in his resting and he was of course of with him on most of the issues when it came to the crunch but Nehru did not make or did not even mince words to support revolutionaries whenever occasion demanded, whether you take the issue of Saunders murder or the issue of Bombay Central Assembly the whole leadership of the congress especially condemn that bombing. They didn't condemn the revolutionary than their spirit but they condemn the option that this is not really the way and all that and violence should be condemned. Motilal Nehru appreciated their courage and sacrifices etc. but that is apart. But Nehru clearly told the British because the British Govt. immediately linked all that to Moscow. He said whatever it was for them anything which come from which should come to like from Moscow.[3] So Nehru went ahead to defend them saying that we have to appreciate the spirit behind it and we just cannot condemn them that these people have actually indulged in violence. So whenever occasion required I don't have to talk about Subhas Bose because he got involvement in NBS and Bhagat Singh and its associate is very well documented and we don't have to put any question on Subhas Bose as just said. For Subhas, the Assembly bomb explosion was a visible expression of the revolutionary movement which excited not only Public interest Public sympathy as well."[4] But Nehru and Gandhi especially we have to go into detail which I tried to do in this book and the cadre if you go back to the state level can talk about Ganesh Shankar Vidyadrthi and so many other people or even the Bandhyopadhyaya congress committee member Yusuf Mehar Ali etc. who spoke publicly in Karachi session where they actually went to the extent of using abusive language for Gandhi which is documented. They said if somebody else had done this like Gandhi has done then he would have been thrown into the Bay of Bengal or Arabian sea. That was the words used. So this language is used so this is all within the congress session so the people, the left congress when it was called who as much congressman and as goes to the congress and the party as they were to the revolutionaries. When Bhagat Singh and his Comrades were on hunger strike. Jawaharlal Nehru went to meet the hunger strikers and saw their agony inside the jail. In a speech at Lahore on August 9, 1929, Jawaharlal Nehru compared the careerist and selfish congressmen with selfless hunger striking prisoners: We should realize the great value of the struggle that the brave young men are carrying on inside the jail. They are not struggling to get honors from the people or laurels from the crowd for their sacrifice. What a contrast this is, compared with the unfortunate wrangles among congressmen and the fighting for securing position in the congress and the reception committee. I am ashamed to hear of these internecine differences amongst the congressmen. But my heart is equally delighted by witnessing the sacrifice of the young men who are determined to die for the sake of the country.[5] So these linkages between the revolutionaries and the congress party are much more complex than though we tried to look at.

References

1. Mr. Jayakar, The story of my life, 1922-25, Bombay, 1959, Vol II, p. 320.
2. Collected Works of Mahatma Gandhi, XXIV, and p. 334.
3. The Tribune April 17, 1929.
4. S.C.Base, the Indian Struggle 1920-42 Calcutta, 1967, p. 160.
5. The Tribune, August, 11, 1929.

12

Role of Mahatma Gandhi in Shaping the Destiny of Bhagat Singh

Dr. Raj Pal Singh

Just as a good piece of poetry renders new meanings and dimensions when read again and again, similarly history revisited is very likely to provide with a new insight into the old facts. There are some historical teasers which continue to call our attention. One of such teasers is the controversy over the attempts and extent of the efforts made by Mahatma Gandhi to save Bhagat Singh from gallows during the course of his discussions with the Governor General and Viceroy, Lord Irwin before signing the Gandhi-Irwin Pact on 5th March 1931. The revolutionaries often interpret it to show that the Congressmen and Gandhiji were afraid of ever increasing popularity of Bhagat Singh and his associates that is why they did not include the commutation of sentence of Bhagat Singh and his two comrades as one of the conditions for arriving at a settlement with the Viceroy. There were many other revolutionary freedom fighters who viewed the role played by the Mahatma as not above board. They opined: "Had Gandhi insisted on the release of all prisoners including Bhagat Singh and other revolutionaries...and on the refusal of this demand had he given the call for a revolution of the "do or die" type of 1942, he would have at least shortened our struggle by a decade."[1]

Head, Department of History, Mukand Lal National P.G. College Yamuna Nagar (Haryana): 135001.

On the basis of the shifts and changes in the stances adopted by the Congressmen and Gandhiji, some writers and researchers also accuse them particularly Gandhiji of not making any serious effort to save Bhagat Singh from the gallows. While others claim that he did make sincere efforts to seek release of Bhagat Singh and his associates. They say that under the circumstances, he could do little to save Bhagat Singh and his associates from falling prey to the imperialists' justice in the political case filled against them. The purpose of the present paper is to make an analysis of the facts of the case as enshrined in the contemporary sources and then to derive some convincing conclusion. The need of such an analysis cannot be over-emphasized to settle the controversy for all times to come because it continues to surface time and again even after elapse of almost eight decades of the event and always threatens to malign the image of our great freedom fighters who belonged to either violent or non violent school of thought. For smooth conduct of the study, the paper has been divided into three sections; Introduction, Discussion and Conclusion.

I

First of all, we take up summarily the court case against Bhagat Singh et al about which intervention of Gandhiji was expected to be more vigorous so as to save him from the gallows. In 1928 Bhagat Singh and Sukhdev killed Saunders, ASP, British police officer to avenge the national shame of the death of Lala Lajpat Rai. Next year he threw bombs in the Central Legislative Assembly at Delhi and gave them up for arrest. Rajguru, Sukhdev and Bhagat Singh were tried by a special tribunal in Lahore. Their trial was historic in the sense that the bold, well thought out and clear statements made before the tribunal gripped the attention of the whole nation. Thousands of youth across the country had been activated and were now bubbling with enthusiasm. This was the sole objective of Bhagat Singh and his associates who had spurned offers of being rescued by their revolutionary friends. When his father S. Kishan Singh made a petition to the tribunal pointing out infirmities in the evidence of the prosecution, Bhagat Singh wrote a terse letter to his father which was published in *The Tribune* on 4 October 1930.It read:

"I was astounded to learn that you had submitted a petition to the members of the special Tribunal in connection with my defence. This intelligence proved to be too severe a blow to be borne with equanimity. It has upset the whole equilibrium of my mind. I have not been able to understand how you could think it proper to submit such a petition at this stage and in these circumstances. In spite of all the sentiments and feelings of a father, I don't think you were at all entitled to make such a move on my behalf without even consulting me. Father, I am quite perplexed. I fear I might overlook the ordinary principles of etiquette, and my language may become a little bit harsh while criticizing or rather censuring this move on your part. Let me be candid. I feel as though I have been stabbed in the back. Had any other person done it, I would have considered it to be nothing short of treachery. But, in your case, let me say that it has been a weakness - a weakness of the worst type ... I want that the public should know all the details about this complication and, therefore, I request you to publish this letter."[2] Obviously Bhagat Singh and his associates had made up their minds to make supreme sacrifice. The judgement was announced on 7 October, 1930. The judgement read as under:

"Whereas Bhagat Singh, Son of Kishan Singh, resident of Khawasrian, Lahore, one of the prisoners in the Lahore Conspiracy case, having been found guilty by us of offences under section 121 and section 302 of the Indian Penal Code and also under Section 4 (b) of the Explosive Substances Act read with Section 6 of that Act and with Section 120-B of the Indian Penal code at a trial commencing from the 5th May 1930, and ending with the 7th October 1930 is hereby sentenced to death. This is to authorize and require you, the said Superintendent, to carry the said sentence into execution by causing the said Bhagat Singh to be hanged by the neck until he be dead at Lahore on the 27th day of October and to return this warrant to the High Court with an endorsement certifying that the sentence has been executed."

After the judgement was announced, the whole nation was in turmoil. People of the country were deeply anguished and came down heavily on Lord Irwin. There was a country-wide clamour for commutation of death sentence into life imprisonment. Under such circumstances and surcharged atmosphere with emotions of one and all, arose the question of intervention on the part of Mahatma Gandhi in the matter.

Next, we would make an attempt to understand as to why people looked towards Mahatma Gandhi to plead either clemency or commutation of sentence awarded by the Court to Bhagat Singh and his associates in the Second Lahore Conspiracy Case. In 1920's Mahatma Gandhi entered Indian freedom movement carrying with him the novel weapons of non-violence and 'Satyagrah' referred to as the Truth force or soul-force in preference to violence in Indian politics to win freedom. After the tragic event of the murder of a number of peaceful persons on the *Baisakhi* day at Jallianwale Bagh in 1919, he courted arrest at Palwal. This was followed by non-cooperation movement and Khilafat movement under his leadership raised him to the status of a great leader. In these movements, freedom fighters believing in revolutionary and pacific methods i.e. believers of both the schools of thought fighting for the attainment of freedom had joined hands and accepted his leadership. Thus he was able to carve a niche in the political horizon of the country as a force to reckon with. Though the abrupt withdrawal of the movement after the incidents of Chaura Chauri had not been to the liking of the all yet the stature of Gandhiji continued to grow. After the announcement of the formation of Simon Commission and its subsequent boycott, the things moved very swiftly culminating in the beginning of Civil Disobedience Movement in the form of Salt *Satyagrah* and the Congress decision to boycott of the First Round Table conference. The Government was forced to initiate dialogue with him for solving the question of question of proposed constitutional reforms. He as a sole representative of the Congress entered into a dialogue with the Viceroy. By that time, the Court had awarded the death penalty on the revolutionary trio mentioned above. The people expected that he would secure the release of all the political workers including the revolutionaries from the British jails before agreeing to reach any sort of agreement with the Viceroy. The Indians looked to the Father of the Nation for help and rescue of Bhagat Singh, Rajguru and Sukhdev. The people expected him to put his foot down in dissuading the British government from awarding capital punishment to the young zealots.

After successful termination of his peace negotiations with the government, Gandhiji started to make public appeals to the revolutionaries to call off their movement and let him try his non-violent methods to secure freedom. At this Sukhdev, a co-accused with Bhagat Singh in the Lahore Conspiracy Case, wrote a letter to Gandhi ji either to negotiate personally with the revolutionary leaders to understand their point of view or stop issuance of appeals to them through public meetings or press, many of whom were awaiting execution at the hands of British. The letter reads:

"Most Gracious *Mahatmaji*,

Recent reports show that since the successful termination of your peace negotiations you have made several public appeals to the revolutionary workers to call off their movement at least for the present and to give you a last chance to try your non-violent cult. As a matter of fact, the calling off of any movement is neither an ideological nor a sentimental act. It is the consideration of the peculiar needs of different times that force the leaders to change their tactics. Let us presume that at the time of peace parley, you did not overlook the fact … that this was not going to be the final settlement … In face of that (Lahore) Resolution, the peace and compromise is but a temporary truce which only means a little rest to organize better forces on a larger scale …As regards the opportunity and the conditions on which any truce can be affected, it rests with the leaders of the movement to decide … Similarly, as is evident from the very name - Hindustan Socialist Republican Party - the revolutionaries stand for the establishment of the Socialist Republic…They are bound to carry on the struggle till their goal is achieved and their ideal is consummated… Since your compromises you have called off your movement and consequently all of your prisoners have been released. But what about the revolutionary prisoners... More than half a dozen prisoners are actually waiting for their execution. What about all of these people? The three Lahore Conspiracy case condemned prisoners, who have luckily come into prominence and who have acquired enormous public sympathy, do not form the bulk of the revolutionary party … As a result their executions are expected to do greater good than the commutation of their sentences. But in spite of all this, you are making public appeals asking them to call off their movement. Why should they do so? You have not mentioned any definite thing …The present policy of the Government towards them is to deprive them of the sympathy and support of the masses which they have won in their movement, and then crush them … Therefore we request you either to talk to some revolutionary leaders - they are so many in jails - and come to terms with them or to stop these appeals …Or if you seriously mean to help them, then have a talk with them to understand their point of view, and discuss the problem in details. Hope you will kindly consider the above request and let your views known publicly.

Yours,

'One of the many' (SUKHDEV)"[3]

Gandhiji published reply of this letter in the *Young India* on 23 April 1931 (i.e. exactly one month after 23rd March when Bhagat Singh, Rajguru and Sukhdev had been martyred in the Lahore Jail by hanging them to death in the evening and putting their dead bodies to fire on the banks of the Ravi River) and identified the writer of the letter as Sukhdev, who had signed the letter as 'one of the many.'[4] This dastardly act of the British Government had shaken the nation to its very foundation. Be what it was. In addition to other things he justified his stand of appealing the members of revolutionary party by making them public appeals become of their style of "work in secret" and lastly said that he could only "give the assurance...when the final settlement comes...all political prisoners must be discharged." In this open letter, Gandhiji had also said that it was not absence of will to get the release of all the political prisoners from the British Jails but the absence of power to get it done that was causing undue delay in their release.

II

Since the above quoted letter dated 23rd April, 1931 written in reply to Martyr Sukhdev's letter by the Mahatma continues to claim that Gandhiji strongly willed to see all the political prisoners released, let us first start to find out the validity of this claim by examining the writings, speeches and other utterances of Mahatma Gandhi on the issue and then study his views on the martyrdom of the revolutionaries and the failure of his earlier efforts to save them from the jaws of death at the British gallows. Under the pall of grief and shock, angry youth and sympathizers of the revolutionary nationalists had gathered at the venue of the session of the Congress at Karachi on 26 March 1931 to know the details as to what the Mahatma had done to save the lives of the trio implicated in a political case. Although Gandhiji as a first speaker on the occasion addressed the delegates on various issues for a long time but he did not utter a single word about it. When Gandhiji was about to close his speech, the question on his role in saving the life of Bhagat Singh was asked. He replied: "*I pleaded with the Viceroy as best as I could. I brought all the persuasion at my command to bear on him." On the day fixed for the final interview with Bhagat Singh's relations I wrote a personal letter to the Viceroy on the morning of 23rd, I poured my whole soul into it, but to no avail. I might have done one thing more, you say. I might have made the commutation a term of the settlement. It could not be so made. And to threaten withdrawal would be a breach of faith. The Working Committee had agreed with me in not making commutation a condition precedent to truce. I could therefore only mention it apart from the settlement. I had hoped for magnanimity. My hope was not to materialize. But that can be no ground for breaking the settlement...But why should that failure worry us? Success is in God's hands. Our failure should spur us to greater effort.*"

The Mahatma's assertion that he pleaded the case of commutation of the sentence with the Viceroy as best as he could and that he "brought all the persuasion at his command to bear on him," is debatable because before he decided to meet the Viceroy he had taken the Congress Working Committee in confidence "not making commutation a condition precedent to truce." Gandhiji himself admits in the next sentence also that instead of making serious efforts to save the lives of Bhagat Singh and his comrades, he "could therefore only mention it apart from the settlement." In the face of this stand, to say that he did all "what was humanly possible" is ante controvertible.

Further, on the concluding day of the session (29th March 1931), the Congress passed a resolution drafted by Gandhiji on the issue. It read: "This Congress, while dissociating itself from and disapproving of political violence in any shape or form, places on record its admiration of the bravery and sacrifice of the late Sardar Bhagat Singh and his comrades Syts. Sukhdev and Raj guru, and mourns with the bereaved families the loss of these lives. The Congress is of the opinion that this triple execution is an act of wanton vengeance and is a deliberate flouting of the unanimous demand of the nation for commutation. This Congress is further of the opinion that Government have lost the golden opportunity of promoting goodwill between the two nations, admittedly held to be essential at this juncture, and of winning over to them method of peace the party which, being driven to despair, resorts to political violence."[5]

Now, let us have a look at the meetings between Mahatma Gandhi and the Viceroy between 16th February to 4th March in which Gandhiji said to have expressed his "Will" or "Pleaded" for the release of all political prisoners and commutation of the sentence passed on the Lahore Conspiracy trio by the tribunal. It is on record, Gandhiji met the Viceroy on 18th February 1931. When the formal meeting was over he mentioned the case of Bhagat Singh. The version of the Viceroy on the issue is:

"In conclusion and not connected with the above, he (Mahatma Gandhi) mentioned the case of Bhagat Singh. He did not plead for commutation, although he would, being opposed to all taking of life, take that course himself. He also thought it would have an influence for peace. But he did ask for postponement in present circumstances. I contented myself with saying that, whatever might be the decision as to exact dates, I could not think there was any case for commutation which might not be made with equal force in the case of any other violent crime. The Viceroy's powers of commutation were designed for use on well-known grounds of clemency, and I could not feel that they ought to be invoked on grounds that were admittedly political."[6]

However, the version of Mahatma Gandhi on this issue is different. He recorded that "I talked about Bhagat Singh. I told him: "This has no connection with our discussion, and it may even be inappropriate on my part to mention it. But if you want to make the present atmosphere more favourable, you should suspend Bhagat Singh's execution." The Viceroy liked this very much. He said: "*I am very grateful to you that you have put this thing before me in this manner. Commutation of sentence is a difficult thing, but suspension is certainly worth considering.*" He went on to add that "I said about Bhagat Singh: "He is undoubtedly a brave man but I would certainly say that he is not in his right mind. However, this is the evil of capital punishment, that it gives no opportunity to such a man to reform himself. I am putting this matter before you as a humanitarian issue and desire suspension of sentence in order that there may not be unnecessary turmoil in the country. I myself should release him, but I cannot expect any government to do so. I would not take it ill even if you do not give any reply on this issue."[7]

After going through both the versions one can clearly visualize that both the Viceroy and the Mahatma agree that the question of commutation of the sentence never cropped up during their discussion. The only question that struck to their minds was the political fall out of the execution of the sentence leading to unnecessary turmoil in the country. However, according to the version of the Viceroy there was a faint hope of postponement of Bhagat Singh's execution whereas Gandhiji gathered wrong impression that the Viceroy certainly was agreeable to his suggestion for suspension of execution of the sentence.

Again, after reaching on an agreement for suspension of the Civil Disobedience Movement when Gandhiji began to address public for garnering support for the success of the truce he addressed a largely attended public meeting at Delhi on 7th March, 1931. On that occasion, some young people distributed pamphlets among the people denouncing the Government and the Mahatma for not doing enough to save the lives of Bhagat

Singh and his comrades. After having spoken on various other issues, Gandhiji took up the issue and made it clear that he had only made a truce with the Government and had not signed a final agreement with it. He also repeated that throughout the negotiations he was not acting on his own free will. Rather the whole Working Committee of the Congress was at his back and thus the terms and conditions finalized in the deal are cumulative in nature. He further assured them that it was still open for them to secure the release of Bhagat Singh and others if they would implement the settlement. He further said, "Let 'Young India' stand by the settlement and fulfill all its conditions, and if, God willing, Bhagat Singh and others alive when we have arrived at the proper stage, they would not only be saved from the gallows but released."[8]

But Gandhiji did not forget to remind the young leaders about the futility of the violent methods adopted by the revolutionaries to secure the freedom of India. He asked them to fulfill the conditions of the settlement and shun violence. Warning them he said: "If you pin your faith to violence, take it from me that you will not only not secure Bhagat Singh's release but will have to sacrifice thousands of Bhagat Singhs. I was not prepared to do so, and hence I preferred the way of peace, of non-violence...I beseech you then, if you want the release of the prisoners, to change your methods, to accept the settlement, and then come and ask me about the Gharwalis and Bhagat Singh. Come to me six months hence, and ask me the question you are asking me today and I promise to satisfy you."[9]

Since the pressure of popular opinion in favour of the commutation of the sentence passed against Bhagat Singh and his associates was mounting and Gandhiji himself was feeling very embarrassed while facing the people in his country wide tour, he was forced to make a last minute effort to appeal to the Viceroy saying therein: "It seems cruel to inflict this letter on you, but the interest of peace demands a final appeal. Though you were frank enough to tell me that there was little hope of your commuting the sentence of death on Bhagat Singh and two others..." and he went on to add: "Popular opinion rightly or wrongly demands commutation. When there is no principle at the stake, it is often a duty to respect it...Political murders have been condoned before now. It is worth while saving these lives, if thereby many other innocent lives are likely to be saved and may be even revolutionary crime also stamped out." Further he appealed the viceroy to save him from a grave crisis in his political standing which loomed large in the face of the present circumstances. Giving a personal touch to the whole matter he exhorted the Viceroy by stating, "Since you seem to value my influence such as it is in favour of peace, do not please unnecessarily make my position, difficult as it is, almost too difficult for future work."[10] It is not known whether this letter dated 23rd March 1931 was ever acknowledged by the Viceroy or not but it is certain that it could be termed as a last-minute desperate attempt on the part of the Mahatma to arouse the conscience of the British Government.[11] But this attempt failed to do so because on the same evening, the trio was hanged to death. Gandhiji was quick to pay his glowing tributes to the martyrs but did not forget to warn the youth of the country against following their example of self sacrifice on the altar of the Mother-land. He wrote: "Bhagat Singh and his companions have been executed and have become martyrs. Their death seems to have been a personal loss to many. I join in the tributes paid to the memory of these young men. And yet I must warn the youth of the country against following their example. We should not utilize our energy, our spirit of sacrifice, our labours and indomitable courage in the way they have utilized theirs. This country must not be liberated through bloodshed."[12]

He was quick to address the Congressmen and asked them not to "swerve from the path it has chalked out for itself.

According to my view, notwithstanding the gravest provocation the Congress should endorse the settlement and test its capacity to secure the result hoped for. We must not put ourselves in the wrong by getting angry. We must realize that commutation of the sentences was not a part of the truce. We may accuse the Government of violence but we cannot accuse it of breach of the settlement. It is my conviction that the grave blunder committed by the Government has increased our power to win freedom and Bhagat Singh and his comrades have embraced death they prefer. Let us not throw away this opportunity by doing anything in anger. It is beyond dispute that there will be a general strike and we cannot honour the deceased patriots better than by taking out absolutely peaceful and dignified processions." [13]

Later speaking at Congress Session at Karachi, Gandhiji said, "By the executions the Government has given the nation grave cause for provocation. It has shocked me too inasmuch as my negotiations and talks had made me entertain a distant hope that Bhagat Singh, Raj guru and Sukhdev might be saved. I am not surprised that young men are angry with me for not having been able to save them...They had a right to do so inasmuch as they thought that I had not done everything in my power to save Bhagat Singh, or that being a believer in ahimsa, I had simply neglected Bhagat Singh and his comrades… then on my arrival at the railway station a young man handed to me flowers made of black cloth…I shall also tell you what I want to do with them. If the young men come and tell me that they should not have been angry and that their suspicions about me were groundless and that therefore they want the flowers returned to them, I shall gladly give them back. But if they do not do so, they will be sent to the Ashram to be preserved as heirlooms." [14]

"And now a message for the young men: If you want my service, do not disown me; come and understand everything from me. You must know that it is against my creed to punish even a murderer, a thief or a dacoit. There can be therefore no excuse for suspicion that I did not want to save Bhagat Singh. But I want you also to realize Bhagat Singh's error. If I had had an opportunity of speaking to Bhagat Singh and his comrades, I should have told them that the way they pursued was wrong and futile... Rowdy demonstrations cannot help us. Could they call Bhagat Singh back to life? They can only retard the advent of *swaraj*. I agree that the Government has given sufficient cause for provocation, but I want the impatient your in the name of God, in the name of our dear Motherland, to throw themselves heart and soul in the non-violent struggle. I ask them to trust my unbroken experience of forty years of the practice of non-violence."[15]

Mahatma Gandhi paid a glowing tribute to Bhagat Singh and his two associates in a write up published in *Navjivan* (Gujarati) on 29th March 1931 and also castigated the revolutionaries on their adopting violent methods to secure their goal of freedom. He squarely blamed them by saying that their violent acts had unnecessarily impeded the early dawn of freedom and sternly warned the young people against adopting their acts as ideals.[16]

While paying a glowing tribute to the bravery and sacrifice of Bhagat Singh and his comrades, he added; "But I want the greater bravery...of the meek, the gentle and the non-violent, the bravery that will mount the gallows without injuring, or harbouring any thought of injury to a single soul."[17] Violence against the foreigner could not be separated from violence against one another. The Kanpur riots, he said, were "the handwriting on the wall...we have harboured violence in our hearts, we have been guilty of using coercion."[18]

Making a passionate appeal to the country for sanity, Gandhiji said: "I have felt deeply ashamed of these deeds of blood, and to whoever my voice may reach I wish to declare that such things may any day prove more than I can bear...as soon as I feel that life is unbearable, I should hope to have the courage to fast myself to death rather than witness those blood feuds."[19]

Dwelling upon the efforts he had made for the commutation of the death sentence of the condemned revolutionaries, Mahatma Gandhi said, "I pleaded with Viceroy as best as I could. I brought all the persuasion at my command to bear upon him." Almost all the biographers of Gandhiji have accepted this public statement of the Mahatma as true version of the negotiations held between him and Lord Irwin between February 18 and March 4 1931 when the Pact was clinched between the two. However, terms of settlement published in the Gazette of India of March 6, 1931 makes no mention of the release of revolutionaries from the jails.[20]

On March 20 Gandhiji had a meeting with Herbert Emerson who, in his note to the Viceroy, recorded what transpired in the meeting between the two regarding the case of Bhagat Singh: "...I then asked him if he had seen in the papers that the Governor-General in Council had rejected the petition for mercy on behalf of Bhagat Singh. He said that he had and that he was apprehensive regarding the consequences. I did not mention the date on which the execution would be carried out, but I did explain to him that the question as to whether it should take place before or after the Karachi Congress had been very seriously considered by Government who realized the difficulties of either course, but thought it would have been unfair to the condemned persons to postpone execution and also not fair to Gandhi to allow the impression to gain ground that commutation was under consideration when this was not the case. He agreed that of the two alternatives it is better not to wait, but he suggested, though not seriously, that the third course of commutation of the sentence would have been better still. He did not seem to me to be particularly concerned about the matter. I told him that we should be lucky if we got through without disorder, and I asked him to do all that he could to prevent meetings being held in Delhi during the next few days and to restrain violent speeches. He promised to do what he could."[21]

Next day, as a follow of to his talks with Gandhiji, Emerson wrote a letter to him soliciting his help in restraining violent speeches of Congressmen criticizing the Government stand on the Bhagat Singh Case in the proposed meeting to be addressed by Subhash Chander Bose in Delhi the same evening.[22] Gandhiji replied to him: "Thank you for your letter just received. I know of the meeting you refer to. I have taken every precaution possible and hope that nothing untoward will happen. I suggest that there should not be display of police force and no interference in the meeting. Irritation is likely to be there. It will be better to allow it find vent through meetings, etc."[23] Here Gandhiji emerges as playing simultaneously the role as savior of Bhagat Singh and also advisor of the Government suggesting them how to tackle the difficult situation of their own creation.

Commenting on the dual role of Gandhiji at this stage, D.P. Das says, "He genuinely believed that the Delhi Pact was much more important than the lives of one revolutionary here or another there. Bhagat Singh and his comrades were the tragic cases that arose at the time which almost stood between a settlement with Irwin by Gandhi. Gandhi had no difficulty in making his choice or option. In the light of his understanding, the course he took was the only one available in the circumstances. It is true it led him to the path of small deception for a cause which he considered to be noble and patriotic."[24]

However, on 23 March, when Tej Bahadur Sapru after meeting the Viceroy informed Gandhiji that the Government was going to execute the death sentence in the case of Bhagat Singh and his associates without further delay. Gandhiji was quick to saw through the emerging gravity of the situation and hoping against all hope, he promptly made a desperate attempt to influence the course of events in the matter. Adding a personal note to the contents of the letter, the Mahatma requested the Viceroy: "Since you seem to value my influence such as it is in favour of peace, do not please unnecessarily make my position difficult as it is, almost too difficult for future work."[25]

Whether this letter was ever acknowledged by the Viceroy or not is not known to us as no reference of the same has come up from the records of the time. But the earnest request of the Mahatma to the Viceroy for commutation of the sentences in this last letter shows that he did write the letter on finding himself pushed in a tight spot on the eve of the Karachi Congress session. Earlier to it, he and the Congress Party seemed to have failed to recognize the real face of the British imperialists who had offered them to talk on the constitutional reforms and release of non-violent prisoners but not agreeing inclusion of the issue of release of revolutionaries in the Gandhi-Irwin Pact was just to divide the public will by separating the revolutionaries from the Congress fold and then use one against the other and punish both if the need to do so ever arose. Therefore, it was an error of judgement on the part of the Congress and Mahatma Gandhi to have agreed to truce with the Government without settling the release of political prisoners of all categories. Be what it was. The fact remains that the Viceroy did not show the minimum courtesy of acknowledging this last appeal of Gandhiji soliciting his help for smooth sailing in the forthcoming Congress session.

Since the day the Pact was signed, the revolutionaries were feeling cheated at the hands of the Congress leadership because they were left high and dry during the course of negotiations on the issue of release of political prisoners under the settlement. Their disillusion with the Congress increased when they found that even after martyrdom of the revolutionary trio, the Congressmen were continuing to adopt stances of getting all political prisoners including revolutionaries released if they contributed to make the successful implementation of the pact possible. This irritated them more than the Government repression. On the other hand, the Congress and Gandhiji, who had shown total reluctance to include as precondition of agreement with the government the release of the revolutionaries, left no stone unturned to take advantage of the sacrifices of the martyrs whose names were stirring the souls of the youth through out the country. This was repudiated as strongly by the revolutionaries as possible as is revealed by the letter of Sukhdev referred to above. The issue of Commutation of the sentence of Bhagat Singh was not included as one of the conditions by the Congress when Mahatma Gandhi's discussions started with the Viceroy for settlement of the issues which had cropped up during the course of Civil Disobedience Movement. However, on February 18 itself, Gandhiji had appealed to the Viceroy to consider on humanitarian ground the postponement of the execution of the sentence of the revolutionary trio. Literally, both the participants had declared that the issue was around the suspension and not the commutation of the death sentence. Gandhiji, in a statement issued on 5th March appealed to the revolutionary organizations to give an opportunity to get the political prisoners released including those being guilty of murder. He reiterated this stand in his speech before a huge public gathering in Delhi on 7th March and sought the cooperation of the youth to make the temporarily arrived at agreement with the Viceroy. The position of Gandhiji in relation to the young revolutionaries was made extremely difficult by the execution of Bhagat Singh, on the eve of the annual session of the Congress at Karachi in the last week of March. He had mildly pleaded for clemency at his very first meeting with the Viceroy, not as a condition for a settlement, but on humanitarian grounds only.

The discussion about the facts of the case leads one to infer that through the means of his writings and public speeches

Gandhiji kept up the public expectations to see the release of their popular heroes from the imprisonment unscathed. But he was a pragmatic politician, who adopted only public postures as far as saving of lives of revolutionaries like Bhagat Singh and his comrades from the British gallows are concerned. He was not as serious on this issue as he was on other issues raised with the Viceroy during the course of negotiations leading to signing of Gandhi--Irwin Pact. In fact from the very beginning, his personal attempts to persuade the Viceroy on the issue were too feeble to evoke any positive response from the latter. This was so as in the very beginning of the peace parleys supported by the Congress Executive Committee, he had raised the issue very casually with the Viceroy and then onwards he was forced to bow before the dictates of the imperial government largely due to the fact that he did not want the "Gandhi-Irwin Pact" to be scuttled midway.

III

The findings of the study have already been given in the preceding pages of the paper; however, a few words by way of conclusion are required for a quick revision of the main points. The contemporary records on the issue make it explicitly clear that both the Congress and Mahatma Gandhi were trying to take credit for those things that they had never done in favour of the revolutionary heroes. They never took up seriously 'the unanimous demand of the nation for commutation' of sentence of Bhagat Singh and his comrades with the British authorities. They very feebly raised the issue with the Government presumably for public consumption. It also emerges out that if at all the Government agreed to their subdued submissions they would be satisfied if they merely agreed to postpone the execution of this sentence for some time so that they could hold their Karachi Session peacefully.

In a nutshell, it can be said that destiny of the martyrs, no doubt, is shaped by none else but themselves. They are the real architects of their fate or destiny. So is true with the great martyr Bhagat Singh. He chose to lay down his life24 along with his comrades to wake the nation up and root out the foreign rule. He knew no compromise and nothing less than freedom for the nation could have stopped him from dying on the gallows. But those Congressmen, who were leading the nation from the front and kept on arousing hopes among the masses for the release of all the political prisoners including the revolutionaries, were expected to rise up to the people's expectations. The people of India had high expectations from Mahatma Gandhi, the then sole unchallenged leader of the Indian National Congress that he would rise to the occasion and succeed in dissuading the Government of the day to execute the special tribunal decision and at least commute death sentence of Bhagat Singh and his comrades to life imprisonment. But he failed to rise to the occasion to do so and unwittingly put his seal to the destiny of the revolutionary trio to fall prey to the British farce of fair trial as the judge "decided to award not only deterrent but a retributive punishment to them."

Notes and References

1. M.N. Gupta, *Gandhi and His Times*. Delhi. 1982. p. 114.
2. The Tribune, Lahore dated 4 October , 1930.
3. *The Collected Works of Mahatma Gandhi*, Volume XLV, published by the Publication Division, Ministry of I and B, Government of India. New Delhi, 1971, Young India, 23 April 1931.
4. *Young India*, 2 April, 1931.
5. *The Collected Works of Mahatma Gandhi*, Interview with Viceroy (Viceroy's Version), Volume, XLV, p. 363.
6. Ibid. pp 196-97.
7. Ibid. p. 200.
8. Ibid. p. 272.
9. Ibid. p. 272-273.
10. Ibid. p. 333.
11. Ibid. p. 348.
12. Ibid.
13. Ibid. p. 349.
14. Ibid. p. 350.
15. Ibid. p. 351.
16. Ibid. pp. 359-60.
17. *The Collected Works of Mahatma Gandhi*, Volume, XLV, p. 344.
18. Ibid. p. 350-351.
19. Ibid. p. 351.
20. Ibid, pp. 432-436; *Gazette of India Extraordinary of 5th March 1931.*
21. *The Collected Works of Mahatma Gandhi*, Volume, XLV, p. 440; also See, p. 316.
22. A.I.C.C. File No. 16-B, 1931. NMML, Delhi. Letter of Emerson to Gandhiji (...With reference to our conversation last night regarding the danger of excitement being worked up in connection with the execution of the sentences passed on Bhagat Singh etc., the Chief Commissioner informs me that notice has been given in the city that Mr. Subhas Chandra Bose will address a meeting of protest tonight at 5.30. I fully realize your difficulties in the matter and I think that you realize the difficulties of Government and also their desire at the present time to avoid, if possible, preventive action, which may, however, be unavoidable if excitement grows. If a meeting is held tonight, it is almost certain to increase feeling, especially if speeches of an

inflammatory character are made. Government will much appreciate any assistance you feel able to give to prevent this and to check the creation of conditions which, if uncontrolled, may have serious consequences."

23. AICC File No. 16-B, 1931; NMML, Delhi. *Collected Works of Mahatma Gandhi*, Vol. XLV, p. 316.

24. *The Mainstream*, dated 15 August 1970.

25. Extracts of Bhagat Singh's last letter as cited by Gandhiji in *Navjivan* dated 29 March 1931 are: "I have been arrested while waging a war. For me there can be no gallows. Put me into the mouth of cannon and blow me off."

13

Relevance of the Ideas of Bhagat Singh in the Present Time

Prof. Brij Kishore Sharma

The contribution of revolutionaries in the freedom movement of India has not been evaluated and analyzed in right perspective. The revolutionary activities from 1857 to 1947 appeared on the political scene of India in the one form or the other. Undoubtedly they contributed immensely to the freedom of the country. Their aims and objectives were not confined only to attain the freedom of country from foreign yoke. They had a definite ideology and philosophy and their aim was to transform India into an independent, self-sufficient and powerful country.

The revolutionary phase of 1924-31 is known as Bhagat Singh era. This era had some specific peculiarities in comparison to the early revolutionary phases and activities. The early revolutionaries believed in individual act of violence and terrorism while the Bhagat Singh's group prepared a detailed strategy for collective action against the foreign rule and its allies. Infact this phase was highly influenced with various new forces of national and international importance. The rise of working class trade unions after the First World War was one of them. In the same manner, the new mass consciousness of

Head, Deptt. of History, V.M. Open University, KOTA (Raj.) - 324007

peasantry, the Russian Revolution, emergence of Communist group in India etc. was important among these. Moreover, the sudden suspension of the Non-Cooperation movement disappointed the youths and revolutionaries. In reaction to this event, the revolutionaries came out of frustration and disappointment very soon by reorganizing themselves with Hindustan Republic Army or Association (HRA) in October 1924.

Since the inception of HRA, Bhagat Singh was associated with its activities. In 1926, he also founded the famous Naujawan Bharat Sabha. He also organized the Lahore Students Union as initially Lahore was the centre of his activities. The establishment of the Hindustan Socialist Republican Association (or Army) during 9th and 10th September 1928 was an important event in the revolutionary movement. Shaheed Bhagat Singh was one of the prominent leaders of HSRA and was among its main founders. He became very popular in the Northern India. Jawaharlal Nehru had also mentioned this fact in his autobiography as follows : *"It is well to appreciate this, for only so can we have some understanding of subsequent events, of the phenomenon of Bhagat Singh, and of his sudden and amazing popularity in North India. It is very easy and very fatuous to condemn persons or acts without seeking to understand the spring of action, the causes that underlie. Bhagat Singh was not previously well known; he did not become popular because of an act of violence and act of terrorism. Terrorists have flourished in India, off and on, for nearly thirty years, and at no time, except in the early days in Bengal, did any of them attain a fraction of that popularity which came to Bhagat Singh".*[1]

In the concluding Para Jawaharlal Nehru had mentioned that Bhagat Singh thus did not become popular because of his act of terrorism, but because he seemed to vindicate, for the moment, the honour of Lala Lajpat Rai, and through him of the nation. He became a symbol; the act was forgotten, the symbol remained, and within a few months each town and village of the Punjab, and to a lesser extent in the rest of northern India, resounded with his name. Innumerable songs grew up about him, and the popularity that the man achieved was something amazing."[2] Pattabhi Sitaramayya, a close associate of Gandhi and the author of the History of the Congress, has said, *"both Gandhiji and Bhagat Singh were equally popular, the first because of his experiments with truth and the second because of his essays in bravery."*

It may also be mentioned here that for some time the popularity of Bhagat Singh seems to have outshone that of Gandhiji. A confidential Intelligence Bureau account, Terrorism in India (1927- 1936), declared that for a *short time Bhagat Singh* had surpassed the popularity of Gandhiji as a foremost politician". While denouncing their cult of violence even Mahatma Gandhi, an apostle of non-violence, unhesitantly appreciated their feelings of intense patriotism and their willingness to sacrifice their all for the emancipation of their country from foreign yoke.

The revolutionary activities in pre-Bhagat Singh era were included terrorist activities such as individual violent actions and plunder. While the Hindustan Socialist Republican Association and its leaders were fast moving towards organized mass actions, but brutal murder of Lala Lajpat Rai compelled them to adopt violent action.[3] The revolutionaries considered it a national humiliation and decided to avenge it. On 17th December 1928, Bhagat Singh, Chandra Shekhar Azad and Rajguru assassinated J.P. Saunders, Assistant Superintendent of Police at Lahore. Next day, a red poster was issued by Bhagat Singh all over Lahore. It was as follow: *It was indeed a great insult to the nation comprising of crores of people when an ordinary British Police official murdered a most respected national leader, Lala Lajpat Rai. It was the foremost duty of each and every youth of India to perform this kind of scared duty........We regret to have had to kill a person but he was part and parcel of that inhuman and unjust order which was to be destroyed.*[4]

The HSRA leadership decided to propagate its objectives and programme among the people of the country through various means. Bhagat Singh and his comrades decided to throw a bomb in the Central Assembly to attract the attention of public, government and Assembly members. Bhagat Singh and Batukeshwar Dutta were entrusted with task. On 8th April, 1929, they threw two bombs in the Central Assembly when the Public Safety Bill and Trade Disputes Bill were introduced. They shouted the slogans of *Inquilab Zindabad, down with the British Imperialism* etc. They could have managed to escape but they did not move from the spot. The objective was to get arrested and to use the trial court as a forum for propaganda so that people would become familiar with their movement and ideology. Bhagat Singh alongwith his comrades were tried for Assembly bomb case and Lahore conspiracy case and were sentenced to death. On 23rd March, 1931, Bhagat Singh, Sukhdev and Rajguru were hanged in Lahore Conspiracy case. Bhagat Singh and his comrades became immortal in the history of India. It was an untimely demise of political future of India.

The ideas of Bhagat Singh were very much matured but could not be implemented due to various reasons. He and his ideology could not reach to the masses at grass-root level. In the view of Bhagat Singh, the movement of Indian National Congress under Gandhi created obstacles in the way of revolutionaries. The theory of so called non-violence was utopian. But the theory of non-violence created confusion in the struggle for India's independence. The theory of non-violence was based on compromise and suited to the imperialists, Indian capitalists and Zamindars, princes and rulers' propertied classes and liberal freedom fighters. The revolutionary ideas of Bhagat Singh are still relevant in India and their implementation is awaited.

Just after the Martyrdom of Bhagat Singh and his comrades, Congress session was held at Karachi to endorse the Gandhi-Irwin Pact. There was anger among the people against Gandhiji, especially the youth, as to why he had not refused to sign the pact on the question of acquaintance of revolutionaries. All along Gandhiji's route to Karachi, he was greeted with black flag demonstrations.[5] In the Congress session of Karachi slogans "Gandhi go back" and "Down with Gandhi" were raised.[6] The Congress passed a resolution drafted by Gandhiji by which it, 'while disassociating himself from and disapproving of political violence in any shape or forms', admired 'the bravery and sacrifice of the three martyrs.[7] In the same session, Subhash Chandra Bose said : *He symbolizes the spirit of revolt that had taken possession of the country.... Before he passed away, he had become the cynosure of millions of eyes and the symbol of the spirit and aspirations of a new India, dauntless in the face of death, determined to smash imperialist rule and raise on its ruins the edifice of a free peoples' state in this great land of ours.*[8]

The contribution of Bhagat Singh and his comrades or even the revolutionaries in the freedom struggle of India cannot be undermined. The attainment of India's independence on 15th August 1947 was outcome of combined efforts of various shades of freedom fighters in which revolutionaries share was of worth mention. But its credit was given to the non-violence path of Gandhiji. But at the same time, the independence given to India was very far from the aspirations of revolutionaries. Infact the struggle for independence could not reach to the right destinations. The ideology of Bharat Singh and his comrades has been rightly briefed by Sumit Sarkar as follows : *As Bhagat Singh clarified in his trial, revolution to him was 'not the cult of the bomb and pistol', but a total change of society culminating in the overthrow of both foreign and Indian capitalism and the establishment of the dictatorship of the proletariat. Revolution is the inalienable right of mankind. Freedom is the imprescriptible birthright of all. The labourer is the real sustainer of society.... To the altar of this revolution; we have brought our youth as incense, for no sacrifice is too great for so magnificent a cause. We are content. We awaited the advent of revolution. Inquilab Zindabad. The Assembly bombs were meant to be purely demonstrative, and the occasion significantly enough, was the anti-labour Trades Disputes Bill. Awaiting execution for the murder of Saunders, the young man of 23 began a systematic study of Marxism, and wrote a profoundly moving piece entitled why I am an Atheist defending total rejection of all religions on grounds of human dignity and rational logic.*[9]

Still the ideas of Bhagat Singh are relevant in Indian political, economic and social context. The British Government in India designated the revolutionaries as terrorist, while they were not terrorists. They had given a definite philosophy and ideology of revolution. Bhagat Singh abandoned his belief in terrorism and individual heroic violent action. He had admitted that in the beginning, he believed in terrorism but as time went on, he realized the killing of persons is senseless, if it target the innocent ones. It only aggravated and side-tracked the issue of social transformation. But force is to be met with force. Force when aggressively used is violence, and is morally unjustifiable but when it is used in the furtherance of a legitimate cause, it has its moral justification.[10]

Bhagat Singh's ideas about revolution are still relevant because these are based on scientific thoughts. In the manifesto of the HSRA, he explained the concept of revolution as follows: *Upheavals have always been a terror to holders of power and privilege (but) Revolution is a phenomenon which nature loves and without which there can be no progress either in nature or in human affairs. Revolution is not a philosophy of despair. Revolution may be anti-government; but it certainly not anti-man. It is a vital living force which is indicative of external conflict between the old and the new……Revolution is Law, Revolution is order and Revolution is Truth.*[11]

Bhagat Singh and his comrades also gave expression to their understanding that revolution meant the development and organization of a mass movement of the exploited and suppressed section of society by the revolutionary intelligentsia.[12] There were three main components of the revolutionary programme of Bhagat Singh viz. Growth of Nationalism, complete independence and establishment of socialist society in India. Bhagat Singh and his comrades defined revolution as 'Independence, social, political and economic aimed at establishing a new order of society in which political and economic exploitations will be impossibility.[13] Their first objectives was national liberation, while their final goal was to establish socialist social order to end exploitation of man by man.[14] Thus, Bhagat Singh envisage to convert the liberation struggle into socialist revolution. He explained his ideology of Revolution before the court in Assembly Bomb Case: *Revolution does not necessarily involve sanguinary strife, nor is there any place in it for individual vendetta. It is not cult of the bomb and the pistol. By 'Revolution' we mean that present order of things, which is based on manifest injustice, must change. Producers or labourers in spite of being the most necessary element of society are robbed by their exploiters of the fruits of their labour and deprived of their elementary rights. The peasant, who grows corn for all, starves with his family, the weaver who supplied the world market with textile fabrics, does not have enough to cover his own and children's bodies, masons, smiths and carpenters who raise magnificent palaces live like pariahs in the slums. The capitalist and exploiters, the parasites of society, squander millions on their whims. The terrible inequalities and forced disparity of chances are bound to lead to chaos. The state of affairs cannot last long, and it is obvious that the present order of society in merry-making is on the brink of a volcano.* 15 In a letter from jail Bhagat Singh wrote: *The peasant have to liberate themselves not only from foreign yoke but also from the yoke of landlords and capitalists.*[16] On 3rd March 1931, he declared that the struggle in India would continue so long - *a handful of exploiters go on exploiting the labour of common people for their own ends. It matters little whether these exploiters are purely British capitalists, or British and Indians in alliance or even purely Indians.*[17]

Bhagat Singh was highly influenced with the Marxist theory of scientific socialism, but at the same time, he was free from sectarian and dogmatic approach of Marxism. His idea of nationalism and national liberation was in absolute term. To him, the demand of the Congress of 'Dominion Status' was so-imperialism. He and his associates never supported this demand of Congress. He had no faith in Congress and Gandhiji. Bhagat Singh and Batukeshwar Dutt after throwing bomb they also commented: *We have only marked the end of an era of utopian non-violence of whose fatality the rising generation has been convinced beyond the shadow of doubts.*[18] Thus, he was in opposition of Gandhism. He criticized Gandhiji for knocking the doors of the government house with baggers bowl in his hand and dominion status of his lips.[19] In his view, the congress policy was week, reformatory and constitutional. They strengthen the hand of enemy. So many pacts were made previously but nothing materialized.[20] He even blamed Gandhiji for destroying the unity of all parties established at the time of boycott of the Simon Commission. The Gandhi-Irwin pact shattered the unity of different political parties and ideologies in India. Apart of all, it may be said that Bhagat Singh phenomenon compelled the Congress to adopt resolution on "complete independence" in December 1929 at Lahore.

Bhagat Singh was a great believer of secularism. He was not in favour of mixing religion with politics or political use of religion and vice-versa. Being fully and consciously secular, he understood, more clearly than many of his contemporaries, the danger that communalism posed to the nation and the national movement. He often told his audience that communalism was a big an enemy as colonialism.[21] In April 1928, at the youth conference Bhagat Singh and his comrade openly opposed the suggestion that youth belonging to religious - communal organizations should be permitted to become members of the Naujawan Bharat Sabha. Religion was one's private concern and communalism was an enemy to be fought, argued Bhagat Singh.[22] Earlier in 1927, condemning communal killings as barbaric, he had pointed out that communal killers did not kill a person because he was guilty of any particular act but simply because the person happened to be a Hindu, Muslim or Sikh. But, wrote Bhagat Singh, a new group of youth was coming forward who did not recognize any difference based on religion and saw a person first as a human being and then as an Indian.[23]

Atheism was an essential part of his political philosophy or his ideology in totality. In his view the concept of God and religion was the root cause of communalism. He also saw the importance of freeing the people from the mental bondage of religion and superstition. In his view there is no logical basis of existence of God. Thus, he denied the existence of God. In an article entitled 'Why I am an Atheist' he explained that how he became an atheist.[24] He advocated for development of scientific thinking and out rightly rejected spiritualism and metaphysical philosophy. The metaphysical philosophy in his view is also an instrument of exploitation and oppression. The common man is being exploited and oppressed to large extent because of his ignorance. By the end of 1926 he was convinced about the futility of believing in the theory of an almighty supreme being who created, guided and controlled the universe. To be a revolutionary, he said, one required immense moral courage, but one also required 'criticism and independent thinking'. In the struggle for self-emancipation, humanity had to struggle against the narrow conception of religion' as also against the belief of God. Any man who stands for progress', he wrote, 'has to criticize, disbelieve and challenge every item of the old faith. Item by item, he has to reason out every nook and corner of the prevailing faith.[25]

Besides, the above ideological foundations and conviction his patriotism, bravery, fearlessness, firm determination, love for humanity, human values, commitment for freedom also characterized his ideology. He never compromised with his opponent the British rule. Thus, he was man of principles, convictions and commitments and there was no scope of convenience.

The ideas of Bhagat Singh were very relevant in the present time. The independence of the country is threatened by the imperialist powers. It cannot be denied that imperialism is present in India in one form or another since independence obviously; India is victims of new imperialism. There is an ardent need to fight the imperialism. In this regard the anti-imperialist and pro-independence ideas of Bhagat Singh are pertinent and relevant. The prevailing social, economic and political inequality and disparity are adversely affecting the national life. Socialist pattern of the society is the need of hour. The ideas of Bhagat Singh pertaining to scientific, socialism are obviously relevant. The problem of communalism is very complicated. This has presented challenges before the Indian society and nation. We have already paid a heavy cost of it in 1947 with the partition of country on communal basis. Besides religious communalism the problem of caste communalism has emerged as a big challenge. The ideas of Bhagat Singh are very much relevant in mitigating such problems. It may be concluded that there is an ardent need to study and implement the ideas and philosophy of Bhagat Singh in the national interest.

Notes & References

1. Jawaharlal Nehru, *An Autobiography*, Delhi, 1962, pp. 174-75.
2. Ibid., pp. 175-76.
3. During the anti- Simon Commission demonstration at Lahore on 30 October, 1928. Lala Lajpat Rai was brutally lathi charged. He breathed his last on 17th November, 1928.
4. Gopal Thakur, *Bhagat Singh: The Man and His Ideas*, New Delhi, 1961, p. 12 and Jagmohan Singh and Chamanlal, *Bhagat Singh Aur Unke Sathiyon Ke Dastavez*, New Delhi 1986, p. 266.
5. Bipan Chandra & others, *India's Struggle for Independence*, New Delhi, 1989, p. 284.
6. Young India, 2 April 1931, Speech by Gandhiji at Karachi Congress.
7. Pattabhi Sitaramayya, *The History of Indian National Congress 1885-1935*, p. 768 Quoted from Bipan Chandra & others, op. cit, p. 284.
8. Ajoy Kumar Ghosh, *Bhagat Singh and his Comrades*, Bombay, 1945 p. 15.
9. Sumit Sarkar, *Modern India 1885-1947*, New Delhi, 1983, p. 268.
10. Delhi Assembly Bomb case Proceedings, statement of Bhagat Singh, 6 June 1929.
11. *The Revolutionary*, A Paper of Hindustan Socialist Republican Association, January, 1925.
12. Bipan Chandra & others, op. cit., p. 255.
13. Shiv Verma (ed.) *Selected Writings of Shaheed Bhagat Singh*, New Delhi. 1986, pp. 190, 198-9.
14. Jagmohan Singh and Chamanlal, op, cit., p. 267.
15. Delhi Assembly Bomb Case Proceedings, *Statement of Bhagat Singh*, 6 June 1929.
16. Bipan Chandra & others, op.cit., p. 256.
17. Ibid., p. 257.
18. National Archives of India, *HOME-Political Deptt. File No. 246/ 1930*.
19. L.P. Mathur, *Bhagat Singh The Prince of Martyrs*, Jaipur, 2002, p. 200.
20. Ibid., p. 203.
21. Bipan Chandra & others, op.cit., p. 257.

22. Ibid; Jagmohan Singh and Chamanlal, op.cit., pp. 1 90-3.
23. Ibid.
24. Virendra Sandhu, *Shaheed Bhagat Singh*, Delhi, 1974, pp. 102-112.
25. Bipan Chandra & others, op.cit.

14

The Life & Ideas of Shaheed Bhagat Singh : A Lesson for Today

Key note Address

Dr. M. A. Lari 'Azad'

Shaheede Azam Bhagat Singh was hanged on alter before 76 years that too in a city of today's Pakistan. Whenever a reference comes of martyrs, everybody utters Bhagat Singh's name within a second. Bhagat Singh has emerged as the most popular personality between patriots & youngmen of the subcontinent.

छियत्तर साल बाद भगत सिंह के क्रांतिकारी विचार मुंबई हवाई अड्डे की झुग्गियों जैसी जगह तक में गूँज रहे हैं।[1] उनके भतीजे, पंजाब वि.वि. के सेवानिवृत्त कम्प्यूटर विज्ञान के प्रो. जगमोहन सिंह 'पूंजीवादी नव साम्राज्यवाद' के विरुद्ध क्रांति का बिगुल फूँक रहे हैं। उन्होंने हवाई अड्डे की 226 एकड़ भूमि पर 85,000 झुग्गीवासियों को पूँजीवादी शोषण के विरुद्ध जाग्रत करने के लिए दो दिवसीय कार्यशाला आयोजित की। झुग्गीवासी और छात्र पंजाब की संस्था 'शहीदे आजम भगत सिंह स्तुति समिति' के मुंबई अध्याय में शामिल हुए हैं। वे नुक्कड़ नाटकों द्वारा झुग्गियों में जागृति फैला रहे हैं, कुछ स्वयंसेवक भगत सिंह के गाँव लायलपुर जिले के खटकड़ कलाँ भी गये थे। नाटक आरम्भ होते हैं, 'ये हक की लड़ाई ये घर की लड़ाई' गीत से। भगत सिंह किसान परिवार से थे परन्तु हक के लिए साम्राज्यशाही से लड़े, इसीलिए वे झुग्गीवाले भी अपनी हक की लड़ाई लड़ना चाहते हैं। भगत सिंह की जयन्ती तक ये अभियान चलेगा।[2]

Head, Dept. of PG. Studies & Research in The NREC College, Khurja-203131 (U.P.).

इतिहास का विनम्र शोधार्थी होने के नाते मैंने भगत सिंह द्वारा अपने जीवन काल में लिखित लेख, उनकी फांसी के बाद प्रकाशित अन्य लेखों तथा पाँचवें दशक के बाद प्रकाशित पुस्तकों का गहन अध्ययन करने का प्रयास किया। अनेक पुस्तकें विश्वविद्यालयी अनुसंधाताओं द्वारा कैरियर अकादमिक प्रतिष्ठा के लिए लिखी गयी और अन्य महंगे प्रकाशनों द्वारा पुस्तकालयों की धूल चाटने को छापी गयीं थीं। आम जनता तक पहुँची अखबारों में छपी और सिनेमा में चित्रित वीर पूजा की वह फोटो जिसे दक्षिणपंथी संगठन भी स्वहित में भुनाने लगे।

भगत सिंह को मात्र एक खून गर्माने वाला शहीद बनाकर भारतीय युवाओं को वीर पूजा की रूमानियत तक ही ले जाया गया जहाँ वतन परस्ती में मर मिटने की महान् घटना थी। दुर्भाग्य से भगत सिंह की महान विचारधारा, गहन चिंतन और स्वतंत्रता की स्पष्ट व्याख्या के पहलू से सरोकार रखा ही नहीं गया। उत्तर भारत का बच्चा-बच्चा वीर भगत के अमर बलिदान को जानता, मानता, गाता है, लेकिन शायद ही लोग भगतसिंह के क्रांतिकारी राजनीतिक विचारों और वर्तमान भारत के लिए उसकी प्रासंगिकता से परिचित हैं।

मेरा यहाँ विनम्र प्रयास है जनसाधारण विशेषकर युवाओं तक ये संदेश पहुँचाने का कि वीर हुतात्मा भगत सिंह ने केवल इन्कलाब के जोश में नौजवानी में फाँसी के फंदे को नहीं चूमा था, बल्कि भगत सिंह अपने युग के महान् व्यक्तित्वों गांधी, सुभाष, नेहरू, एम.एन. रॉय से भी आगे जाकर युवावस्था में ही एक ठोस राजनीतिक दर्शन और स्वतंत्रता के दिशा निर्देशन के स्पष्ट प्रतिपादक थे और आज उनके इस पहलू से अधिक प्रेरणा ली जा सकती है।

इतिहास लेखन की दृष्टि से भगत सिंह पर पाचवें दशक में गोपाल ठाकुर की पुस्तिका से लेकर गत वर्ष तक प्रकाशित भगत सिंह के अब तक उपलब्ध दस्तावेज़ों के बीच आठवें दशक में उनकी भतीजी वीरेन्द्र सिन्धु द्वारा सम्पादित पुस्तक में महान् विचारक भगत सिंह की राजनीतिक अवधारणा का परिचय मिलता है।[3] आठवें दशक के पूर्वार्द्ध में दिल्ली के युवा वामपंथियों ने भी भगत सिंह पर एक संकलन छापकर उनके ऊपर साम्यवादी प्रभाव को जताया।[4] प्रो. बिपन चन्द्रा ने आठवें दशक के उत्तरार्द्ध में भगत सिंह के दो लेखों की भूमिका लिखी तो स्थापित हो गया कि भगत सिंह मात्र एक वीर क्रांतिकारी ही नहीं थे बल्कि अपने समय के एक प्रखर राजनीतिक चिंतक थे और गहन अध्ययन एवं उत्तरोत्तर विकसित हो रही राजनीतिक विचारधारा से सम्पन्न थे। इतिहासकारों में सुमित सरकार, इरफान हबीब व हरबंस मुखिया प्रभृति ने माना कि भगत सिंह में मात्र भावनात्मक बहादुरी नहीं थी बल्कि गम्भीर अध्ययन मनन से उपजी परिपक्व विचारधारा भी थी। नवें दशक के पूर्वार्द्ध

में मन्मथनाथ गुप्त की कृति[5] के बाद भगत सिंह और साथियों के 10 दस्तावेज़ों[6] के निकलने के बाद 1986 में शिव वर्मा ने 28 दस्तावेज छापे। बापू के निबंध *'कल्ट आफ दि बम'* के उत्तर में भगत सिंह के जेल में लिखित लेख को भगवती चरण वोहरा ने अन्तिम रूप दिया था।[7] भगत सिंह की दुर्लभ जेल नेट बुक नवें और अंतिम दशक में सामने आयी।[8] इसका प्रथम उल्लेख 1968 में मिलता है। जब इसे भगत सिंह के अनुज कुलवीर सिंह (फरीदाबाद) के पास देखा गया था,[9] पूरे एक दशक बाद एक रूसी विद्वान ने इसका उल्लेख किया,[10] 1979 के बाद कई शोध अध्येताओं ने नेहरू मेमोरियल म्यूज़ियम लायब्रेरी, तीन मूर्ति में इसकी फोटोप्रति देखी थी। फिर इसका उल्लेख अक्सर होता रहा,[11] इसकी एक फोटोप्रति डॉ. प्रकाश चतुर्वेदी ने मास्को अभिलेखागार में भी देखी थी। इसकी प्रथम प्रकाशित प्रति की मूल प्रति गुरुकुल कांगड़ी के कुलपति रहे जी.बी. कुमार हूजा को 1981 में वहां के मुख्य अधिष्ठाता स्वामी शक्तिवेश से मिली थी।[12] अन्तिम दशक में भगत सिंह के ऊपर कई पुस्तकें आयीं[13] और नई सदी में भी प्रकाशन जारी है,[14] मेरे शिष्य चन्द्रमणि ने भी एक नाटक लिखा जिसकी भूमिका स्वयं मैंने लिखी,[15] मनोज कुमार के तर्ज पर दो रूमानी चलचित्र भी आये; प्रसार भारती द्वारा प्रथम बार अभी-अभी राजशेखर व्यास ने भगत सिंह की सौवीं जयन्ती पर एक वृत्तचित्र भी तैयार किया है;[16] *ऐसे अनेक प्रामाणिक, अप्रामाणिक अभिलेखों से गुजरते हुए मुझे ये लगा कि फांसी के फंदे को चूमने वाले युवा क्रांतिवीर भगत सिंह के जोशीले व्यक्तित्व को राष्ट्रभक्ति को बढ़ावा देने के लिए चित्रित किया गया है और वास्तविक महान युगद्रष्टा, मेधा सम्पन्न चिन्तक, वैचारिक दर्शन के प्रखर प्रतिपादक भगत सिंह को पीछे छोड़ दिया गया है जिसका गहन अध्ययन व लेखन वर्तमान भारत के देश प्रेमियों को एक ठोस राजनीतिक दृष्टि प्रदान करता है।*

यहाँ मेरा प्रयास प्रामाणिक अभिलेखों के आधार पर उसी बहुमूल्य उपयोगी राजनीतिक विचारक भगत सिंह के मूल बिन्दुओं को रेखांकित करना है जहाँ से भारत के युवा एक स्पष्ट दृष्टि प्राप्त कर सकते हैं। आज की महती आवश्यकता है कि भगत सिंह के विचारों की यथार्थ अन्तर्वस्तु जन-जन तक पहुँच सके क्योंकि वे आज के भारत के लिए अत्यंत प्रासंगिक हैं।

जेल में लिखित प्रपत्रों में भगत सिंह की विचारधारा का विकास हुआ; उस समय तक उन्होंने कांग्रेस के बुर्जुआ नेतृत्व को पहचान लिया था और किसानों-मजदूरों की एक जनसेना के निर्माण की आवश्यकता महसूस कर रहे थे। मार्क्स, एंजेल्स, लेनिन, गोर्की से लेकर फ्रेंच और रूसी क्रांति के इतिहास का गहन विश्लेषण करके स्वदेश के राष्ट्रीय आन्दोलन के लिए उन्होंने अमूल्य निष्कर्ष निकाले थे। उनकी इतिहास-दृष्टि

में साम्राज्यशाही से मुक्ति ही लक्ष्य मात्र न था बल्कि सर्वहारा वर्ग के विचारात्मक राजनीतिक वर्चस्व का स्वप्न सर्वोच्च बन गया था। मैं समझता हूँ कि भारतीय जनता विशेषतया करोड़ों विद्रोही संभावना संपन्न युवाओं को यह तथ्य बताना हमारा युगधर्म है। यदि हमने ये ऐतिहासिक दायित्व निभाया होता तो दक्षिणपंथी सांप्रदायिक प्रतिक्रियावादी भगतसिंह के नायक-रूप को भुना नहीं पाते। उस महावीर की जन्म शताब्दी तक जन-मुक्ति के कुछ वैचारिक प्रतिबद्धता वालों को छोड़ आयोजित लेखकों ने इस दिशा में तनिक भी कोशिश नहीं की।

कानपुर में गणेशशंकर विद्यार्थी के 'प्रताप' में कार्यरत रहते हुए भगत सिंह ने 'प्रताप', 'महारथी', (दिल्ली), 'चांद', (इलाहाबाद), 'अर्जुन', (दिल्ली), 'मतवाला' में गुप्त नामों से लिखा; 'किरती' में 'विद्रोही' के छद्मनाम से पंजाबी में तथा उर्दू पत्रिकाओं में भी लिखते थे। वर्नाक्यूलर पत्रों के प्रयोग का चलना इतिहास लेखन में अभी कम और प्रतिबन्धित प्रपत्रों की मात्रा विपुल है; राष्ट्रीय अभिलेखागार, इण्डिया ऑफिस लन्दन और पाकिस्तान में उपलब्ध प्रपत्रों में भी काफ़ी कुछ शेष होगा। शिव वर्मा ने लिखा है कि जेल में भगत सिंह ने चार पुस्तकें भी लिखी थीं, 'आत्मकथा', 'समाजवाद का आदर्श', 'भारत में क्रांतिकारी आन्दोलन' एवं 'मृत्यु के द्वार पर'[17] चमनलाल ने इनकी पाण्डुलिपियों के अस्तित्व पर ही संदेह किया है।[18]

12 सित. 1929 से भगत सिंह को जेल में पढ़ने-लिखने की सुविधा मिलने लगी थी; उनके पास समय बहुत कम था परन्तु सशस्त्र क्रांति की धारणा से ऊपर किसानों-मजदूरों की जनसेना के निर्माण का दृष्टिकोण सुनिश्चित हो चुका था, मुक्ति-मार्ग के बारे में उनकी अवधारणा भी निश्चित होने लगी थी, उन्होंने इस मध्य अवधि में तीव्र गति से अध्ययन किया। भगत सिंह ने भारतीय राष्ट्रीय आंदोलन पर जो आलोचनात्मक टिप्पणियाँ लिखी थीं; एवं मेहनतकश देशवासियों, युवाओं, क्रांतिकारियों के समक्ष क्रांति का जो रास्ता उन्होंने बताया था, उसकी प्रासंगिकता आज के भारत में निर्विवाद है। आज देश में सत्ता लोभी राजनीतिज्ञ जाति-धर्म-भाषा-क्षेत्र वाद का विष घोल रहे हैं, कामरेड वाजपेयी और पण्डित नम्बूदरीपाद के समीकरण आग लगाये जा रहे हैं, एन.डी.ए., यू.पी.ए. की खिचड़ी छद्म वामपंथी भी खाये जा रहे हैं, विदेशी पूँजी के आगे श्रमिक रौंदा जा रहा है, अमेरिकी साम्राज्यवाद एटमी करार का वेष धरे घुसा आ रहा है, भगत सिंह की आशंकाएं तथा भविष्यवाणी सत्य सिद्ध होती जा रही हैं; साम्राज्यवाद के खिलाफ संघर्ष के इस निर्णायक मोड़ पर मेहनतकश जनता और क्रांतिवादी युवाओं को संपूर्ण क्रांति के नये पथ पर आगे भगत सिंह की तरह अडिग बढ़ना होगा। फांसी के तीन दिन पहले पंजाब के गवर्नर को पत्र में भगत सिंह ने लिखा था कि, "यह युद्ध तब तक चलता रहेगा, जब तक कि

शक्तिशाली व्यक्ति भारतीय जनता और श्रमिकों की आय के साधनों पर अपना एकाधिकार जमाये रखेंगे। चाहे ऐसे व्यक्ति अंग्रेज पूंजीपति, अंग्रेज शासक अथवा सर्वथा भारतीय ही हों। उन्होंने आपस में मिलकर एक लूट जारी कर रखी है। यदि शुद्ध भारतीय पूँजीपतियों के द्वारा ही निर्धनों का खून चूसा जा रहा हो तब भी इस स्थिति में कोई फ़र्क नहीं पड़ता।.....निकट भविष्य में यह युद्ध अंतिम रूप में लड़ा जायेगा और तब यह निर्णायक युद्ध होगा। साम्राज्यवाद एवं पूँजीवाद कुछ समय के मेहमान हैं।"

भगत सिंह की इतिहास-मेधा में राष्ट्रीय मुक्ति संग्राम मानव मुक्ति संग्राम तक की यात्रा का मध्य पड़ाव था जिसका अंतिम बिन्दु साम्राज्यवाद-पूँजीवाद के खिलाफ संघर्ष था। इस निर्णायक मुक्ति संग्राम का नायक सर्वहारा ही होगा और पूँजीवाद का अकेला उत्तर समाजवाद ही होगा। भगत सिंह का भारतीय पूंजीपतियों के बारे में स्पष्ट दृष्टिकोण था कि स्वतंत्रता का अर्थ बहुसंख्य श्रमिक जन को सत्ता की प्राप्ति थी न कि गोरे अंग्रेजों के स्थान पर काले अंग्रेजों का सत्तारूढ़ हो जाना। अगर देशी शोषक मेहनतकशों का शोषण करते रहेंगे तो उनका संघर्ष जारी रहेगा। भगत सिंह मानते थे कि कांग्रेसी राजनीति का परिणाम अभिजातों को सत्तासीन करना होगा।[19] भगत सिंह का निष्कर्ष था कि किसान-मजदूरों-युवाओं के संगठन बना कर समग्र जन संघर्ष के बिना क्रांति को निर्णायक मोड़ तक नहीं ले जाया जा सकता है। भगत सिंह ने लिखा, "इस समय हम नौजवानों से यह नहीं कह सकते कि वे बम और पिस्तौल उठायें। आज विद्यार्थियों के सामने इससे भी महत्वपूर्ण कार्य हैं।. ...नौजवानों को क्रांति का यह संदेश देश के कोने-कोने तक पहुँचाना है, फैक्टरी-कारखानों के क्षेत्रों में, गंदी बस्तियों और गाँवों की जर्जर झोपड़ियों में रहने वाले करोड़ों लोगों में इस क्रांति की अलख जगानी है जिससे आजादी आयेगी और तब एक मनुष्य द्वारा दूसरे मनुष्य का शोषण असंभव हो जायेगा।"[20] उन्होंने अंतिम दिनों में लिखा था कि, "आतंकवाद हमारे समाज में क्रांतिकारी चिन्तन की पकड़ के अभाव की अभिव्यक्ति है या एक पछतावा। इसी तरह यह अपनी असफलता का स्वीकार भी है।... आतंकवाद अधिक से अधिक साम्राज्यवादी ताकत को समझौते के लिए मजबूर कर सकता है। ऐसे समझौते, हमारे उद्देश्य-पूर्ण आजादी से हमेशा ही कहीं दूर रहेंगे।"[21] भगतसिंह वैचारिक यात्रा के आखिरी मोड़ पर पहुँच कर क्रांतिकारी उग्रवाद की सीमाओं को समझ गये। जीवन संध्या में उनकी प्रखर मेधा एक जनक्रांति की तैयारी एवं पूर्वाधार के सवालों से सघनता से जूझ रही थी।

भगत सिंह ने स्पष्ट लिखा था कि "क्रांति राष्ट्रीय हो या समाजवादी, जिन शक्तियों पर हम निर्भर हो सकते हैं, वे हैं किसान और मज़दूर।" उन्होंने सक्रिय

युवाओं को राय दी थी कि वे मार्क्स व लेनिन को पढ़ें, उनकी सीखों को दिग्दर्शक बनायें, मजदूरों-किसानों व शिक्षित मध्यवर्गीय युवाओं के मध्य काम करें, उन्हें राजनीतिक सीख दें और उन्हें संगठित करें। वे सर्वहारा क्रांति के पक्षधर थे। वे मात्र राष्ट्रवादी क्रांतिकारी न होकर पूर्ण अन्तर्राष्ट्रीयतावादी थे। वे भाषा-जाति-धर्म की कट्टरता से पूर्णतः मुक्त थे, और रहस्यवाद व भाग्यवाद की मानसिक दासता से मुक्त हो चुके थे। भगत सिंह के चिन्तन की वर्तमान समय में प्रासंगिकता पर मनन करने से उनकी अनवरत विकासशील भौतिकवादी जीवन दृष्टि और संघर्षपूर्ण विश्लेषण, साम्राज्यशाही के खिलाफ वैश्विक युद्ध के प्रति दृष्टि, राष्ट्रीय मुक्ति संग्राम को साम्राज्यशाही के खिलाफ संग्राम का भाग मानने की दृष्टि, कांग्रेस व गांधी के वर्ग चरित्र का मूल्यांकन, क्रांतिकारी उग्रवाद के विश्लेषण से आगे सर्वहारा क्रांति की अनिवार्यता पर बल तथा धर्म-जाति भाषा की संकीर्णता की खिलाफत को माना जायेगा। आज जब क्रांतिकारी हरावलों को एक बार पुनः संगठित होकर साम्राज्यवाद तथा देशी पूँजीवाद के खिलाफ संग्राम का रास्ता खोजना है तो भगत सिंह की चिन्तन-प्रक्रिया और निष्कर्षों से अमूल्य सीखें मिलती हैं। भगत सिंह की विकासमान वैज्ञानिक भौतिकवादी विचार-परंपरा हमारी परंपरा बन सकती है। संपूर्ण कृतित्व का अध्ययन आज उनके लिए अपरिहार्य है जो मुक्ति की नयी परियोजना बनाने को संकल्पित हैं।

लाला लाजपत राय की 'द्वारकादास लाइब्रेरी' के अध्यक्ष राजाराम शास्त्री ने बताया था कि 1924 से 1928 तक भगत सिंह पुस्तकों को पढ़ते नहीं निगलते थे, फिर भी उनकी ज्ञान-पिपासा अनबुझी ही रहती थी। पुस्तकों को पढ़ कर नोट बनाना, साथियों से वाद-विवाद करना और नये ज्ञान की वेदी पर उस समझ को परखना, इस प्रक्रिया में अपनी त्रुटियों को सुधारना भगत सिंह की आदत थी।[22] फलस्वरूप 1928 के प्रारम्भ में उन्होंने अराजकतावाद को त्याग समाजवाद को लक्ष्य बना लिया। उनकी वैचारिक प्रगति फांसी पर चढ़ने के दिन तक जारी रही। उनकी फांसी के कुछ घंटे पूर्व तक उनसे मिले वकील प्राणनाथ मेहता ने 23 मार्च 1931 को लेनिन की जीवनी दी थी तो वे बोले कि 'आज रात को ही इसे खत्म कर दूंगा'; संतरी ने बताया था कि जब द्वार खुला तो वे लेनिन को ही पढ़ रहे थे, बोले, 'ठहरिये, यहाँ एक क्रांतिकारी दूसरे क्रांतिकारी से मिल रहा है।' कुछ पंक्तियाँ और पढ़कर ही उठे।[23]

भगत सिंह को अपने विचारों को सुस्थिर करने का समय ही नहीं मिला, उनका चिन्तन तूफानी विचार-यात्रा है; साहित्य, इतिहास, दर्शन के तीव्रगामी अध्ययन से उसमें निरन्तर परिवर्तन होता रहा, यह अनवरत वैज्ञानिक दृष्टि की ओर बढ़ा और अधिक से अधिक अन्तर्विरोधमुक्त होता गया। उन्होंने प्रथम लेख सत्रह साल की

उम्र में पंजाब की भाषा व लिपि की समस्या पर लिखा था, सित0 1929 के बाद उन्होंने सारा समय गहन अध्ययन व लेखन में लगाया; उनका अध्ययन क्षेत्र अत्यन्त व्यापक था, 23 मार्च 1931 तक अध्ययन की अवधि मात्र डेढ़ साल थी, जिसमें उन्होंने असीम प्रतिभा से वैचारिक परिपक्वता पायी; सत्रह से तेइस साल की वय की लघु अवधि में उनकी चिन्तन-यात्रा युगान्तकारी थी। उनकी युगद्रष्टा प्रतिभा की तुलना चौबीस साल जीने वाले रूसी क्रांति चिन्तक दोब्रोल्यूबोव से की जाती है।[24] भगत सिंह के निष्कर्ष को इतिहास ने सत्य भी सिद्ध किया। अंतिम समय में लिखित लेखों में वे परिपक्व चिन्तक के शिखर पर पहुँच गये थे।[25] उनकी राजनीतिक-वैचारिक समझ रूस की लाल क्रांति से प्रकाशित हुई थी; उन्होंने प्लेखानोव एवं वेरा ज़ासूलिच की पीढ़ी की तरह नरोदवाद की क्रांतिकारी जनवादी परंपरा से आगे मार्क्सवाद तक सोचा। उनका प्रयास लघु और अनगढ़ था परन्तु उसकी मौलिकता और उसके विकास की तेज गति ऐतिहासिक थी। अन्तर्राष्ट्रीय अन्धानुकरण के बजाय उनके मौलिक विचारों की विकास प्रक्रिया माओ त्से तुङ्ग व हो ची मिन्ह के निकट दिखायी देती है जिन्होंने अपने देश की ठोस परिस्थितियों का अध्ययन कर क्रांति की आम रणनीति का रास्ता तय किया। भगत सिंह की आज यही प्रासंगिकता है कि प्रगतिशील युवा उसकी भविष्यवाणी के अनुसार साम्राज्यवाद व पूंजीवाद के खिलाफ़ निर्णायक लड़ाई के इस ऐतिहासिक समय में जन-जन तक यह विचार फैलायें कि पूँजीवादी शासन के रूप में हमें प्राप्त अधूरी आज़ादी की त्रासदी के विरुद्ध बकौल भगत सिंह के 'क्रांति की तलवार विचारों की सान पर तेज़' करके कारख़ानों-झोपड़ियों तक श्रमिकों को सत्ता दिलानी होगी।

सन्दर्भ

1. Hindustan Times, New Delhi, 13-9-2007.
2. sonbhik.Mitra@hindustantimes.com, 12-9-07.
3. *युगद्रष्टा भगत सिंह और उनके मृत्युंजय पुरखे*, संपा. वीरेन्द्र सिंधु
4. Introduction to *'why I am an Atheist?* Sardar Bhagat Singh easearch committe, New Delhi, 1979.
5. *भगत सिंह एण्ड हिज टाइम्स, मन्मथ नाथ गुप्त*
6. जगमोहन सिंह व चमनलाल (संपा.) :*भगत सिंह और उसके साथियों के दस्तावेज, 1986.*
7. *बम का दर्शन*. भगवती चरण वोहरा,
8. संपा भूपेन्द्र हूजा : *इण्डियन बुक कार्निकल* (1991).

9. संपा. जी. देवल : *'पीपुल्स पाथ'* (1968).

10. एल.वी. मित्रोखिन : *लेनिन एण्ड इण्डिया* (1977).

11. *भगतसिंह और उसके साथियों के दस्तावेज़,* संपा. जगमोहन सिंह व चमनलाल, द्वितीय संस्करण, भूमिका 1991.

12. भूपेन्द्र हूजा, इण्डियन बुक कार्निकल 1991.

13. हंसराज रहबर, *विष्णु प्रभाकर तथा पत्रों का संकलन* (परिकल्पना प्रकाशन, 1998).

14. कुलदीप नैयर, *'मार्टियर भगत सिंह : एक्सपेरिमेंट्स इन रिवॉल्यूशन'* तथा ए. जी. नूरानी, *दि ट्रायल ऑफ़ भगत सिंह',* 2004-5.

15. चन्द्रमणि ब्रह्मदत्त, *क्रांति की लपटें* (शहीद दाताराम स्मृति न्यास, खुर्जा, 2005)

16. श्रीनन्द झा, *'हिन्दुस्तान टाइम्स'* 27-9-07, पृ. 7.

17. शिव वर्मा, *क्रांतिकारी आंदोलन का वैचारिक इतिहास,* प्रस्तावना, पृ. 15.

18. *'भगत सिंह के संपूर्ण दस्तावेज'* (2004) संपादकीय.

19. भगत सिंह का पत्र : 2-2-1931.

20. पंजाब छात्र संघ, लाहौर के द्वितीय अधिवेशन में प्रेषित संदेश, 19-10-1929.

21. ऐतिहासिक मसविदा दस्तावेज, फरवरी 1931.

22. शिव वर्मा, *'क्रांतिकारी आंदोलन का वैचारिक विकास',* प्रस्तावना, पृ. 16.

23. एल.वी. मित्रोखिन, भगतसिंह की जेल नोट बुक : *एक महान विचार यात्रा का दुर्लभ साक्ष्य* (1981), पृ. 15.

24. संपा. चमनलाल, *'भगतसिंह के संपूर्ण दस्तावेज़',* प्रस्तावना.

25. *मैं नास्तिक क्यों हूँ* (अक्टू. 1930), *क्रांतिकारी कार्यक्रम का मसविदा* (2-2-1931).

15

भगत सिंह-व्यक्तित्व एवं विचारधारा

डॉ. वर्षा आलोक

भगत सिंह के जन्म के समय भारत की राजनीतिक स्थिति

जिस समय सरदार भगत सिंह का जन्म हुआ समस्त भारत में विशेष रूप से पंजाब का वातावरण कोलोनाइजेशन (Colonigational) बल के विरुद्ध चलाये जा रहे आंदोलन के कारण तनावपूर्ण था। भगत सिंह के दादा सरदार अर्जुन सिंह राजनीतिक रूप से सक्रिय थे। दादी जयकौर एक साहसी महिला थी। उनके तीनों पुत्रों सरदार किशन सिंह, अजीत सिंह, एवं स्वर्ण सिंह ने किसी न किसी रूप में अपने जीवन को राष्ट्र को समर्पित कर दिया था। इसी अनुकूल पृष्ठभूमि में जब सारा परिवार अंग्रेजो के विरुद्ध संघर्ष में लगा हुआ था, भगतसिंह का जन्म हुआ।

उनका जन्म 28 सितम्बर 1907 अश्विन शुक्ला त्रयोदशी संवत् 1964 विक्रमी शनिवार प्रातः लगभग 9 बजे हुआ था। भगत सिंह का जन्म ग्राम बंगा, जिला लायलपुर (अब पाकिस्तान) में हुआ था।

भगतसिंह के जन्म से पूर्व उनके चाचा अजीत सिंह को अंग्रेजों ने लाला लाजपतराय के साथ निष्कासित करके बर्मा भेज दिया था उनके पिता किशन सिंह लाहौर जेल में बंद थे। दूसरे चाचा स्वर्ण सिंह भी जेल में सजा काट रहे थे।

लेकिन भगतसिंह के जन्म के साथ सभी लोग रिहा होकर घर आ गए।

"उस वक्त परिवार में दोहरी खुशी हो गयी। एक तो लड़का पैदा हुआ और दूसरा ऐसे नसीबो वाला कि सब लोग घर आ गए। इसलिए दादी जयकौर ने नाम रखा भागों वाला जो आगे चल कर भगतसिंह हो गया। उनकी पैदाइश ही ऐसे समय में हुई जब सारा परिवार ही आज़ादी की जद्दोजहद में जुटा था। स.भगतसिंह को देशभक्ति की भावना परिवार से ही मिली।"[1]

प्रवक्ता—गांधी अध्ययन केन्द्र, आगरा

भगतसिंह को अपने माता-पिता से रूपवान और बलिष्ठ व्यक्तित्व-विरासत में मिला था। घर का वातावरण आरम्भ से ही राष्ट्र प्रेम की भावना से ओत-प्रोत था।

सारे समय घर में देश भक्ति की बातें होती रहती थीं।

इसका असर नन्हे भगत पर भी पड़ा। उनका भविष्य उनके बचपन में ही सबके समक्ष प्रत्यक्ष रूप में आ गया।

व्यक्तित्व

स. भगत सिंह एक अत्यन्त आकर्षक व्यक्तित्व के स्वामी थे। उनका व्यक्तित्व उनके विचारों एवं उद्देश्य का दर्पण था। भगतसिंह की अत्यन्त निकट सहयोगिनी क्रान्तिकारिणी दुर्गा देवी के अनुसार–

भगत सिंह का अपना निखरा हुआ, मंजा हुआ व्यक्तित्व था जो सर्वथा उसके सादे लिबास और भावपूर्ण व्यवहार में फूट पड़ता था।[2]

भगतसिंह के व्यक्तित्व को संवारने व निखारने में उनके द्वारा पढ़ी गयी विभिन्न प्रसिद्ध पुस्तकों का योगदान रहा है। वह व्यक्तित्व को बाहरी आकर्षण जैसे पोशाक आदि से संवारने के स्थान पर विचारधारा द्वारा व्यक्तित्व को आकर्षित बनाने के विचार से अधिक सहमत थे। भगतसिंह के पास हमेशा कोई न कोई मूल्यवान व प्रसिद्ध पुस्तक अवश्य होती थी।

अपने इसी तेजस्वी व्यक्तित्व व ओजस्वी विचारधारा के कारण मात्र 23 वर्ष की अल्पायु में भगतसिंह ने जिस प्रकार अपने को योग्य और अनुकरणीय बना लिया था, वह सराहनीय है। इसके अतिरिक्त स. भगत सिंह सफल लेखक व प्रभावशाली वक्ता भी थे।

स. भगत सिंह उद्देश्यवादी लेखक थे। वह उद्देश्य था जनता को क्रान्ति के लिए तैयार करना।[3] उनके लेखन का उद्देश्य भी यही था। अपने इसी ध्येय की पूर्ति के लिए उन्होंने अपनी कार्य प्रणाली को तीन भागों में विभाजित कर रखा था। यह उनके द्वारा लिखे गए लेखों को पढ़ने से ज्ञात होता है।

पहला भाग था–जनता के सोये विचारों पर हल्की चोट देकर उन्हें जागरूक बनाना;

द्वितीय भाग था–जनता को समस्त जानकारी देना।

तीसरा व अंतिम भाग था जनता को प्रेरणा देना कि जो कुछ करके दूसरों ने हासिल किया वह तुम भी कर सकते हो।

बहुत सीमा तक भगत सिंह अपने इस उद्देश्य में सफल भी हुए। उनके द्वारा लिखित छद्म नामों से (उदाहरण निर्भय गौतम) अपने समकालीन क्रान्तिकारियों की यशोगाथा अपने आप में इतिहास का एक स्वर्णिम पृष्ठ है।

सरदार भगत सिंह का हिन्दी, उर्दू, अंग्रेजी और गुरुमुखी पर समान अधिकार था। भगतसिंह ने गुरुमुखी और उर्दू की पत्रिका 'कीरती' में नियमित रूप से क्रान्तिकारी शहीदों की जीवनियां लिखी थीं। 'चांद' के प्रसिद्ध फांसी अंक में भी इनका प्रकाशन हुआ था।

'मेरे क्रान्तिकारी साथी' नामक लेख में उन्होंने लिखा—"आज लोग इन हुतात्माओं को भूल चुके हैं। उन्हें मूर्ख और पथ भ्रष्ट तथा आदर्शवादी बताते हैं। परन्तु आज कहाँ है वह उत्साह? कहाँ है वह निर्भीकता और तत्परता? आज कितने लोग हैं जो उसी प्रकार फांसी के तख्ते पर प्राण दे सकेंगे"।[4]

उपरोक्त उदाहरण उनकी सटीक व सधी हुई लेखनी का अनुपम उदाहरण है। कोई ऐसा विषय नहीं भगवान, साहित्य, सौन्दर्य, संस्कृति जिस पर उन्होंने न लिखा हो। उनकी विचार धारा स्पष्ट थी।

जेल में भगत सिंह ने चार पुस्तकें लिखीं। दुर्भाग्य वश केवल एक पुस्तक (Why I am an atheist) को छोड़कर अन्य तीन नष्ट हो गयीं। वे चार पुस्तकें थीं—

1) क्रान्तिकारी आंदोलन का इतिहास।

2) Why I am an atheist

3) किसी पुस्तक का अनुवाद।

4) आत्म कथा।

सरदार भगत सिंह के प्रतिदिन के जीवन का कार्यक्रम था केवल अध्ययन। ऐसा अध्ययन जो इन्हें सर्वांग और संपूर्ण बना सके। राजनीति, इतिहास तथा अन्य विषयों पर भी इन्हें समान अधिकार था।

यहाँ तक अपने जीवन के अन्तिम समय में भी वह लेनिन की जीवनी पढ़ रहे थे। अपनी अंतिम इच्छा में भी उन्होंने यही कहा—

"मैं लेनिन की जीवनी पढ़ रहा हूँ। मैं इसे पूरी करना चाहता हूँ।"

उनके मित्रों का विचार है यदि वह क्रान्तिकारी न बनते तो वह किताबी कीड़ा होने के साथ-साथ किसी विश्वविद्यालय में प्रोफेसर बन जाते।[5]

विचार धारा

सरदार भगत सिंह के गहन अध्ययन का ही फल था कि उन दिनों के विवाद ग्रस्त मसलों जैसे--क्रांति का क्षेत्र तथा साधन, हिंसा तथा अहिंसा, कांग्रेसी नेताशाही का रूप और आदर्श राज्य-व्यवस्था आदि के बारे में उनके विचार निश्चित हो गये थे। उनकी विचारधारा स्पष्ट रूप में देश की जनता के समक्ष आयी थी।

भगत सिंह से पूर्व क्रान्तिकारियों का उद्देश्य केवल-स्वतन्त्रता प्राप्ति ही था। किन्तु स्वतन्त्रता के वास्तविक रूप से यह क्रान्तिकारी परिचित नहीं थे। इसके अलावा क्रान्तिकारियों ने अपने विचारों से जनता को अवगत कराने की चेष्टा भी नहीं की थी। फलस्वरूप उनके साथ जनता की सहानुभूति नहीं के समान थी।

भगत सिंह पहले क्रान्तिकारी थे जिन्होंने जो प्रमुखता बम को दी वही बुलेटिन (समाचारों) को भी दी तथा अपने कार्य एवं अपनी विचारधारा को समाचारों के द्वारा जनता तक पहुँचाया।[6]

भगत सिंह प्रथम क्रान्तिकारी हैं जिन्होंने क्रान्ति को परिभाषित किया। इसके अतिरिक्त समाजवाद, धर्म, राजनीति तथा अन्य विषयों में अपने स्पष्ट विचार जनता के समक्ष रखकर क्रान्तिकारियों को सम्मिलित करके "नौजवान भारत सभा" की स्थापना की।

यह सभा क्रान्तिकारियों का खुला मंच थी। भगवती चरण वोहरा और भगत सिंह द्वारा बनाये गए सभा के नियम आज ऐतिहासिक दस्तावेज बन गए हैं।[7]

क्रान्ति संबंधी दृष्टिकोण

जैसा कि विदित है कि भगत सिंह से पूर्व कोई क्रान्तिकारी ऐसा नहीं आया जिसने क्रान्ति पर जनता के समक्ष अपने विचार स्पष्ट रूप से रखे हों। जनता के हृदय में इनकी छवि आपराधिक थी। क्रान्तिकारी कार्य के बाद गुमनामी के अंधेरो में खो जाते थे। सान्डर्स वध के बाद भगत सिंह ने "हिन्दुस्तान समाजवादी प्रजातन्त्र सेना" के नाम से जो पर्चा बांटा उसमें लिखा था–"मनुष्य का रक्त बहाने के लिए हमें खेद है। परन्तु क्रान्ति की वेदी पर कभी-कभी रक्त बहाना अनिवार्य हो जाता है। हमारा उद्देश्य एक ऐसी क्रान्ति से है जो मनुष्य द्वारा मनुष्य के शोषण का अंत कर देगी।"

उपरोक्त कथन से स्पष्ट है कि भगत सिंह के अनुसार मनुष्य द्वारा मनुष्य का शोषण करने के विरुद्ध उठाया गया कोई भी क्रान्तिकारी कदम भले ही उसमें रक्त क्यों न बहाना पड़े, वही क्रान्ति की शुरुआत है।

प्रायः यह समझा जाता है कि भगत सिंह का क्रान्ति से तात्पर्य था रक्त रंजित संघर्ष। परन्तु यह कथन सत्य नहीं है। दिल्ली के सेशन जज द्वारा आजन्म कैद की सजा के फैसले के खिलाफ अदालत में उन्होंने कहा–

"क्रान्ति संसार का नियम है, वह मानवीय गति का रहस्य है। लेकिन उसमें रक्त रंजित संघर्ष बिल्कुल लाजिमी नहीं है और न उसमें व्यक्तिगत प्रतिहिंसा की कोई जगह है। वह बम और पिस्तौल का सम्प्रदाय नहीं है।"

इस प्रकार हम देखते हैं कि भगत सिंह के विचार से क्रान्ति का उद्देश्य स्पष्ट रूप से अन्याय पर खड़ी हुई वर्तमान व्यवस्था को बदलना था। अपने इस उद्देश्य की पूर्ति के लिए वह कोई भी मार्ग अपनाने को तैयार थे।

आतंकवाद के प्रति दृष्टिकोण

"सरदार भगत सिंह का विशेष क्रान्तिकारी दृष्टिकोण यही है कि उनके समय से क्रान्तिकारियों का आदर्श समाजवादोन्मुख हो गया तथा उनका मानसिक धरातल भी परलोकापेक्षी धार्मिक होने के स्थान पर अब इहलोकापेक्षी सामाजिक ही विशेषतः हो गया।"[8]

भगत सिंह के अनुसार आतंक के बिना क्रान्ति असंभव है। अतः केवल आतंक के माध्यम द्वारा ही हम उच्चवर्गीय शासकों के सन्मुख अपनी स्वतन्त्रता प्राप्ति के उद्देश्य को रख सकने में सफल हो सकते हैं।

एक अन्य क्रान्तिकारी भगवती चरण बोहरा के साथ जारी किए गए 'बम का दर्शन' नामक पर्चे में आंतकवाद को परिभाषित करते हुए लिखा–

"आतंकवाद क्रान्ति का एक दौर है। एक आवश्यक दौर। आतंकवाद एक पूर्ण क्रान्ति नहीं है और आतंकवाद बिना क्रान्ति पूर्ण नहीं होती।

उनके अनुसार आतंकवाद एक गलत शब्द था जो क्रान्तिकारियों के लिए उपयोग में लाया जाता था। उस समय में उनके काम करने का मुख्य तरीका अंग्रेजों और उनके भारतीय सहयोगियों में आतंक फैलाना एक उपाय था लक्ष्य नहीं था।

क्रान्तिकारियों का यह भी विश्वास था कि आतंकवाद अन्यायी शोषक के हृदय को दहलाता है। इसके अतिरिक्त पीड़ित तथा दलित जनता को प्रतिकार द्वारा आत्मविश्वास, उत्साह और साहस देता है।

ड्रीमलैंड नामक एक अंग्रेजी काव्य पुस्तिका की भूमिका में भगत सिंह ने लिखा

यह प्रसिद्ध है कि मैं आतंककारी रहा हूँ; परन्तु मैं आतंककारी नहीं हूँ। मैं एक क्रान्तिकारी हूँ जिसके कुछ निश्चित आदर्श हैं जिसके सामने एक लम्बा प्रोग्राम

"देश को स्वतन्त्र कराना है। स्वतन्त्रता के पश्चात् एक नवीन भारत का निर्माण होगा। झोपड़ियों के स्थान पर आलीशान बिल्डिंगों का निर्माण होगा। नग्न व भूखे लोगों को भोजन व कपड़े दिए जायेंगे।[9]

इस प्रकार स. भगत सिंह का उद्देश्य क्रांति द्वारा मजदूर वर्ग की परिस्थितियों में भी क्रान्तिकारी परिवर्तन लाना शामिल था।

समाजवाद के प्रति दृष्टिकोण

भगत सिंह की एक प्रमुख देन यह भी है कि उनके समय से क्रान्तिकारियों का आदर्श समाजवादोन्मुख हो गया था।

स्वतन्त्रता प्राप्ति के बाद इस देश का भविष्य कैसा होगा? क्या जनता को आर्थिक व सामाजिक स्वतन्त्रता प्राप्त होगी? क्या मनुष्य द्वारा मनुष्य के शोषण का अंत हो सकेगा? इस बारे में स. भगत सिंह ने सबसे पहले सोचा। इसी कारण *नौजवान भारत सभा* का संगठन मूलतः कम्युनिस्ट सिद्धान्तों पर ही किया गया।[10]

नौजवान भारत सभा का उद्देश्य समाजवादी विचारधारा का प्रचार एवं किसानों तथा मजदूरों को संगठित करना था। कामरेड शिव वर्मा के अनुसार–

"समाजवाद उस समय युग की आवाज थी। क्रान्तिकारियों में भगत सिंह ने सबसे पहले उस आवाज को सुना और पहचाना, इसीलिए वह अपने दूसरे साथियों से बड़ा था।" स. भगत सिंह का कहना था कि–

अंग्रेजी दासता के विरुद्ध संघर्ष तो हमारे युद्ध का पहला मोर्चा है। अंतिम लड़ाई तो हमें शोषण के विरुद्ध ही लड़नी पड़ेगी। चाहे वह शोषण मनुष्य द्वारा मनुष्य का हो या एक राष्ट्र द्वारा दूसरे राष्ट्र का हो।[11]

भगत सिंह ने सोशलिस्ट शब्द की व्याख्या करते हुए कहा–"सोशलिस्ट शब्द इस बात का प्रतीक होगा कि हम किस प्रकार का शासन देश में चाहते हैं।...क्योंकि शनैः शनैः अपने आंदोलन को हम जनता का आंदोलन बना देना चाहते हैं। यही हमारा अंतिम लक्ष्य भी है।[12] जस्टिस फोर्ड तक ने भगत सिंह की प्रशंसा करते हुए कहा था–

"भगत सिंह एक विश्वसनीय क्रान्तिकारी है, उसे विश्वास है कि वर्तमान सामाजिक ढांचे को समाप्त करके ही विश्व को बेहतर किया जा सकता है।"[13]

अर्थात् अंग्रेज सरकार भी भगत सिंह की समाजवादी विचारधारा से परिचित हो गयी थी।

भगत सिंह ने अपना जीवन समाजवाद को समर्पित कर दिया था। फांसी से कुछ दिन पहले उन्होंने जेल अधीक्षक के द्वारा पंजाब गर्वनर के नाम अपने पत्र में लिखा–

"अतिशीघ्र अंतिम संघर्ष के आरम्भ की दुदुंभी बजेगी साम्राज्यवाद और पूंजीवाद अपनी अंतिम घड़ियाँ गिन रहे हैं। हमने संघर्ष में हाथ बँटाया था और हमें अपने कार्य पर गर्व है।"[14]

हिंसा और अहिंसा पर विचार

स. भगत सिंह एवं उनके दल के कार्यक्रम में हिंसा व अंहिसा का प्रश्न नगण्य था। स. भगत सिंह ने असेम्बली में बम फेंकने के पश्चात कोर्ट में दिए गए अपने ऐतिहासिक बयान में कहा—"हमने उस काल्पनिक अहिंसा की समाप्ति की घोषणा की है जिसकी निरुपयोगिता के बारे में नई पीढ़ी के मन में किसी प्रकार का संदेह नहीं बचा है।"[15]

हिंसा व अहिंसा के दर्शन पर भगत सिंह लिखते हैं—"यदि आवश्यकता हो तो ऊपर से उग्र एवं भयानक बनो। लेकिन अपने दिल में हमेशा नम्र रहो, फुफकारो यदि आवश्यकता हो, किन्तु काटो मत, दिल से प्यार करो और ऊपर से लड़ो।"

ईश्वर तथा धर्म के प्रति दृष्टिकोण

भगत सिंह अपने जीवन के प्रारम्भिक काल से नास्तिक नहीं थे। डी.ए.वी. स्कूल में प्रातः व शाम की प्रार्थना के साथ-साथ गायत्री मंत्र का जाप भी करते थे।

जैसे-जैसे भगत सिंह की क्रान्तिकारी गतिविधियाँ बढ़ती गयीं उनकी विचार धारा बदलने लगी।

भगत सिंह ने विश्व प्रसिद्ध क्रान्तिकारियों का इतिहास पढ़ा जिसमें बेकूनिन, मार्क्स, लेनिन शामिल हैं। ये सभी नास्तिक थे।

भगत सिंह के अनुसार—"...बाद में मैं निरालम्बा स्वामी की पुस्तक *'कागन रोग'* के संपर्क में आया। यह केवल एक प्रकार की रहस्यमयी वास्तिकता थी। यह विषय मेरे लिए रूचिपूर्ण बन गया। 1926 के अंत तक मुझे उस ईश्वर जिसने संसार को बनाया, निर्देशित व नियंत्रित किया, के निराधार सिद्धान्त पर विश्वास हो गया। ...मैं एक नास्तिक बन गया।[16]

स. भगत सिंह के नास्तिक विचारों को और बल मिला जब मई 1927 को निर्दोष होने के बाद भी दशहरा बम कांड में उन्हें गिरफ्तार कर लिया गया। जेल से उन्हें भारी यातनाएँ दीं गयीं। लेकिन उन्होंने ईश्वर को एक बार भी याद नहीं किया। उनके अनुसार—

"यह वास्तविक परीक्षा थी और मैं सफल हो गया।[17] भगत सिंह के अनुसार देश-प्रेम व देश-भक्ति की भावना धर्म, जाति, ऊँच-नीच व अन्य सामाजिक कुरीतियों

से कहीं अधिक सर्वोपरी थी। इसीलिए उनकी 'नौजवान भारत सभा' धर्म निरपेक्षता के सिद्धान्त पर आधारित है। यहाँ प्रत्येक सदस्य को यह शपथ लेनी होती थी कि वह राष्ट्र को जाति एवं धर्म से ऊपर रखेगा।

भगत सिंह व इन्कलाब

वंदे मातरम्, इनकलाब जिंदाबाद और जयहिन्द के नारे स्वतन्त्रता के लिए किए गए संघर्ष के विभिन्न पक्षों के प्रतीक हैं जो कि स्वयं साम्राज्यवाद के विरुद्ध भगत सिंह एंव उनकी हिन्दुस्तान सोशलिस्ट *रिपब्लिकन-एसोसिएशन पार्टी* के योगदान को दर्शाते हैं।[18]

भगत सिंह के हर नारे के पीछे मात्र जोश नहीं बल्कि एक संपूर्ण विचारधारा थी। जस्टिस फोर्ड की अदालत में अपने द्वारा लगाए गए नारे इंकलाब जिंदाबाद की व्याख्या करते हुए स. भगत सिंह ने कहा–

"...इन्कलाब जिन्दाबाद से हमारा वह उद्देश्य नहीं था जो आमतौर में गलत अर्थ में समझा जाता है। पिस्तौल और बम इंकलाब नहीं लाते हैं, बल्कि इंकलाब की तलवार विचारों की शान पर तेज होती है...हमारे इंकलाब का अर्थ पूंजीवादी युद्धों की मुसीबतों का अन्त करना है... ।"[19]

स. भगत सिंह के इन्कलाब का अर्थ एक ऐसे समाज की रचना से था जिसका निर्माण पुरानी रुढ़िवादी समाज-व्यवस्था के स्थान पर हुआ हो।

भगत सिंह के अनुसार चूंकि प्रत्येक नारा एक उद्देश्य लिए होता था इसीलिए वह चाहते थे कि नवयुवक नारा लगाने से पूर्व उस पर भली भांति विचार कर लें। 2 फरवरी 1931 को काल कोठरी से देश के नवयुवकों को उन्होंने लिखा–

"...आप लोग 'क्रान्ति चिरंजीवी हो' की पुकार करते हैं। यह नारा हमारे लिए बहुत पवित्र है। इसका इस्तेमाल बहुत सोच समझ कर होना चाहिए"[20]

सरदार भगत सिंह द्वारा किए गए प्रत्येक कार्य ने ऐतिहासिक रूप धारण किया। इसका प्रमुख कारण यह है कि उनसे पूर्व किसी भी क्रान्तिकारी ने कोई भी कार्य इतनी जागरूकता, साहस एवं विचार-विनिमय के पश्चात् नहीं किया।

इसके अतिरिक्त उनकी एक महान उपलब्धि यह भी है कि उन्होंने क्रान्तिकारी स्वतन्त्रता संग्राम को धार्मिक मनोभूमि से भी ऊपर उठाया तथा उसे राष्ट्रीयता की ओर उन्मुख किया।

भगत सिंह से पूर्व क्रान्तिकारी विदेशी दासता विरोधी राष्ट्रीयता को अपने साम्प्रदायिक और धार्मिक विश्वासों से अनुप्राणित कर रहे थे। लेकिन भगत सिंह

व उनके क्रान्तिकारी साथियों का मानसिक धरातल परलोकापेक्षी धार्मिक होने के स्थान पर इहलोकापेक्षी सामाजिक ही हो गया।

इसके अतिरिक्त उन्होंने साम्प्रदायिकता समाप्त करने की भी पहल की। वह स्वयं को भारतीय कहलाना अधिक पसंद करते बजाए इसके कि लोग उन्हें सिक्ख समझें। उन्होंने राष्ट्रीय भावना को भूगोल, भाषा, प्रान्तीयता की परिधि के बाहर की मानववादी भावना के लिए बहुत पीछे छोड़ दिया।

इस प्रकार स. भगत सिंह के अल्पकालीन जीवन में किया गया कोई भी कार्य जिसमें सान्डर्स वध, असेम्बली कम कांड एवं ऐतिहासिक भूख हड़ताल शामिल हैं–केवल नौजवानी जोश अथवा आदर्शवाद की क्षणिक प्रेरणा से नहीं किया गया था। इसके पीछे भगत सिंह के ठोस जीवन-दर्शन में पूर्ण आस्था के साथ-साथ उनके व्यावहारिक ज्ञान व दृढ़ इच्छाशक्ति तथा व्यापक दृष्टिकोण का होना शामिल था।

स. भगत सिंह जब फांसी पर झूले तब उनकी आयु मात्र 23 वर्ष थी। उनके बलिदान की तत्कालीन सभी प्रसिद्ध नेताओं ने प्रशंसा की। नेताजी सुभाष चन्द्र बोस ने कहा–

"आज भगत सिंह केवल एक व्यक्ति नहीं बल्कि प्रतीक है। वह क्रांति की आत्मा को प्रदर्शित करते हैं जो कि राष्ट्र की निधि है।"[21]

पं. जवाहर लाल नेहरू ने कहा

"भगत सिंह की पौरुषिक साहसिक मृत्यु से उन्हें (लोगों को) प्रेरणा लेनी चाहिए ताकि भारत का अस्तित्व रहे।"[22]

ब्रिटिश सरकार भी उनके साहस के आगे झुक गयी। एक सरकारी रिपोर्ट में कहा गया–

"वह आज भारत का एक नायक, शहीद व सबसे प्रख्यात सपूत है।"[23]

जिस आदर्श व उद्देश्य के लिए वह जिस सरकार से लड़े उसी ने उन्हें प्रख्यात सपूत की संज्ञा दी इससे अधिक भगत सिंह की लोक प्रियता का क्या सबूत हो सकता है?

आज भगत सिंह व उनके द्वारा किए गए कार्य व दर्शन मात्र इतिहास का विषय बन कर रह गए हैं। यह सोचना भी निराधार है कि उनके विचार जितने उस समय प्रासंगिक थे उससे अधिक आज प्रासंगिक है।

देश के विधान ने परोक्ष रूप में उन्हें न स्वीकारा हो पर उनके द्वारा प्रतिपादित स्वतन्त्र भारत में वर्ग विहीन समाजवादी शोषण रहित राष्ट्र के सिद्धान्त को अवश्य स्वीकार कर लिया गया है।

समाजवादी व्यवस्था कायम करना सरकार का उद्देश्य घोषित हो चुका है और धर्मनिरपेक्ष राज्य हमारे संविधान व दैनिक जीवन की महत्वपूर्ण पृष्ठभूमि बन चुका है।

क्रांति प्रयास के इस विकास मार्ग में हम स. भगत सिंह को एक "मोड़ सूचक पाषाण चिह्न (कारनर स्टोन) कह सकते हैं। यह कथन सर्वथा उचित भी है।

स्रोत-सामग्री

I

ग्रन्थ सूची

1. बनारसी दास चतुर्वेदी (संपादक) *यश की धरोहर,* आत्माराम एंड संस, 1966
2. चन्द्रशेखर शास्त्री, *भारतीय आतंकवाद का इतिहास,* कानपुर 1939
3. गोपाल ठाकुर,*भगत सिंह व्यक्तित्व एवं विचार धारा,* पीपुल्स पब्लिशिंग हाऊस दिल्ली, 1979
4. कन्हैया लाल मिश्र प्रभाकर, *उत्तर प्रदेश स्वतन्त्रता संग्राम की एक झाँकी,* उ. प्र. सूचना एवं प्रसारण विभाग, 1972
5. मन्मथनाथ गुप्त–*भारतीय क्रान्तिकारी आंदोलन का इतिहास,* आत्माराम एंड संस, 1966
6. मनमोहन, *एक क्रान्तिकारी के संस्मरण,* इंडियन प्रेस, इलाहाबाद 1960
7. रामशरण विद्यार्थी, मन्मथनाथ गुप्त–*भूले बिसरे क्रान्तिकारी,* प्रकाशन विभाग, सूचना एवं प्रसारण मंत्रालय भारत सरकार, 1976
8. शिव वर्मा, *संस्मृतियाँ,* समाजवादी साहित्य सदन, लखनऊ, 1969
9. सत्यभक्त–*क्रांति के पथिक,* संस्कृत संस्थान बरेली।
10. वीरेन्द्र सिन्धु–*युगद्रष्टा भगत सिंह और उनके मृत्युञ्जय पुरखें,* भारतीय ज्ञान पीठ प्रकाशन, वाराणसी, 1968
11. यशपाल, *सिंहावलोकन,* भाग (1.2.3), साथी प्रेस लखनऊ, 1966

12. A.C. Guha *Spark of Revolution*, Delhi 1971.
13. S. Bhagat Singh *'Why I am athiest* 'Suchita Gupta University Ret. Delhi 1979.'
14. G.S. Deol 'Shaheede Azam Sardar Bhagat Singh, The Man and His Ideology, Deep. pub. Nabha, 1979.
15. Dr Sitaramayya, *The History of the Indian National Congress* Vol I. Padma pub. Bombay, 1946.

II

सरकारी रिपोर्ट व रिकार्ड

1. लाहौर षड्यन्त्र केस (प्रथम) फैसला 13 सितम्बर 1915
2. गृह विभाग (पुलिस) भारत सरकार 1920-1931
3. असेम्बली बमकांड फैसला 12 जून 1929
4. गृह विभाग, अदालत, भारत सरकार 1925-1931

III

अखबार व पत्रिकाएँ

1. The Tribune, लाहौर 1928-31
2. The Hindustan Times, दिल्ली 1928-31
3. The Tribune, अंबाला, 23, 25 मार्च 1967
4. राष्ट्रधर्म, अप्रैल 1981
5. 50th Martyrdom Day of Sardar Bhagat Singh (PR Dept) Punjab 23 March 1980.

IV

साक्षात्कार

1. श्री कुलतार सिंह (लघुभ्राता स. भगत सिंह)
2. श्रीमती दुर्गा देवी बोहरा,
3. श्री जयदेव कपूर
4. श्री शिववर्मा

संदर्भ

1. स. कुलतार सिंह (लघु भ्राता स. भगत सिंह) द्वारा अपने निवास स्थान सहारनपुर में दि. 20.3.1981 को दिए गए साक्षात्कार से उद्धृत।
2. श्रीमती दुर्गा देवी वोहरा द्वारा 27.6.1981 को लखनऊ में दिए गए साक्षात्कार से उद्धृत अंश।
3. वीरेन्द्र सिंधु, *युग द्रष्टा भगत सिंह और उनके मृत्युञ्जय पुरखे*– पृ. 320, भारतीय ज्ञान पीठ प्रकाशन वाराणसी।
4. *मेरे क्रान्तिकारी साथी–स. भगत सिंह* (संकलन वीरेन्द्र सिन्धु) पृ. 14 आत्माराम एंड संस, 1977।
5. मन्मथनाथ गुप्त, *Bhagat Singh, and His Times*, पृ. 83, लिपि प्रकाशन, 1977।
6. क्रान्तिकारी जयदेव कपूर से 23 मार्च 1981 को सहारनपुर में लिए साक्षात्कार से उद्धृत।
7. स. कुलतार सिंह *A Revolutionary Shaheed (They) died So, that India May Live,* पृष्ठ 1, सूचना एवं प्रसारण विभाग चढ़ीगढ, 1981।
8. भगवानदास माहौर, *यश की धरोहर (अमर शहीद स. भगत सिंह),* पृष्ठ 25, आत्माराम एंड संस, 1966।
9. *भारत सरकार, गृह विभाग* (राजनीतिक), 1930 पृष्ठ 1।
10. जितेन्द्र नाथ सान्याल, *अमर शहीद स. भगत सिंह,* पृष्ठ 37।
11. श्री जयदेव कपूर द्वारा दिए गए साक्षात्कार से उद्धृत, दिनांक 23 मार्च 1981 स्थान सहारनपुर।
12. *विश्वनाथ अमर शहीद चन्द्र शेखर आजाद,* पृष्ठ 62, ललित्त प्रेस वाराणसी 1967।
13. डा.जी.एस देवल *Shaheed-e Azam sardar Bhagat-Singh The Man and his Ideology,* पृष्ठ 133।
14. स्मारिका, पृष्ठ 187, राष्ट्रभाषा प्रेस आगरा 1981।
15. स्मारिका, पृष्ठ 178, राष्ट्रभाषा प्रेस आगरा 1981।
16. स. भगत सिंह, Why I am an atheist, पृष्ठ 11, सुचिता गुप्ता, यूनीवर्सिटी रोड दिल्ली, 1979।

17. वही, पृष्ठ 13।

18. प्रो. हजारा सिंह, *Historic Martyrdom (They Died) So that India May Live,* पृष्ठ 39 सू. प्र. विभाग चंड़ीगढ़ 1981।

19. स्मारिका, पृष्ठ 384, राष्ट्र भाषा प्रेस आगरा 1981।

20. वीरेन्द्र सिन्धु, स. भगत सिंह पत्र और दस्तावेज, संकलन पृष्ठ 46, राजपाल एंड संस दिल्ली 1977।

21. गृह विभाग (राजनीतिक), भारत सरकार, फाइल न. 18-111, 26 मार्च 1931 न-2 पृष्ठ 2।

22. जवाहर लाल नेहरू, *आत्मकथा,* पृष्ठ 193, एलाइड प्रकाशन दिल्ली, 1962।

23. *गृह विभाग (राजनीतिक)* भारत सरकार 1931 फा. न. 18-111 साप्ताहिक रिपोर्ट 25 मार्च 1931 न 12, पृष्ठ1-2।

16

शहीद भगत सिंह की क्रांति की अवधारणा

डॉ. (श्रीमती) कमलेश शर्मा (भारद्वाज)

"शहीदों के मजारों पर जुड़ेंगे हर बरस मेले,
वतन पर मरने वालों का यही बाकी निशां होगा।"

भारतीय स्वतंत्रता आन्दोलन के इतिहास में क्रांतिकारियों का महत्वपूर्ण स्थान है, जो अंग्रेजों की दमनकारी नीतियों और कार्यों का जवाब क्रांति के माध्यम से देना जानते थे। इनमें भगतसिंह, चन्द्रशेखर आजाद, सूर्यसेन, रामप्रसाद बिस्मिल, सुखदेव, अशफाकउल्ला खाँ, राजेन्द्र सिंह लाहिड़ी, रोशनसिंह, गणेश शंकर विद्यार्थी जैसे शहीदों के नाम विशेष रूप से उल्लेखनीय हैं। इन्होंने स्वतन्त्रता की बलिवेदी पर अपने प्राणों का उत्सर्ग किया। इन्हें मात्र क्रांतिकारी ही नहीं कहा जा सकता, वरन् ये महान् विचारक भी थे, जिनके विचारों में एक नवीन भारत की तस्वीर दिखाई देती है। इनकी क्रांति की अवधारणा अत्यन्त व्यापक थी। यद्यपि इनका राजदर्शन विवाद का विषय रहा है, लेकिन देश के प्रति इनकी निष्ठा, प्रेम, त्याग व वीरता, लक्ष्य के प्रति समर्पण-प्रतिबद्धता निर्विवाद है। इनकी कुर्बानी व ब्रिटिश हुकूमत की क्रूरता ने सारे देश को हिला दिया था। शहीदों के रक्त से ही भारत की वह भूमि तैयार हुई, जिस पर महात्मा गांधी आजादी के लिए अहिंसा को लेकर आगे बढ़े थे। शहीदों के बलिदान ने आमजन में स्वतंत्रता के जज्बे को जीवंत कर दिया। वे अपने बलिदान के माध्यम से क्रांतिकारी जनता को स्वतंत्रता का महत्व समझाना चाहते थे।

शहीद भगतसिंह के समक्ष दो ही प्रमुख उद्देश्य थे--पहला देश की स्वतन्त्रता, दूसरा स्वतंत्रता के बाद शोषण मुक्त समाज का निर्माण। भगतसिंह समाजवाद की कल्पना को साकार रूप देना चाहते थे। समाज में किसी भी प्रकार के शोषण से वह

अध्यक्ष, भारतीय संस्कृति एवं परम्परा विभाग, वर्धमान खुला विश्वविद्यालय कोटा, राज. 324010

घृणा करते थे। देशवासियों की उन्नति एवं उनके उत्थान का ही सपना वह देखते थे।

क्रांतिकारी नवयुवक साहसी और दृढ़संकल्पी तो थे ही, फिर भी मानवीय स्वभाववश उन्हें भी भावनाएँ उद्वेलित करती थीं, जिन्हें उन्होंने अपने खतों में व्यक्त किया है। भावनात्मक पहलू के साथ-साथ इन खतों में उनके राजनीतिक व सामाजिक चिंतन पर भी प्रकाश पड़ता है। इन पत्रों के अलावा असेम्बली बम केस के प्रकरण क्रमांक 306 में दिनांक 6.6.1929 को न्यायालयीय लिखित कथन में उद्घोषित वक्तव्य, असेम्बली में फेंके बम के साथ गुलाबी पेम्पलेट में घोषित वक्तव्य व तत्कालीन अखबारों व उनके परिवारजनों के कथनों आदि के माध्यम से भगतसिंह के क्रांति संबंधी विचारों की जानकारी मिलती है।

भगतसिंह बमों का प्रेमी या खून-खराबे को पसंद कदापि नहीं करता था, उसका लक्ष्य तो भारतीय जन-समूह में क्रांति की नई चेतना का विकास करना था। देश-प्रेम के भाव को क्रांति के माध्यम से विकसित कर समाज का एक शोषणमुक्त व्यवस्थित रूप प्रस्तुत करना था।

1920 से खिलाफत आंदोलन व असहयोग आंदोलन आरंभ हो गया था, लेकिन 5 फरवरी 1922 को चोरी-चौरा घटना से आंदोलन स्थगित कर दिया गया। राष्ट्रीय कांग्रेस के इस आत्मसमर्पण से ब्रिटिश शासकों को स्वाधीनता संघर्ष के पहले राष्ट्रव्यापी उभार का दमन करने में सफलता मिली। इससे स्वतंत्रता के लिए चल रहे जन आंदोलनों को भारी क्षति पहुँची।

पंजाब में क्रांतिकारी गतिविधियाँ तेज हो रही थीं, जब उन्हें गिरफ्तार करने का षड्यंत्र रचा जा रहा था, तब भगतसिंह के समक्ष विदेशी शासन के विरुद्ध संघर्ष की व्यापक योजना थी। प्रथम बार 1923 में जब घर से फरार हुए तो अपने पिता सरदार किशन सिंह के नाम एक पत्र छोड़ गये थे—"मेरी जिंदगी मक्सदे आला यानी आजादी-ए-हिन्द के असूल के लिए वक्फ (दान) हो चुकी है। इसलिए मेरी जिंदगी में आराम और दुनियावी खाइशात (इच्छाएँ) बायसे कशिश (आकर्षण) नहीं है। आपको याद होगा कि जब मैं छोटा था तो बापूजी ने मेरे यज्ञोपवीत के वक्त ऐलान किया था कि मुझे खिदमते वतन के लिए वक्फ कर दिया गया है। लिहाजा मैं उस वक्त की प्रतिज्ञा पूरी कर रहा हूँ।"[1]

प्रस्तुत पत्र में भगत सिंह का अपने देश के प्रति प्रेम प्रकट होता है, उन्होंने अपने सारे युवा स्वप्न व महत्वाकांक्षाएँ देश के नाम कर दी। काकोरी केस. में रामप्रसाद बिस्मिल, राजेन्द्रसिंह लाहिड़ी, अश्फाकउल्ला खां और रोशन सिंह को फांसी

देने से देश में मातम छा गया था। शचीन्द्रनाथ सान्याल तथा मन्मथनाथ गुप्त को आजीवन कारावास देकर अंडमान भेज दिया गया। अब आंदोलन को भगतसिंह को ही संभालना था। उन्होंने खुद लिखा, "फिर सारी जिम्मेदारी अपने कंधों पर उठाने का समय आया।"

काकोरी षडयन्त्र के समय क्रांतिकारी संगठन का नाम हिन्दुस्तान रिपब्लिकन एसोसियेशन था। भगतसिंह ने नया नाम सोशलिस्ट रिपब्लिकन एसोसियेशन कर दिया। सितम्बर, 1928 में दिल्ली के फिरोजशाह कोटला में उत्तर भारत के क्रांतिकारियों की बैठक में प्रथम बार समाजवाद का लक्ष्य स्वीकार गया।

साइमन कमीशन के विरोध के समय लाला लाजपतराय की मृत्यु पुलिस की लाठियों से हुई। इस घटना से सम्पूर्ण देश में क्रोध की लहर फैल गयी। भगतसिंह व राजगुरू ने सांडर्स को मार दिया। राष्ट्र के अपमान का प्रतिशोध लेने के लिए लालाजी के हत्यारे को मारना आवश्यक है। यह प्रस्ताव भगतसिंह का ही था। भगतसिंह क्रांतिकारी थे, लेकिन रक्त के प्यासे नहीं थे। दिल्ली असेम्बली में बम फेंकने के बाद जो गुलाबी पर्चे बाँटे गये, उनमें भगतसिंह ने यह स्पष्ट रूप से उद्घोषित किया था—"हम मनुष्य के जीवन को पवित्र मानते हैं। हम ऐसे उज्ज्वल भविष्य में विश्वास करते हैं, जिसमें प्रत्येक व्यक्ति को पूर्ण शांति और स्वतन्त्रता का अवसर मिल सके। हम इन्सान का खून बहाने की अपनी विवशता पर दुःखी हैं, परन्तु क्रांति द्वारा सबको समान स्वतन्त्रता देने और मनुष्य द्वारा मनुष्य के शोषण को समाप्त कर देने के लिए क्रांति में कुछ न कुछ रक्तपात अनिवार्य है, लेकिन मानवता को प्यार करने में हम किसी से पीछे नहीं है।"[2]

समाजवादी आधार पर भगतसिंह समाज का पुनर्गठन करना चाहते थे। उनकी क्रांति की अवधारणा का स्वरूप न्यायालय के माध्यम से प्रसारित कथनों में मिल जाता है। भगतसिंह उच्च वर्ग द्वारा निम्न वर्ग के शोषण के विरोधी थे। उन्होंने घोषणा की कि भारतीय क्रांतिकारी संघर्ष तब तक चलता रहेगा जब तक मुट्ठीभर सत्तारूढ़ लोग चाहे भारतीय हो, चाहे ब्रिटिश या चाहे दोनों ही मिलकर खड़े हो, तो भी इस संघर्ष को कोई नहीं रोक सकेगा, जब तक शोषण की समाज-व्यवस्था में परिवर्तन नहीं होगा।[3] समाज की विभिन्न श्रेणियों में फैले भेदभाव को वे बिल्कुल पसंद नहीं करते थे। उन्हें ढोंग से घृणा थी व जमींदारी व्यवस्था को वे नापसंद करते थे। कपड़े बुनने वाले जुलाहे, मकान बनाने वाले मिस्त्री एवं कृषि करने वाले श्रमिक किसानों को वे सबकी तरह समान श्रेणी पर लाना चाहते थे। वे ऐसी स्वतन्त्रता में विश्वास नहीं रखते थे कि बड़ा जमींदार छोटे जमींदार का शोषण करे। भगतसिंह का दर्शन गाँधीजी से भिन्न था। महात्मा गांधी बड़े जमींदार को समाप्त करने के पक्ष में नहीं

थे। फैक्ट्री मालिक व दूसरे पूँजीपतियों की समाप्ति के भी वे इच्छुक नहीं थे। इनसे लड़ने के लिए सहायता लेने की उनकी विशेष नीति थी। अंग्रेजों से सत्ता बड़े लोगों के हाथ आनी थी, ताकि पहले भारतीय निर्धन जनता का शोषण अंग्रेज कर रहे थे और स्वतंत्रता के पश्चात् धनवान पूँजीवादी भारतवासी अपनी निर्धन भारतीय जनता का शोषण करें। ऐसी स्वतन्त्रता की अवधारणा भगतसिंह की नहीं थी।

भगतसिंह ने जब नेशनल कॉलेज लाहौर में प्रवेश किया, तो उन्हें विश्व के सभी क्रांतिकारियों के बारे में पढ़ने का अवसर मिला। फ्रांस की क्रांति के साहित्य को पढ़कर वे बहुत प्रभावित हुए। कार्ल मार्क्स, बर्क आदि को उन्होंने पढ़ा।[4] सोवियत क्रांति एक युगान्तकारी घटना थी, जिसने सभी क्रांतियों को पीछे छोड़ दिया। सोवियत क्रांति ने समाजवाद की रूपरेखा को व्यावहारिक रूप दिया। भगतसिंह ने सोवियत क्रांति व लेनिन के बहुत से लेखों का अध्ययन किया। भगतसिंह ने जनता के समक्ष जब-जब मौका मिला व न्यायालय के कथनों व कार्यवाहियों के द्वारा सोवियत क्रांति का प्रचार किया।

"सांडर्स मर्डर" अपने लाहौर के प्रसिद्ध प्रकरण में भगतसिंह ने लेनिन और सोवियत क्रांति के प्रभाव का खुलकर उपयोग किया। प्रकरण में पैरवी के दौरान भगतसिंह एवं उनके साथियों ने अपने गले में लाल रूमाल बाँधे थे। "लांग लिव रिव्यूलेशन और लांग लिव रसियन रिव्यूलेशन" के भी नारे लगाये थे।[5] अदालत में क्रांतिकारियों के नारे "इंकलाब जिंदाबाद", "वंदेमातरम्" व राष्ट्रीय गीतों की गूँज होती थी। पूरा वातावरण बलिदान के रंग से रंग जाता था। क्रांति के दीवाने गा उठते थे—

"सरफरोशी की तमन्ना अब हमारे दिल में है।
देखना है जोर कितना बाजुए कातिल में है।।
वक्त आने दे बता देंगे तुझे ऐ आसमां।
हम अभी से क्या बताएं, क्या हमारे दिल में है।।"

भगतसिंह ने कारावास के एकांत को भी गहन अध्ययन में बदल दिया था। कारावास से लिखे गये वक्तव्यों, न्यायालयीय वक्तव्यों से, अपने आचरण एवं लेखों से जनसाधारण में क्रांति की ज्वाला को प्रस्फुटित करने का कार्य भगतसिंह ने किया। "इंकलाब जिन्दाबाद" का नारा सर्वप्रथम भगतसिंह ने ही दिया, जिसमें क्रांति की भावना समाहित थी।

भगतसिंह को जेल की काल कोठरी में देशवासियों की ही चिंता सताती रहती थी। वे नवनिर्माण के मार्ग खोजने में व्यस्त थे। समाज की कैसी व्यवस्था हो जिसमें

सभी लोग सुखी हों। उन्होंने निम्न ग्रंथों की रचना की—(1) आत्मकथा, (2) मौत के दरवाजे पर, (3) समाजवाद के आदर्श, (4) स्वाधीनता की लड़ाई में पंजाब का पहला उभार। समाज और राष्ट्र के नवनिर्माण में ये पुस्तकें बहुत ही उपयोगी सिद्ध होती, परन्तु जेल से सुरक्षित बाहर भिजवा देने पर भी यह साहित्य प्रकाशित हुए बिना ही नष्ट हो गया।[6]

स्वयं को मिटाकर वे देशवासियों के मध्य क्रांति की गूँज पहुँचाना चाहते थे, स्वयं उनके शब्दों में—"क्रांतिकारी पार्टी में आते समय मैंने सोचा था कि अगर मैं "इन्कलाब-जिन्दाबाद" का नारा देश के कोने-कोने तक पहुँचा सका तो समझूंगा, मेरे जीवन का मूल्य मुझे मिल गया, पर आज तो मैं फांसी की कोठरी में भी अपने उस नारे की गूंज सुन रहा हूँ। मैं समझता हूँ इस छोटी सी जिन्दगी का इससे अधिक मूल्य और हो भी क्या सकता है?"[7] भगतसिंह के कुछ क्रांतिकारी साथी उन्हें लाहौर सेन्ट्रल जेल से बचाना चाहते थे, लेकिन भगतसिंह स्वयं मृत्यु को गले लगाने को उतावले थे, जैसा कि उस पर्चे से स्पष्ट है, जो उन्होंने चौदह नम्बर बैरक के कैदियों को लिखा—"जिन्दा रहने की ख्वाइश कुदरती तौर पर मुझमें भी होनी चाहिए। मैं इसे छिपाना नहीं चाहता, लेकिन मेरा जिन्दा रहना एक शर्त पर निर्भर करता है—

"मेरा नाम भारतीय क्रांतिकारी पार्टी का मध्यबिन्दु बन चुका है और भारतीय क्रांतिकारी दल के आदर्शों और बलिदानों ने मुझे बहुत ऊँचा उठा दिया है, इतना ऊँचा कि जिन्दा रहने की सूरत में इससे ऊँचा मैं हरगिज नहीं हो सकता। आज मेरी कमजोरियाँ लोगों के सामने नहीं है। अगर मैं फांसी से बच गया, तो वह जाहिर हो जायेगी और क्रांति का निशान मद्धिम पड़ जाएगा या शायद मिट ही जाए। लेकिन मेरे दिलेराना ढंग से हँसते-हँसते फांसी की सूरत में भारतीय माताएँ अपने बच्चों के भगतसिंह बनने की आरजू किया करेंगी और देश की आजादी के लिए बलिदान होने वालों की तादाद इतनी बढ़ जाएगी कि क्रांति को रोकना साम्राज्यवाद की सम्पूर्ण राक्षसी शक्तियों के वश की बात न रहेगी।"

"हाँ, एक ख्याल आज भी चुटकी लेता है। देश और इन्सानियत के लिए जो कुछ करने की हसरतें मेरे दिल में थी, उनका हजारवाँ हिस्सा भी पूरा न कर पाया। अगर जिन्दा रह सकता तो शायद इनको पूरा करने का मौका मिलता और मैं अपनी हसरतें पूरी कर सकता।"

"इसके सिवा कोई लालच मेरे दिल में फांसी से बचे रहने का अभी नहीं आया। मुझसे ज्यादा खुशकिस्मत कौन होगा? मुझे आजकल अपने आप पर बहुत नाज है मुझमें अब कोई ख्वाहिश बाकी नहीं है। अब तो बड़ी बेताबी से आखिरी इम्तहां का इन्तजार है। आरजू है कि यह और करीब हो जाए।"

अपनी फांसी से पूर्व सुखदेव व राजगुरु के साथ भगतसिंह प्रसन्नचित्त थे, तीनों ने गाना शुरू किया--

"दिल से निकलेगी न मर कर भी वतन की उलफत,
मेरी मिट्टी से भी खुशबू-ए-वतन आएगी।"

गर्जना की--

"इन्कलाब-जिन्दाबाद, साम्राज्यवाद मुर्दाबाद"

भगतसिंह क्रांति के द्वारा देशवासियों को जाग्रत करना चाहते थे। फांसी से पूर्व अंग्रेज डिप्टी कमिश्नर को कहे शब्दों से यह स्पष्ट है--

"मजिस्ट्रेट महोदय, आप भाग्यशाली है कि आज आप अपनी आँखों से यह देखने का अवसर पा रहे हैं कि भारत के क्रांतिकारी किस प्रकार प्रसन्नतापूर्वक अपने सर्वोच्च आदर्श के लिए मृत्यु का आलिंगन कर सकते हैं।"

भगतसिंह दूरद्रष्टा थे, उन्होंने गर्वनर को लिखे पत्र में लिखा था कि "निकट भविष्य में यह युद्ध अंतिम रूप से लड़ा जाएगा, तब यह निर्णायक होगा। साम्राज्यवाद और पूँजीवाद कुछ समय के मेहमान हैं। मैं आती हुई क्रांति की आवाज सुन रहा हूँ और क्षितिज पर नये युग का प्रभात देख रहा हूँ।"

भगत सिंह, सुखदेव एवं राजगुरू को 23 मार्च 1931 की शाम फांसी पर चढ़ा दिया गया। रात को अंग्रेजों ने उसी रात सतलुज नदी के तट पर हुसैनीवाला पुल के निकट तीनों शहीदों के शवों को जला डाला। छिपकर रात को यह कार्य किया गया ताकि लोगों को खबर न हो। अपने भाई कुलतार सिंह को लिखे पत्र के शब्दों को उन्होंने सच कर डाला--

"उसे फिक्र है हरदम नया तर्जे जफा क्या है
हमें यह शौक देखें सितम की इन्तहा क्या है।
दहर से क्यों खफा रहे चर्ख का क्यों गिला करें,
सारा जहाँ अदूसही आओ मुकाबिला करें।।
कोई दम का मेहमां हूँ ए एहले महफिल
चरागे सहर हूं बुझा चाहता हूं
मेरी हवा में रहेगी ख्याल की बिजली
यह मुश्ते खाक है फानी रहे न रहे।।

अर्थात् अरूणोदय हो रहा है, तब नियति का मार्ग कौन अवरूद्ध कर सकता है? यदि सारा संसार भी हमारे विरुद्ध हो जाए, तब भी चिंता किस बात की है? मेरे जीवन

का अन्त आ गया है। जिस प्रकार भोर होते ही दीपों की लौ बुझ जाती है, उसी प्रकार उषा काल होते होते मैं विलीन हो जाऊँगा। हमारी आस्था तथा हमारे विचार सारे संसार को बिजली की एक कड़क के समान चौंका कर आलोकित कर देंगे। इस बात की क्या चिन्ता है, यदि एक मुट्ठी भर धूल धूल में मिल जाती है।

भगतसिंह के मन मस्तिष्क में अंतिम क्षण तक भारत को आजाद कराने की योजनाएं घूम रही थीं। देश की आजादी का लक्ष्य हासिल करते हुए वे क्रांति द्वारा साम्राज्यवाद व पूँजीवाद का खात्मा करना चाहते थे। उन्होंने अपने बलिदान से देश की जनता को क्रांति की मशाल लेकर आगे बढ़ने का रास्ता बताया। क्रांति को वैचारिक आधार प्रदान कर सुदृढ़ता प्रदान की। उनकी क्रांति की अवधारणा सिर्फ भारतवर्ष तक ही सीमित नहीं थी। वे साम्राज्यवाद व पूँजीवाद को पूरी तरह नष्ट करना चाहते थे और एक समाजवादी समाज की स्थापना करना चाहते थे, जिसमें किसी भी तरह का भेदभाव व शोषण न हो।

संदर्भ

1. मिश्र, विनोद, *'शहीदों के खत'*, पृ. 2
2. असेम्बली में फेंके बम के साथ वितरित किये, गुलाबी पेम्पलेट में घोषित वक्तव्य।
3. सरदार भगतसिंह का देहली असेम्बली बम के प्रकरण में न्यायालयीय लिखित कथन दिनांकित 06.06.1929, नेशनल आर्काइव्ज देहली से प्राप्त फौजदारी प्रकरण पत्रिका क्रमांक 306 के अनुसार।
4. भगतसिंह लाहौर की द्वारकादास लाईब्रेरी के पाठक थे।
5. सुधीर भसीन, *शहीद भगतसिंह : भारत सोवियत मित्रता को जनसाधारण में सक्रिय करने वाली पहली कड़ी शोध समवेत,* वोल्यूम नं. XVI पृ. 42
6. वीरेन्द्र सिंधु, *भारतीय क्रांति के अग्रदूत, अमर शहीद भगतसिंह,* पृ. 47
7. दिसम्बर 1930 की रात भगतसिंह के साथ शिव वर्मा से उनकी मुलाकात।

17

1928 से 1931 के मध्य क्रांतिकारी एवं कांग्रेस : एक दृष्टि

डॉ. के.डी. शर्मा

भारतीय स्वाधीनता संग्राम मुख्यतः दो समानान्तर धाराओं से प्रवाहित हुआ है। एक थी ब्रिटिश साम्राज्यवाद के विरुद्ध सशस्त्र क्रांति और संग्राम की धारा तथा दूसरी अंग्रेजी सरकार द्वारा प्रदत्त संवैधानिक धरातल पर लड़ी जाने वाली सुधारात्मक समझौतावादी एवं अहिंसक लड़ाई। इन दोनों धाराओं का उद्देश्य एक ही था देश के लिये आजादी हासिल करना। यह तथ्य है कि भारत के लिये आजादी प्राप्त करने की दिशा में पहला राष्ट्रव्यापी प्रयास सशस्त्र संग्राम के माध्यम से ही किया गया था, जिसका महत्त्वपूर्ण अध्याय 10 मई 1857 को मेरठ छावनी में रचा गया और अंतिम दक्षिण पूर्व एशिया में नेताजी सुभाष चंद्र बोस के नेतृत्व में 1943 ई. में।

बीसवीं शताब्दी के प्रारम्भ तक भारतीय राष्ट्रीय कांग्रेस देश की प्रमुख राजनीतिक पार्टी का रूप ले चुकी थी जिसकी कमान आगे चलकर महात्मा गांधी के हाथों में आयी। महात्मा गांधी ने स्वतंत्रता प्राप्ति के लिये हिंसा के मार्ग को न अपनाकर अहिंसा का मार्ग देश के सम्मुख रखा। सत्याग्रह और अहिंसा गांधीजी के ही प्रमुख हथियार थे जबकि क्रांतिकारी उन्हें नैराश्य से उत्पन्न दर्शन मानते थे।[1] गांधी जी के मार्ग पर विश्वास न करते हुए भी क्रांतिकारी उनकी ओर सद्भाव से देखते थे। चंद्रशेखर आजाद प्रायः अपने साथियों से कहा करते थे कि क्रांतिकारी दल के कार्य कांग्रेस के कार्य के पूरक होंगे, विरुद्ध नहीं होंगे। आखिर दोनों ही स्वाधीनता की लड़ाई लड़ रहे हैं। दोनों अपने-अपने मार्गों द्वारा एक ही ध्येय की प्राप्ति के लिए प्रयासरत है।[2]

बी-157, शास्त्री नगर, मेरठ

1920-21 में अंग्रेजी राज के विरुद्ध असहयोग आन्दोलन प्रारंभ करते समय गांधी जी ने सी.आर. दास के माध्यम से क्रांतिकारियों से अपील की कि वे एक वर्ष के लिये अपनी गतिविधियों को रोक दें, और उनके साथ सहयोग करें। ब्रिटिश साम्राज्यवादियों के विरुद्ध अनवरत संघर्ष में जुटे क्रांतिकारियों ने गांधी जी को अहिंसा के उनके प्रयोग के क्रियान्वयन में सहयोग देने के लिये अपनी गतिविधियों को स्थगित कर दिया। परन्तु गांधी जी का यह प्रयोग चौरी-चौरा में लोगों के हिंसा के मार्ग के अपनाने से असफल हो गया और उन्होंने उस प्रयत्न को 'हिमालय पर्वत के समान भूल' कहकर स्थगित कर दिया। इस स्थिति को एक राष्ट्रीय आपदा मानते हुए सुभाष ने लिखा–

"To sound the order of retreat just when public enthusiasm was reaching the boiling-point was nothing short of a national calamity."[3]

सचिन सान्याल ने गांधी जी को पत्र लिखते हुए सूचित किया कि क्रांतिकारियों ने उन्हें दिया गया अपना वचन पूरा कर दिया है कि वे एक वर्ष तक कोई हिंसा नहीं करेंगे। अब क्रांतिकारी अपनी गतिविधियाँ फिर से जारी करने के लिये स्वतंत्र हैं–

"Now the experiment is over and therefore the revolutionaries are free from their promise, or, as a matter of fact, they promised to remain silent only for a year and so more."[4]

क्रांतिकारियों द्वारा गांधी जी को दिये गये सहयोग के बावजूद भी उनके प्रति गांधी जी के दृष्टिकोण में कोई परिवर्तन देखने को नहीं मिला। इसके विपरीत गांधी जी उन्हें न केवल गुमराह ही मानते रहे अपितु यह भी मानते रहे कि उनकी गतिविधियों ने देश को जितनी बड़ी हानि पहुँचायी है, उतनी अन्य किसी ने नहीं क्योंकि उन्होंने देश की प्रगति में बाधा डाली है।[5] जवाहरलाल नेहरू क्रांतिकारियों की इस प्रकार की गई आलोचना को अनुचित मानते थे। क्रांतिकारियों की मनोदशा को 1928 ई में देश में घटने वाली घटनाओं से जोड़ते हुए उन्होंने लिखा–

"हिन्दुस्तान के मन में इसी राष्ट्रीय अपमान का खयाल काम कर रहा था और जब उसके कुछ दिनों बाद ही लाला जी की मृत्यु हुई तब लोगों ने लाजिमी तौर पर उसका ताल्लुक उन पर किये गये हमले से जोड़ा और इस खयाल से लोगों के दिलों में जो गुस्सा और रोष आया, वह खुद-ब-खुद एक प्रकार के अभियान के रूप में बदल गया। इस बात को समझ लेना जरूरी है, क्योंकि इसको समझ कर ही हम पीछे होने

वाली बातों को, भगत सिंह की कहानी, उत्तरी भारत में भगत सिंह को यकायक जो आश्चर्यजनक लोकप्रियता मिली, उसको, समझ सकेंगे। उन कामों की तह में जो मूल स्रोत होते हैं, उनको जो बातें प्रेरित करती हैं, उनको समझ लेने की कोशिश किये बिना किसी शख्स या किसी काम की निन्दा करना बहुत ही आसान और वाहियात है।"[6]

भगत सिंह की प्रशंसा करते हुए उनकी लोकप्रियता के विषय में नेहरू ने आगे लिखा–

"इस तरह भगत सिंह ने अपने हिंसात्मक कार्य के लिये लोकप्रियता प्राप्त नहीं की, बल्कि इस लिये प्राप्त की कि कम-से-कम उस समय लोगों को ऐसा मालूम हुआ कि उसने लालाजी की और लालाजी के रूप में कौम की इज्जत रखी है। भगत सिंह एक प्रतीक बन गये। उनके काम को लोग भूल गये, केवल प्रतीक उनके मन में रह गया, जिसके फलस्वरूप पंजाब के हरएक गाँव व कस्बे में और उससे कुछ कम बाकी के उत्तरी भारत में उनका नाम घर-घर में गूंजने लगा। उनकी बाबत बेशुमार गीत बने और उन्होंने जो लोकप्रियता पाई वह सचमुच अजीब थी।"[7]

क्रांतिकारियों ने लाजपत राय की हत्या का बदला अंग्रेज अधिकारी सांण्डर्स को मारकर लिया। जिसने लोगों के उबलते जोश और क्रोध को कुछ शान्ति दी। उसके वध से केवल लाहौर या पंजाब में ही नहीं अपितु समस्त भारत में सनसनी फैल गई। 18 सितम्बर, 1928 को साण्डर्स की हत्या के दूसरे दिन सारे लाहौर में सी.आई.डी. की आँखों में धूल झोंक कर एक लाल पर्चा बांटा गया, जिसमें लिखा था कि साण्र्डस को मारकर क्रांतिकारी दल ने लाला लाजपत राय की मृत्यु का बदला ले लिया है और साथ ही ब्रिटिश साम्राज्य को चेतावनी भी दी है।[8]

साण्डर्स काण्ड के बाद नेहरू की प्रतिकिया अप्रत्याशित और उत्साहवर्धक थी। भगत सिंह द्वारा गठित नौजवान भारत सभा को भेजे गये एक संदेश में उसके सदस्यों को आश्वस्त करते हुए नेहरू ने लिखा, "इस सभा (नौजवान भारत सभा) और इसके सदस्यों के बारे में जहाँ तक मैं जानता हूँ, मुझे यकीन है कि पुलिस के दमन या जोर-जुल्म से उनका जोश ठण्डा नहीं पड़ेगा। ये बहादुर लोग हैं, जिन्हें अपने कामों के अंजाम का पता होगा, और उनसे वे घबराते भी नहीं हैं। उन्हें कहीं बाहर से अपनी दिलेरी के लिये बढ़ावा पाने की जरुरत नहीं है, लेकिन वे इतमिनान रखें कि हिन्दुस्तान में बहुतों की हमदर्दी उनके साथ है और जहाँ तक मुमकिन है वे उनकी मदद करने को तैयार हैं। मुझे यकीन है कि नौजवान भारत सभा जिन्दा रहेगी और उसकी ताकत बढ़ती ही जायगी, ताकि वह एक राष्ट्रवादी भारत को गढ़ने में आगे बढ़कर हिस्सा लेती रहे।"[9]

अप्रैल 1929 को केन्द्रीय असेम्बली बम काण्ड भारत में क्रांतिकारी आन्दोलन का अविस्मरणीय अध्याय है। असेम्बली में अंग्रेजी सरकार की ओर से दो बिल रखे गये थे, एक था 'Trade Disputes Act'–'औद्योगिक विवाद कानून', और दूसरा 'Public safety Bill' 'सार्वजनिक सुरक्षा कानून'। इन दोनों कानूनों का अभिप्राय था जनता की स्वतंत्रता की भावना को कुचलना और उसके असन्तोष को दबाना। 8 अप्रैल 1929 को भगत सिंह एंव बटुकेश्वर दत्त ने असेम्बली में सरकारी पक्ष के सदस्यों के समीप बम फेंका फिर दोनों जोर से चिल्लाए, 'इंकलाब जिंदाबाद'। 'साम्राज्यवाद का नाश हो', 'दुनियाँ के मजदूरो एक हो जाओ', 'एच.एस.आर.ए. जिंदाबाद'। साथ ही उन्होंने लाल पर्चे हॉल में फेंके। उन पर्चो का आशय था, 'बहरों को सुनाने के लिये विस्फोट के बहुत ऊँचे शब्दों की आवश्यकता होती है।'

'हम मनुष्य के जीवन को पवित्र समझते हैं। हम ऐसे उज्ज्वल भविष्य में विश्वास रखते हैं जिसमें प्रत्येक व्यक्ति को पूर्ण शान्ति और स्वतंत्रता का अवसर मिल सके। हम मानव के रक्त को बहाने और अपनी विवशता के लिये दुखी हैं, परन्तु क्रांति द्वारा सबको समान स्वतंत्रता देने और मनुष्य द्वारा मनुष्य के शोषण को समाप्त करने के लिये क्रान्ति में कुछ न कुछ रक्तपात अनिवार्य है।'[10]

असेम्बली बम काण्ड ने साम्राज्यवाद की जड़ों को हिला डाला था लेकिन महात्मा गांधी ने खुले रूप से इस कृत्य को निन्दनीय ही नहीं माना अपितु कहा कि इस कृत्य ने स्वतंत्रता प्राप्ति के प्रयास को बदनामी दिलाई है। उन्होंने कांग्रेसियों को भी आगाह किया कि वे गुप्त रूप से भी क्रांतिकारियों के इस कृत्य को समर्थन देने से बचें।[11] इतना ही नहीं गांधी जी ने भगत सिंह के इस कार्य को पागलपन की संज्ञा दी जिसे उसने राष्ट्रीय कार्य के लिये इस्तेमाल किया था।[12] गांधी जी की सलाह को नजर अंदाज करते हुए नेहरू ने 'कांग्रेस बुलेटिन' में भगत सिंह और बटुकेश्वर दत्त के बयान को प्रकाशित कराया जिस पर उन्हें गांधी जी की नाराजगी भी झेलनी पड़ी। नेहरू ने क्रांतिकारियों की देशव्यापी लोकप्रियता का उल्लेख करते हुए गांधी जी को लिखा, "मुझे अफसोस है कि भगत सिंह और दत्त के बयान का मेरे द्वारा कांग्रेस बुलेटिन में दिया जाना आपने नापसन्द किया। मैं खुद उसे उसमें देने के बारे में कुछ दुविधा में था लेकिन जब मुझे पता चला कि कि कांग्रेस के क्षेत्रों में उसे ज्यादातर सराहा जा रहा है तो मैंने उसके उद्धरण देने का फैसला कर डाला।[13] सुभाष चन्द्र बोस के अनुसार असेम्बली बम की घटना भारत में क्रांतिकारी अन्दोलन की स्पष्ट अभिव्यक्ति थी जिसने न केवल जन चेतना को ही जाग्रत किया अपितु जनमानस की सहानुभुति भी अपने पक्ष में हासिल की थी।"[14]

भगत सिंह और बटुकेश्वर दत्त के एक साथ लिये गये चित्र सारे देश में वितरित किये गये थे। दोनों का नाम देश भर में बड़े गर्व के साथ लिया जाने लगा था। लाहौर षडयंत्र केस के समय जेल में बंद भगत सिंह और उनके साथियों ने अपने साथ होने वाले आम कैदियों जैसे व्यवहार के विरुद्ध भूख हड़ताल आरम्भ की तो सारा देश उत्तेजना से भर उठा, ऐसे में नेहरू ने लिखा, "कोई भी हिन्दुस्तानी उनकी दिलेरी की तारीफ किये बिना नहीं रह सकता और अब तो उनके द्वारा बड़ी और अपनी इच्छा से तकलीफ सहने में हमारे दिल पूरी तरह उनके साथ होंगे। ये लोग अपने किसी स्वार्थ कि लिये नहीं बल्कि सभी सियासी कैदियों की हालत में सुधार कराने की गरज़ से उपवास कर रहे हैं। जैसे-जैसे दिन बीतेंगे, उनके इस कठोर इम्तिहान की तरफ हमारी आंखे लगी रहेंगी और अपने दिलों को थामे हम यही उम्मीद करते रहेंगे कि हमारे ये दोनों बहादुर भाई इस इम्तिहान में कामयाब हों"[15] 3 अगस्त, 1929 को नेहरू लाहौर गये और जेल में भगतसिंह, बटुकेश्वर दत्त और जतिन्द्रनाथ दास से मुलाकात की। इस मुलाकात से वह बेहद भावुक हो उठे थे। इसी दिन अपने एक वक्तव्य में उन्होंने कहा–

"इन अनोखे बहादुर नौजवानों से मुलाकात करना और उन्हें अपनी आंखों से इतना दुःख-दर्द झेलते देखना मेरे लिये बहुत ही तकलीफदेह रहा। उनसे बात करके मुझे यही पता लगा कि उनमें से एक-एक को चाहे जो भुगतना पड़े, अपनी आन पर वे डटे रहेंगे।"[16] जेल में इन क्रांतिकारी नौजवानों से मिलकर नेहरू को लगा कि कांग्रेस के मंच पर बैठ कर स्वयं अपने को गौरवान्वित करने वाले कांग्रेस जन कितने बेमानी हैं; लाहौर में ही दिये गये अपने एक भाषण में उन्होंने कहा–

"इन नौजवानों की कुर्बानी ने हमारे अंदर सियासी जिन्दगी की एक नई चेतना पैदा कर दी है और एक बार फिर अपने देश को आजाद कराने की तमन्ना जगा दी है। जेलों के अंदर ये बहादुर नौजवान जो जंग छेड़े हुए हैं उसकी अहमियत कितनी ज्यादा है, यह हमें समझना होगा। ये लोग अपनी कुर्बानी के बदले में जनता की वाहवाही पाने या बड़ी-बड़ी भीड़ों से गले में हार डलवाने के लिये नहीं लड़ रहे हैं। कहाँ इन लोगों की यह कुर्बानी और दूसरी ओर, कितने अफसोस की बात है कि कांग्रेस और स्वागत-समिति के अंदर ओहदे पाने के लिए कांग्रेसजनों के बीच तू-तू मैं-मैं चल रही है। कांग्रेस जनों के बीच चलने वाले इन आपसी झगड़ों की बात सुनकर मेरा सिर शर्म से नीचा हो गया है। पर साथ ही मेरे दिल में उतनी ही खुशी इन नौजवानों की कुर्बानी को देखकर हुई है, जो कि देश की खातिर अपनी जान देने पर तुले हुए हैं।"[17]

नेहरू की नैतिक एवं मौखिक सहानुभूति से बहुत आगे बढ़कर सुभाष चन्द्र बोस खुले रूप से क्रांतिकारियों के समर्थन में खड़े हो गये। कलकत्ता में क्रांतिकारियों की मांगों के समर्थन में प्रदर्शन करते हुए उन्हें गिरफ्तार कर लिया गया और राजद्रोह का मुकदमा चलाया गया। जेल में भूख हड़ताल करते हुए जतिन दास की 13 सितम्बर को मृत्यु हो गई। जतिन के इस आत्म बलिदान ने देशभर में लोगों को रोमांचित कर दिया। इस पर सुभाष ने लिखा,

"His martyrdom acted as a profound inspiration to the youth of India and everywhere youth and student organisations began to grow up. Among the many messages that were received on the occassion was one which touched the heart of every Indian. It was a message from the family of Terence Mc Swiney, the Lord Mayor of Cork, who had died a martyr under similar conditions in Ireland. The message ran thus : Family of Terence Mc Swiney have heard with grief and pride of the death of Jatin Das. Freedom will come"[18]

23 दिसम्बर, 1929 को क्रांतिकारियों ने वाइसराय लार्ड इरविन की ट्रेन को बम से उड़ाने का प्रयास किया, जिसमें वाइसराय बाल-बाल बच गये। इस घटना के कुछ दिन बाद हुई लाहौर कांग्रेस में महात्मा गांधी ने वाइसराय को बधाई देने सम्बन्धी प्रस्ताव कांग्रेस के सम्मुख रखा। माहौल बेहद गर्म था। प्रतिनिधियों की बहुत बड़ी संख्या ने गांधी जी के प्रस्ताव का कड़ा विरोध किया। यह प्रस्ताव 823 के विरोध में केवल 904 प्रतिनिधियों का ही समर्थन प्राप्त कर सका।

वाइसराय की ट्रेन घटना पर महात्मा गांधी ने यंग इंडिया में एक लेख *'कल्ट आफ दि बोम्ब'* पर लिखते हुए क्रांतिकारियों को बुरा भला कहा तथा उनको डरपोक और गुमराह की संज्ञा दी।[19] गांधी जी के इस लेख के जवाब में 26 जनवरी 1930 को क्रांतिकारियों ने देश भर में *'फिलोसॉफी आफ दि बोम्ब'* शीर्षक से एक पर्चा बांटा जिसमें कहा गया था–

"क्रांतिकारी हिंसा, हिंसा की खातिर नहीं करते। वे तो अपने विश्वास के अनुसार न्याय चाहते हैं और अपने उद्देश्य की पूर्ति में अपना सब कुछ बलिदान कर देते हैं।" क्रांति का अभिप्राय समझाते हुए पर्चे में लिखा था–

"हम अपने देश के नौजवानो, मजदूरों, किसानों और बुद्धिमानों से अनुरोध करते हैं कि अपने देश की आजादी के झण्डे के नीचे एकत्रित होकर हमारा साथ दें। देश में ऐसी व्यवस्था लाने का प्रयत्न करें जिसमें राजनैतिक और सामाजिक दासता और आर्थिक शोषण असम्भव हो जाए।"

"अहिंसा के नाम पर समझौतावादी नीति को ठोकर मार दीजिये। हमारी संस्कृति और गौरव का कोई अर्थ उस समय तक नहीं होगा, जब तक अहिंसा के नाम पर विदेशी दासता के सम्मुख सिर झुकाए रहेंगे।"[20]

23 मार्च 1931 को भगत सिंह, राजगुरु और सुखदेव की शहादत से देश भर में गांधीजी के प्रति अपार रोष फूट पड़ा। लोगों को आशा थी कि वे वाइसराय से वार्ता करके इन तीनों क्रांतिकारियों की मौत की सजा को कारावास में परिवर्तित करा लेंगे। "देश भर से यह मांग उठी थी कि उन्हें फाँसी लगने से बचा लेना चाहिए। लाखों करोड़ों लोग जो सविनय अवज्ञा-आन्दोलन के नेता के रूप में गांधी जी के प्रति श्रद्धा भाव रखते थे, वही लोग राष्ट्रीय संघर्ष का एक प्रतीक मानकर भगतसिंह को भी पूजते थे। इसलिये लोगों को उस समय बहुत बेचैनी हुई जब गांधीजी ने उसी वाइसराय के साथ समझौता कर लिया जिसने भगत सिंह और उसके साथियों की सजा रद्द करने से इन्कार किया था। उन लोगों के एक वर्ग ने तथा वामपंथी राजनीतिक कार्यकर्ताओं ने इस तरह के समझौते के लिये गांधी जी की सार्वजनिक तौर पर आलोचना की। और जब गांधी जी तथा नव निर्वाचित अध्यक्ष वल्लभ भाई पटेल कांग्रेस अधिवेशन में भाग लेने कराची पहुंचे तो जनता के एक वर्ग ने अपना विरोध प्रकट करने के लिए उनका स्वागत काले फूलों और काली मालाओं से किया।"[21]

सन्दर्भ

1. सचिन सान्याल का पत्र-गांधी को *यंग इण्डिया* के 12 फरवरी 1925 के अंक में प्रकाशित।
2. एन.के. निगम, *बलिदान (चंद्रशेखर आजाद की रोमांचकारी जीवनी)*, पृ. 54, दिल्ली 1968.
3. सुभाष चंद्र बोस, *"दि इण्डियन स्ट्रगल"* कलकत्ता, 1948, पृ. 108.
4. सचिन सान्याल का पत्र गांधी को, *यंग इण्डिया* के 12 फरवरी, 1925, के अंक में प्रकाशित.
5. *'यंग इण्डिया'* 9 अप्रैल, 1925, क्रांतिकारियों को महात्मा गांधी का उत्तर.
6. जवाहरलाल नेहरू, *'मेरी कहानी'* पृ. 216.
7. उपरोक्त, पृ. 217.
8. एन. के. निगम, पूर्वोक्त, पृ. 30.
9. *'दि सर्चलाइट'* 11 जनवरी 1929, *जवाहरलाल नेहरू वाङ्मय,* वाल्यूम 4, पृ. 1.

10. एन. के. निगम, पूर्वोक्त, पृ. 40-41.

11. *यंग इण्डिया,* अप्रैल 18, 1929.

12. उपरोक्त.

13. *जवाहरलाल नेहरू वाङ्मय,* वाल्युम 4, पृ. 159.

14. सुभाष चंद्र बोस, पूर्वोक्त, पृ. 225.

15. *जवाहरलाल नेहरू वाङ्मय,* वाल्युम 4, पृ. 9.

16. 9 अगस्त 1929 को लाहौर में दिया गया नेहरू का वक्तव्य, उपरोक्त पृ. 13.

17. उपरोक्त, पृ. 14.

18. सुभाष चन्द्र बोस, पूर्वोक्त, पृ. 227.

19. एन. के. निगम, पूर्वोक्त, पृ. 54.

20. उपरोक्त, पृ. 58.

21. ई.एम.एस. नंबूदरीपाद, *भारत का स्वाधीनता संग्राम,* पृ. 321, दिल्ली, 2004.

18

सरदार भगत सिंह और आतंकवाद

डॉ. राजेन्द्र कुमार

भारत माँ के उस अमर लाल को, जो केवल तेईस वर्ष की आयु में उस राज्य के सत्ताधीशों को हिला गया, जिनके राज्य में कभी सूर्यास्त नहीं होता था, भारत का इतिहास भगत सिंह के नाम से याद करता है। भगत सिंह क्रांतिकारी थे, गांधीजी के अहिंसापूर्ण विचारों से उनका मतभेद था, किन्तु आजादी तक और उसके बाद के तीन-चार दशक तक जब तक ग्लोबल विलेज कल्चर ने हमारी संस्कृति पर हमला नहीं किया था, उत्तर भारत में, विशेष रूप से देहात में भगत सिंह गांधी जी से भी अधिक लोकप्रिय थे। इस बात का यह प्रमाण है कि गांवों में लगभग प्रत्येक घर में दीवार पर महापुरुषों के चित्र लगाने की परम्परा थी और उनमें भगत सिंह का चित्र अवश्य लगा होता था। उनका लगाया हुआ नारा 'इन्कलाब जिन्दाबाद' आज भी सार्थक है।

भगत सिंह युवकों के आदर्श रहे हैं। वे न केवल वीरता, साहस, देशभक्ति, दृढ़ता और आत्म बलिदान के सर्वोत्तम उदाहरण हैं, बल्कि वे अपने लक्ष्य के प्रति स्पष्टता, वैज्ञानिक-ऐतिहासिक दृष्टिकोण से सामाजिक समस्याओं के विश्लेषण की क्षमता वाले अद्भुत बौद्धिक क्रांतिकारी व्यक्तित्व के प्रतिरूप भी थे। भगत सिंह तथा उनके साथियों के बारे में यह प्रचारित किया जाता था कि वे आतंकवादी हैं। जनता को सच्चाई पता न चल जाये इसीलिए भगत सिंह पर 1931 में लिखी गयी सबसे पहली किताब अंग्रेज सरकार ने जब्त कर ली थी। उस किताब को लिखने के आरोप में गिरफ्तार उनके साथी जितेन्द्र नाथ सान्याल ने जिला मजिस्ट्रेट के सामने दिये गये बयान में उस पुस्तक के उद्देश्य पर रोशनी डालते हुए कहा था—"सबसे पहले मैं उन परिस्थितियों का वर्णन करूंगा, जिनसे प्रभावित होकर मैंने यह पुस्तक लिखी है। मैं करीब डेढ़ वर्ष तक सरदार भगत सिंह के साथ रहा हूँ। मेरे साथ उनका जितना ही अधिक सम्पर्क होता गया, मेरे हृदय में उनके प्रति उतनी ही श्रद्धा उत्पन्न होती

प्रगति प्रेस, महावीर चौक, मुजफ्फरनगर (उ.प्र.)

गयी। जब मैं जेल से बाहर आया, मैंने देखा, जैसा कि मुझे आशा थी, कि सरदार भगत सिंह की प्रशंसा करने वाले एक-दो नहीं, हजारों-लाखों की संख्या में हैं। किन्तु जब मैंने उनकी प्रशंसा करने वालों में से कुछ से पूछताछ की, तो पता लगा कि बहुत कम लोगों को सरदार भगत सिंह के सम्बन्ध में सच्चा ज्ञान है। साधारण जनता तो सिर्फ यही जानती थी कि सरदार भगत सिंह का सांडर्स हत्याकाण्ड और असेम्बली बमकाण्ड–इन दो घटनाओं से ही सम्बन्ध है, किन्तु मैं जानता था कि सरदार भगत सिंह न तो आतंकवादी थे और न अराजकतावादी, अतएव अपने स्वर्गीय मित्र के प्रति कर्तव्यपालन के उद्देश्य से मैंने उनका सच्चा और ऐतिहासिक चित्र प्रस्तुत करने का विचार किया। मैं यह दिखाना चाहता था कि वे एक साम्यवादी और अन्तर्राष्ट्रीयतावादी थे और जनता उन्हें गलत समझे हुए थी।"[1]

भगत सिंह के बारे में ब्रिटिश सरकार के कुप्रचार के साथ-साथ समकालीन कांग्रेसी नेताओं ने भी उन्हें आतंकवादी क्रांतिकारी के रूप में प्रचारित करने का प्रयास किया, और विचित्र बात यह है कि अभी तक भी एक वर्ग, जिसमें सरकारी अमला भी है, उन्हें आतंकवादी मानता है। इसका ताजा उदाहरण पिछले अक्तूबर में दिल्ली के एक प्रकाशन एवं वितरण दानिश बुक्स की मालकिन सुनीता नारायण के साथ घटी घटना है जिसका उल्लेख समाचार पत्रों और पत्रिकाओं में "भगत सिंह को क्यों पढ़वाना चाहती हो?" शीर्षक के अन्तर्गत हुआ था। सुनीता महाराष्ट्र के चन्द्रपुर के किसी मेले में अपनी पुस्तकों का स्टाल लगाने गयी थी। पुलिस को किसी तरह गलतफहमी हो गयी कि सुनीता नक्सलवादी आन्दोलन से जुड़ी हुई सुनीता हैं। अतः उनके स्टाल की तलाशी ली गयी और उसमें क्रान्ति, विद्रोह, मार्क्स, भगत सिंह, नारी स्वतंत्रता आदि टाइटलों की किताबें देखकर पुलिस भड़क उठी, उनका स्टाल तहस-नहस कर दिया और उन्हें गिरफ्तार कर लिया। उनकी कोई बात नहीं सुनी गयी। खैर, उनके साथ जो हुआ, वह तो हुआ ही, पूछताछ के दौरान एस.पी. ने कहा–'वह इतिहास क्यों पढ़वाना चाहती हो जिस पर खून के छींटे पड़े हैं? आप क्यों लोगों को टेररिज्म पढ़ाना चाहती हैं, क्यों भगत सिंह को पढ़वाना चाहती हैं? अब तो हमारा देश आजाद है, हमारा अपना संविधान है, अपनी सरकार है, अंग्रेज तो चले गये, अब भगत सिंह की क्या जरूरत है?"[2] एस.पी. रैंक के अधिकारी के मुँह से जब इस तरह की नसीहतें निकलती हैं तो आश्चर्य होता है। इस गलतफहमी को तोड़ना आवश्यक है। भगत सिंह क्रांतिकारी विचारक थे, उनके पास एक दृष्टि थी और देश को स्वतंत्र कराने के बाद स्वराज्य चलाने के लिए उनके पास एक कार्यक्रम था, जबकि उस समय तक किसी भी भारतीय नेता, यहाँ तक कि गांधी जी ने भी इस बारे में कुछ विचार नहीं किया था। किन्तु स्वभावतः उनका झुकाव आतंकवाद की ओर न था। इसलिए आवश्यक हो जाता है कि अब तक इस अल्प परिचित पक्ष

को भी सामने लाया जाये ताकि लोगों को भगत सिंह के विचारों की सही जानकारी मिल सके, और हमारे देश के युवक भगत सिंह के विचारों की रोशनी में अपने आंदोलन को दिशा दे सकें। जिन युवकों को देश और जनता के भविष्य के लिए कार्य करना है, अनेक गुणों व सिद्धान्तों से परिचित कराने के लिए भगत सिंह ने बहुत काम किया, बहुत कुछ लिखा।

भगत सिंह युवावस्था में चले गये, उनकी भावनाओं की कल्पना उनके कार्यों, अदालत में दिये गये उनके बयानों, पत्र-पत्रिकाओं में छपे उनके लेखों, पर्चों तथा जेल में लिखी 404 पृष्ठों की उनकी डायरी, जिसमें महत्वपूर्ण राजनीतिक और दार्शनिक टिप्पणियाँ हैं, से की जा सकती है।[3]

फांसी से एक दिन पहले भगत सिंह ने कहा था—"मैं क्रांति का मूल मन्त्र बन गया हूँ।" इससे उनका क्या आशय था, इसे आज अधिक गहराई से समझने की जरूरत है। भगत सिंह ने देश के इतिहास, परिस्थितियों और आदर्शों के गम्भीर, परिश्रमी व ईमानदार विद्यार्थी के रूप में क्रान्ति तथा उसके उद्देश्यों का अध्ययन किया और उसकी ऐतिहासिक समझ हमारे साथ साझी की है। उन्होंने भारत के क्रांतिकारी आन्दोलनों, आतंकवादी कार्रवाइयों, यहां तक कि गांधी जी की अहिंसा के अनुभवों की गहराई से विवेचना की और दुनिया-भर में हुए क्रान्तिकारी आंदोलनों और विचारों का भी वहाँ की परिस्थितियों के आधार पर विस्तृत विश्लेषण किया। उन्होंने लोगों और समय की जरूरतों को गंभीरता से समझने का प्रयास किया। इसी रास्ते पर चलते हुए भगत सिंह रोमाण्टिक विचारवादी क्रान्तिकारी, (अर्थात् आतंकवाद समर्थक) से वैज्ञानिक क्रान्तिकारी में परिवर्तित हुए। 'काकोरी कांसपिरेसी केस' के देशभक्त वीरों के अकारण फांसी पर लटका दिये जाने की प्रतिक्रियास्वरूप वे कुछ दिनों के लिए आतंकवाद, जिसे उन दिनों त्रासवाद कहा जाता था, से प्रभावित अवश्य हुए थे, लेकिन अपने मूल विचारों से वे दृढ़ राजनीतिक, सामाजिक और आर्थिक क्रान्तिकारी थे। यह बात उन्होंने स्वयं स्वीकार की थी। उन्होंने कहा था—"मैं अपनी पूरी ताकत से यह कहना चाहूंगा कि क्रान्तिकारी जीवन के पहले कुछ दिनों के सिवाय न तो मैं आतंकवादी हूँ और न ही था। मुझे पूरा विश्वास है कि इन तरीकों से हम कुछ भी हासिल नहीं कर सकते।"[4] एक और जगह उन्होंने कहा था—"आतंकवाद हमारे समाज में क्रान्तिकारी चिंतन की पकड़ के अभाव की अभिव्यक्ति है, या एक पछतावा है। यह अपनी असफलता की स्वीकृति है।" भगत सिंह का कहना था—"शुरु-शुरु में आतंकवादी विचारधारा का कुछ लाभ था। इसने राजनीति को आमूल बदल दिया। नवयुवक बुद्धिजीवियों की सोच को चमकाया, आत्मत्याग की भावना को ज्वलंत रूप दिया और दुनिया व अपने दुश्मनों के सामने अपने आन्दोलन की सच्चाई और शक्ति को जाहिर करने का अवसर दिया। लेकिन यह अपने आप

में पर्याप्त नहीं है। सभी देशों में आतंक का इतिहास असफलता का इतिहास है. ... इसकी पराजय के बीज इसके भीतर ही छिपे होते हैं। साम्राज्यवादियों को अच्छी तरह पता है कि 30 करोड़ लोगों पर शासन के लिए प्रतिवर्ष 30 व्यक्तियों की बलि दी जा सकती है। शासन करने का स्वाद बमों या पिस्तौलों से किरकिरा तो किया जा सकता है, लेकिन शोषण के व्यावहारिक लाभ उसे बनाये रखने पर विवश करेंगे।"[5]

आगे चलकर आतंकवाद की कमियों पर उन्होंने अपना स्पष्ट मंतव्य प्रकट करते हुए लिखा है–"भले ही हमारी उम्मीद के अनुसार हथियार आसानी से मिल जायें, और यदि हम पूरे जोर से लड़ें, इतने जोर से जैसा कि इतिहास में पहले कभी न घटा हो, तो भी आतंकवाद अधिक से अधिक साम्राज्यवादी ताकत क़ो समझौते के लिए ही मजबूर कर सकता है। ऐसे समझौते से सुधारों की एक ही किश्त प्राप्त की जा सकती है, इससे आगे कुछ नहीं। इसके पीछे उनका तात्पर्य यह था कि आतंकवादी कार्रवाई से यदि सरकार मजबूर हो भी गयी तो बदले में एक-दो शर्त मानेगी और आतंकवाद का उद्देश्य खत्म हो जायेगा। गांधीजी के आंदोलन पर टिप्पणी करते हुए भगत सिंह ने कहा कि गांधीवाद असहयोग आंदोलन से दबाव बना कर ऐसे ही समझौते करने के लिए ताकत लगा रहा है। वह दावे के साथ आजादी के लिए 'स्टैण्ड' नहीं लेता, बल्कि गोरों की सत्ता में भूरों की हिस्सेदारी लेना चाहता है और वर्तमान ढांचे में ही थोड़ी सी सुविधाएँ मांगने की फिराक में है। जबकि आजादी के बाद शासन-व्यवस्था में आमूल-चूल परिवर्तन की आवश्यकता है। एक ऐसे सामाजिक ढांचे का निर्माण करना होगा जिसमें श्रमिकों के शोषण के लिए कोई स्थान न हो।"

भगत सिंह ने क्रान्ति सम्बन्धी विचारधारा के परिपक्व होने के पश्चात् आतंकवादी रास्ते को खारिज तो किया, किन्तु उसकी भूमिका को पूरी तरह से नकारा नहीं, बल्कि विवेकपूर्ण तरीके से उसका इस्तेमाल करने का सुझाव दिया। वे लिखते हैं–"आतंकवाद के शैतान को दाद देने की जरूरत नहीं है। आतंकवादियों ने काफी काम कर लिया है, काफी कुछ सिखा दिया है। यदि हम अपने उद्देश्यों और तरीकों सम्बन्धी भूल न करें तो उग्रवाद अभी भी कुछ लाभप्रद हो सकता है। विशेषतः निराशावाद के समय में आतंकवादी तरीका हमारे प्रचार अभियान में सहायक हो सकता है।... ... क्रांतिकारी को निरर्थक आतंकवादी कठिनाइयों और व्यक्तिगत आत्म बलिदान के दूषित चक्र में न डाला जाये। सभी के लिए उत्साहवर्धक आदर्श, किसी उद्देश्य के लिए मरना न होकर उस उद्देश्य के लिए जीना–और वह भी लाभदायक तरीके से जीना-होना चाहिये।"[7]

भगत सिंह क्रान्ति के दृष्टिकोण से आतंकवादी कार्रवाइयों का मूल्यांकन चाहते हैं। जो नवयुवक परिपक्व तरीके से संगठन के काम में फिट नहीं होते, जो कम

विचारशील हैं, जिनमें दूरदृष्टि का अभाव है, तथा अधिक जोशीले होते हैं, उन्हें शोर-शराबे के कामों में लगाया जा सकता है। किन्तु हत्या, तोड़फोड़, आगजनी और लूटमार जैसी सिर्फ आतंक फैलाने की गतिविधियों को भगत सिंह निरुद्देश्य गतिविधियाँ कह कर खारिज करते हैं। इन गतिविधियों से क्रान्ति का लक्ष्य, जो पवित्र होता है, नष्ट-भ्रष्ट हो जाता है। साथ ही जनता की सहानुभूति और समर्थन मिलना भी बन्द हो जाता है। उनका विचार था कि जब तक किसी देश की जनता स्वयं अपनी मांगों के लिए लड़ने को तैयार नहीं हो जाती, तब तक किसी ठोस लाभ की आशा नहीं की जा सकती।[8] इसलिए जनता को जगाना और समझाना आवश्यक है और आतंकवाद द्वारा यह काम नहीं किया जा सकता।

भगत सिंह ने हिंसा की वकालत कभी नहीं की। हिंसा-अहिंसा के प्रश्न पर उन्होंने कहा—'किसी विशेष हालत में हिंसा जायज हो सकती है, लेकिन जन आंदोलनों का मुख्य हथियार अहिंसा होगी'[9] इसके बावजूद गांधीजी के अहिंसावादी विचारों को शक्तिहीन मानकर वे इनका विरोध करते थे, लेकिन गांधीवाद की ऐतिहासिक भूमिका को उन्होंने एक वैज्ञानिक यथार्थवाद की तरह आंका। बिना उसकी गहराई में जाये उन्होंने उसे खारिज नहीं किया। उनका कहना था—'गांधीजी एक उदार हृदय, परोपकारी मनुष्य हैं, परन्तु केवल परोपकार से ही जनता का कल्याण नहीं हो सकता। यहाँ तो ऐसी संचालन शक्ति की आवश्यकता है, जो सारे समाज में क्रान्ति तथा नवजीवन की ज्वाला फूंक दे। उनके अनुसार निःस्वार्थ भाव से काम करने वाला नवयुवकों का दल ही सामाजिक क्रान्ति का संगठन तथा संचालन कर सकता है।[10]

भगत सिंह के विचार से नवयुवक समाज अपनी स्वाभाविक जड़ता दूर फेंक कर देश सेवा के इस पवित्र अनुष्ठान में तब तक आगे नहीं बढ़ सकता, जब तक उसे फांसी की टिकटी पर से खड़े होकर ललकारा न जाये। उन्होंने यह काम अपने हाथ में लिया। 8 अप्रैल 1929 में लेजिस्लेटिव असैम्बली में बम फेंका, गिरफ्तार हुए और मुकदमे के सिलसिले में दिए गये अपने बयान द्वारा उन्होंने जनता में इसी प्रकार की जागृति फैलाने का प्रयास किया था और उसका समुचित प्रभाव भी जनता पर, आजादी के आंदोलन पर पड़ा।

मुकदमे के दौरान भगत सिंह से नीचे की अदालत ने पूछा था कि क्रान्ति से आप लोगों का क्या मतलब है? इस प्रश्न के उत्तर में उन्होंने कहा था कि क्रान्ति से हमारा अभिप्राय है—अन्याय पर आधारित मौजूदा समाज व्यवस्था में आमूल परिवर्तन, और परिवर्तन के लिये खूनी लड़ाइयाँ अनिवार्य नहीं हैं, और न ही उसमें व्यक्तिगत प्रतिहिंसा के लिए कोई स्थान है। वह बम और पिस्तौल का सम्प्रदाय नहीं है।

भगत सिंह के क्रान्तिकारी चिन्तन में 'सेवा करना, कष्ट सहना और कुर्बानी देना' के सिद्धान्त पर चलते हुए अपने उद्देश्य की ओर बढ़ना मुख्य बात थी। उनके अनुसार 'क्रान्ति, जो जनता के लिए हो और जिसे जनता ही पूरी करे।' तथा क्रान्ति का इस सदी में एक ही मतलब हो सकता है—'जनता के लिए जनता द्वारा राजनीतिक सत्ता पर कब्जा करना।' अपने क्रान्तिकारी कार्यक्रम के मसौदे में उन्होंने लिखा—'साम्राज्यवादियों को गद्दी से उतारने का भारत के पास एकमात्र हथियार श्रमिक क्रान्ति है। कोई और चीज इस उद्देश्य की पूर्ति नहीं कर सकती।'[11]

इस प्रकार भगत सिंह जहां हमें निःस्वार्थ दृढ़ निश्चय और बहादुरी के साथ सच्चाई के लिए खड़े होने की प्रेरणा देते हैं, वहीं वे हमें विचारधारात्मक परिपक्वता व तर्कशील वैज्ञानिक दृष्टिकोण से इतिहास की, आसपास की और भविष्य की समस्याओं के विश्लेषण का तरीका भी सिखाते हैं। वे नवयुवकों से कहते हैं—'इसे आंख मूंद कर न पढ़ें। यह न समझें कि इसमें जो लिखा है, वह सही है। इसे पढ़ो, इसकी आलोचना करो, सोचो और इसकी मदद से अपने विचार बनाने की कोशिश करो।'[12] यह प्राचीन भारतीय दर्शन के सूक्त 'वादे-वादे जायते तत्वबोधः' पर आधारित है।

सन्दर्भ

1. जितेन्द्र नाथ सान्याल : *अमर शहीद सरदार भगत सिंह*, दिल्ली, 2006, पृ. 11.
2. *'हंस'* मासिक, दिल्ली दिसम्बर 2006 अंक, पृ. 721.
3. जगमोहन सिंह, चमन लाल, सं. : *भगत सिंह और उनके साथियों के दस्तावेज*, नई दिल्ली, 1997, पृ. 11.
4. वही, पृ. 10.
5. वही, पृ. 399.
6. वही, पृ. 399.
7. वही, पृ. 400.
8. जितेन्द्र नाथ सान्याल : *अमर शहीद सरदार भगत सिंह*, दिल्ली, 2006, पृ. 69.
9. जगमोहन सिंह, चमन लाल, सं. : *भगत सिंह और उनके साथियों के दस्तावेज*, नई दिल्ली, 1997, पृ. 10.
10. जितेन्द्र नाथ सान्याल : *अमर शहीद सरदार भगत सिंह*, दिल्ली, 2006, पृ. 69.
11. दस्तावेज, उपरोक्त, पृ. 9-10.
12. वही, पृ. 12.

19

शहीद भगतसिंह राष्ट्रीय चेतना के सचेतक और संवाहक

डॉ. रामस्वरूप ढेंगुला

हंसते-हंसते देश के लिये स्वयं को बलिदान कर देना जीवन की सर्वोच्च उपलब्धि है। शहीद भगतसिंह आत्मबलिदान करने वाले महामानवों में से एक थे। मात्र 23 साल की उम्र में, राष्ट्रीय आन्दोलनों की क्रान्ति की कड़ी में क्रान्तिकारी के रूप में, वे राष्ट्रीय चेतना के प्रतीक बन गये थे। राष्ट्रीय आन्दोलन के अहिंसक एवं नरम नेताओं के आन्दोलनों को भी भगतसिंह के बलिदान ने गति प्रदान की थी। युवकों के जैसे प्रेरणास्रोत भगतसिंह बीसवीं सदी के दूसरे-तीसरे दशक में थे, वैसे वे आज भी हैं। भगतसिंह की चर्चा करते ही आज भी युवकों के रोंगटे खड़े हो जाते हैं, भुजायें फड़क उठती हैं, देश के लिये बलिदान देने को तैयार हो जाते हैं। सन् 1930 में अज्ञात कवि द्वारा लिखी गई कविता की दो पंक्तियाँ आज भी युवकों में लोकप्रिय हैं।

हाथ में हो हथकड़ी और बेड़ियां हों पांव में,
गाएंगे उनको बजाकर गीत वंदे मातरम।

बचपन में भगतसिंह को क्रान्तिकारियों का परिवार मिला, विद्यालय में क्रान्तिकारी विचारों वाले साथी और शिक्षक मिले। चूंकि भगतसिंह चिंतनशील, मननशील, अध्ययन में गहरी पैठ रखने वाले और तत्कालीन समय से आगे सोचने वाले थे। उनका मानना था कि शोषण मुक्त समाज के स्वरूप के गठन के लिये, समाजवादी शासन की स्थापना होनी चाहिये, साम्राज्यवादी शक्तियों का वे पूर्ण पराभाव देखना चाहते थे। उनके लेखन में यह बात झलकती है। पंजाब में अंग्रेज सरकार द्वारा तत्समय किये गये अत्याचारों के वे प्रत्यक्ष साक्षी थे। भगतसिंह के 23 मार्च, 1931

कुंजपुरा दतिया (म.प्र.)

में शहीद हो जाने के बाद, वे देश की लोक आस्था के केन्द्र बन गये। लोककवियों, राष्ट्रीय कवियों एवं राष्ट्रीय फिल्म निर्माताओं ने शहीद भगतसिंह को पूरा सम्मान दिया। राष्ट्रीय आन्दोलनों में क्रान्तिकारियों और अहिंसक-नरमवादी आन्दोलनकारियों दोनों ने एक-दूसरे के पूरक के रूप में कार्य किया। और देश के राष्ट्रीय आन्दोलनों में भाग लेने वाला कोई भी व्यक्ति एक दूसरे के विचारों का न विरोधी था, न प्रतिस्पर्धी। क्रान्तिकारियों में शहीद भगतसिंह की प्रसिद्धि का मूल कारण उनके द्वारा छोड़े लिखित विचार हैं।

सन् 1857 के स्वतन्त्रता समर के बाद देश में राष्ट्रीय चेतना का भाव व्यापक रूप से जन-जन के बीच जाग्रत हो उठा था। भारतीय संस्कृति में मातृभूमि को स्वर्ग से बढ़कर देवभूमि और माता के समान माना गया है।[1] भगतसिंह के मन में भी यही विचार थे। बैशाखी (13 अप्रैल) के पवित्र दिन सन् 1919 में अमृतसर के जलियांवाला बाग में अंग्रेज जरनल डायर द्वारा हजारों निर्दोष लोगों को गोलियों से भून देने की घटना ने भगतसिंह के बाल मन पर गंभीर असर किया था, वे वहां से खून से सनी मिट्टी इकट्ठी कर लाये थे। वे उस मिट्टी को बड़े श्रद्धाभाव से देखते थे। पंजाब के क्रान्तिकारी करतारसिंह सराभा के प्रति भगतसिंह के मन में पूजा के भाव थे, करतारसिंह का मात्र उन्नीस वर्ष की उम्र में किया गया बलिदान उनके मन को सदैव प्रेरित करता था, वे करतारसिंह का चित्र सदैव अपनी जेब में रखते थे। भगतसिंह पूर्व में शहीद हो चुके क्रान्तिकारियों के चित्र सामने रख उनकी पूजा कर, अपने खून से तिलक करते थे, खादी की माला पहनते थे और बाद में अपने क्रान्तिकारी विचारक साथियों के साथ जुलूस निकाल भाषण देते थे। भगतसिंह लाहौर के नेशनल कालेज के छात्र के रूप में राष्ट्रीय-क्रान्तिकारी अध्यापकों, छात्रों और विद्यालय के संरक्षक लाला लाजपतराय के सम्पर्क में आये, यहीं उन्होंने राष्ट्रनायक राणाप्रताप, चन्द्रगुप्त मौर्य नाटक का सफल मंचन किया। इंकलाब जिन्दाबाद का नारा, जो स्वतन्त्रता आन्दोलन का सबसे लोकप्रिय नारा हुआ, जिसे बाद में सुप्रसिद्ध क्रान्ति के पुजारी सुभाष बोस ने भी अपनाया, यह लोकआस्था का नारा देश को भगतसिंह की ही देन है। आज के आन्दोलनकारी भी इस नारे को वाणी दे भगतसिंह की याद करते रहते हैं।[2] सुभाष बोस ने 20 मार्च, 1931 के अपने भाषण में, भगतसिंह को "उस भावना का प्रतीक बताया जो सारे देश के लिये थी।" इसी क्रम में भगतसिंह की शहादत के बाद, बोस ने दि0 8 अप्रैल, 1931 में अमृतसर में भाषण देते हुये भगतसिंह को देश की स्वतन्त्रता के लिये बलिदान देने वाला देशभक्त और विश्व का प्रसिद्ध सिख बलिदानी कहा तथा आशा व्यक्त की, कि देश अनेक भगतसिंह पैदा करेगा।[3]

शहीद भगतसिंह की बलिदानी आत्मा बड़ी प्रबल थी, उनके विश्वास दृढ़ और अडिग थे, वे मानते थे कि अंग्रेज जब तक देश से निकाले नहीं जाते तब तक भगतसिंह अनेक बार पृथ्वी पर अवतरित हो अंग्रेजों से युद्ध करता रहेगा, तत्समय के एक कवि ने लिखा है–

यह न समझो कि भगतसिंह फांसी पर लटकाया गया

सैकड़ों भगत बना जायेंगे मरते-मरते।[4]

इन सब तथ्यों के प्रकाश में यह बात सामने आती है कि शहीद भगतसिंह राष्ट्रीय चेतना को संगठित, जाग्रत एवं व्यापक संदर्भ में परिभाषित करने वाले देश के क्रान्तिवीर योद्धा थे।

देश के अनन्य भक्त भगतसिंह का जन्म 28 सितम्बर, 1907 को लायलपुर जिले के बंगा नामक गांव में क्रान्ति समर्थक सरदार किशनसिंह के यहां हुआ था। भगतसिंह की जननी माता का नाम विद्यावती था, विद्या की देवी का पुत्र भगतसिंह भी बचपन से कुशाग्र बुद्धि का और पढ़ने लिखने में रुचि रखने वाला था। भगतसिंह की लिखावट उत्तम थी, उन्हें गणित, भूगोल, इतिहास में गहन रुचि थी, भगतसिंह ने इटली, रूस, और आयरलैन्ड के क्रान्ति आन्दोलनों को पढ़ा था। वे लाला लाजपतराय के द्वारकादास पुस्तकालय में पढ़ने जाते थे और उन्होंने एक बार पंजाब हिन्दी साहित्य सम्मेलन की प्रतियोगिता जीती थी। भगतसिंह उर्दू, पंजाबी, संस्कृत, हिन्दी के ज्ञाता थे, सत्रह वर्ष की आयु से वे लेखक के रूप में प्रतिष्ठित हो गये थे। गणेशशंकर विद्यार्थी के 'प्रताप' अखबार में भगतसिंह ने सहयोगी के रूप में काम किया था, उर्दू के "किर्ती" अखबार में भी उन्होंने काम किया था। वे अपने दल में नीति निर्धारण करने वाले नेता थे और उन्होंने सबसे बढ़कर अपनी प्रतिभा के बल पर अदालत का जनमंच के रूप में उपयोग किया था और अब तो उनकी लिखी जेल जीवन की डायरी भी सामने आ चुकी है।[5] लेखन और अध्ययन मानव को विचारवान, चिन्तनशील बना देता है। भगतसिंह की लेखन, अध्ययन, भाषण की उपलब्धि असाधारण हैं। यही उपलब्धि आज के युवाओं और चिंतकों को भगतसिंह के विषय में गंभीरता से मनन कर क्रान्तिकारियों के विषय में सत्ता के स्वाद वाली प्रवृतियों के एकपक्षीय लेखन को अस्वीकृत करने को बाध्य करती है। गांधीजी यदि राष्ट्रपिता और महात्मा हैं, तो भगतसिंह राष्ट्रपुत्र और राष्ट्रपूज्य से कम नहीं हैं। यहां मैं विचारक के रूप में यह कहना चाहता हूँ कि शहीद होने वाला प्रत्येक क्रान्तिवीर राष्ट्र पुत्र है। वह किसी अहिंसक और नरम नीति वाले राष्ट्रीय नेता से कम नहीं है। अगर यदि गांधीजी के विषय में पढ़ाये जाने की बात उठती है, तो भगतसिंह और उनके क्रान्तिवीर साथियों को भी पूरे आदरभाव से पढ़ाया जाना चाहिये। याद रखना होगा

कि आजादी सदैव बलिदान माँगती है और बलिदान भगतसिंह से प्रेरणा प्राप्त करने वाले वीर ही दे सकते हैं।

भगतसिंह राष्ट्रीय चेतना के बहुत बड़े संवाहक थे और आज भी हैं। वह पवित्र गंगा नदी के समान व्यक्तित्व वाले थे। भगतसिंह ने मार्क्सवादी साहित्य को बड़े चाव के साथ पढ़ा था और वे समान नागरिक सुविधाओं वाले समाजवाद की स्थापना चाहते थे। पर यह दूर की बात थी, तात्कालिक रूप से देश को अंग्रेजों के चंगुल से मुक्त कराने की समस्या उनके सामने थी। अतः भगतसिंह के सारे क्रियाकलाप देश की जनता में जागृति पैदा करने के लिए थे। अपने वैचारिक प्रकटीकरण से, अपने कार्यों से, अपने आत्मबलिदान से भगतसिंह का एक ही संदेश था कि भारत माता को अंग्रेजों के खूनी और नापाक पंजों से आजाद कराना है। अतः यह कहना सही होगा कि भगतसिंह केवल देशभक्त थे, भारतमाता के अनन्य भक्त थे। उनका यह वैचारिक संवाहन या वैचारिक प्रकटीकरण उनके शहीद होने के बाद देश में अनेक प्रकार की, अनेक स्वरूपों में राष्ट्रीय जागृति को उत्पन्न कर गया। भगतसिंह का वैचारिक संवाहन आज भी युवकों के लिये प्रेरणा स्रोत है, नवीन-नवीन स्फूर्ति का संदेश है। भगतसिंह ने अपने साथियों सहित फांसी के फंदे की ओर बढ़ते हुए गाया था–

मर के भी दिल से न जायेगी वतन की उल्फ़त
अपनी मिट्‌टी से भी खुशबू ए वफ़ा आयेगी।[6]

राष्ट्रीय आन्दोलन के समय के कवि माखनलाल चतुर्वेदी ने शहीद भगतसिंह की विचारधारा को अपने भावों में ढालकर लिखा था–

मजबूत कलेजों को लेकर इस न्याय दुर्ग पर चढ़े चलो,
माता के प्राण पुकार रहे, संगठन करो, बस चढ़े चलो।[7]

भगतसिंह के चिंतन को युवकों के संदर्भ में वाणी देने वाली एक और प्रेरणा–

सुनो आज भारत के तुम नौजवानो।
मेरे बाद तुम्हारा भी इम्तहान होगा।[8]

फांसी लगने के पूर्व भगतसिंह ने अंग्रेज सरकार से मांग की थी कि उनके साथियों को फांसी पर न चढ़ाया जाकर गोली से उड़ा दिया जाय। इससे यह बात सामने आती है कि उनका वैचारिक संवाहन कितना राष्ट्रवादी और प्रखर था।

भगतसिंह के अंतिम समय के सारे भाषण, अदालत में दिये बयान देश की जनता में जनजागृति पैदा करने के लिये थे। भगतसिंह और उनके साथियों ने पूरे आत्मबल,

साहस का परिचय देते हुए, हंसते-गाते, फांसी का फन्दा चूमकर जो शहीदी दर्जा प्राप्त किया वह देश के युवकों और विचारक नागरिकों को इतना भाया कि भगतसिंह शहादत के बाद लोकआस्था का केन्द्र बन गये। भगतसिंह की यह भी अवधारणा थी कि क्रान्तिकारी आन्दोलन जनता की सहानुभूति के बगैर सफल नहीं हो सकता है।[9] आज ही ग्वालियर से प्रकाशित दैनिक पत्र में यह पढ़ने में आया कि भगतसिंह को फांसी का निर्णय हो जाने के बाद देश के दो लाख नागरिकों ने अंग्रेज सरकार से अपील की थी कि भगतसिंह को फांसी न दी जाय। इस दृष्टिकोण से भगतसिंह और उनके क्रान्तिकारी साथियों पर शोध करने की अभी आवश्यकता है। पर ये तथ्य इस बात के परिचायक हैं कि भगतसिंह के विचारों और सोच को कितना बड़ा जनसमर्थन मिल रहा था और तत्समय जनता में उनकी बड़ी पहचान बन गई थी।

प्रेरणास्पद व्यक्ति लोकआस्थाओं में सदैव अमर रहता है। यही अमरता जीवन का प्रधानतत्व है। भगतसिंह ने स्वयं कहा था, मेरे मरने से क्या होगा आप मेरे विचारों को नहीं मार सकते हैं। भगतसिंह की शहादत के बाद पूरे उत्तर भारत में उबाल आ गया था, युवाओं का आक्रोश जुलूस-आन्दोलनों के जरिये सामने प्रकट हो रहा था। भगतसिंह के विषय में अनेक कवितायें लिखीं गई और लोग उन्हें गा-गाकर जनसमूहों, राजनीतिक सम्मेलनों और धार्मिक मेलों में सुना कर जनजागृति करने लगे। वे भगतसिंह के प्रति जनआस्था की कवितायें और लोकगीत में सुना कर जनजागृति करने लगे। भगतसिंह के प्रति जनआस्था की ये कवितायें और लोक-गीत हिन्दी, उर्दू, अवधी, बुन्देली और पंजाबी में जो उस काल में लिखे गये थे, आज भी प्रचलित हैं।[10] अज्ञात कवि द्वारा लिखित लोक में प्रचलित एक कविता के बोल इस प्रकार हैं–

आजादी का दीवाना था सरदार, भगतसिंह।
फांसी पे गया झूल वो सरदार, भगतसिंह।।[11]

भोजपुरी बोली की लोकअभिव्यक्ति भगतसिंह के विषय में इस प्रकार है–

देसवा के करनवां, झूलते फांसी पर झुलनवां, मोर भगतसिंह ललना।
दिहलें देसवा खातिर जनवां, मोरे भगतसिंह ललना।।[12]

आल्हा गायकी की तर्ज पर गाये जाने वाला गीत, इसके बोल इस प्रकार हैं–

विदा करो मां, जाते हैं हम विजय ध्वजा फहराने आज,
देश स्वतन्त्र बनाने जाते, हम निज शीश चढ़ाने आज।।[13]

आज भी भगतसिंह के विषय में यह दो लाइनें बड़े जोर-शोर से सुनाई दे रहीं हैं–

यूं पैदा दोस्तो भगतसिंह, जोरावर लोकमान्य नहीं होते।

यूं ही मुट्ठियां बांध लेने से इंकलाब नहीं होते।।

भगतसिंह ने स्वयं अनेकों कवितायें लिखी हैं। उनका आत्मबल बड़ा प्रबल था। भगतसिंह के आज उपलब्ध नवीन साहित्य, पत्र, डायरी के पृष्ठ यह सब जनआस्था को पुनर्जागरण कर आज युवाओं के सामने प्रेरित करने के उदाहरण प्रस्तुत कर रहा है।

अहिंसक आन्दोलन के समर्थक नरमवादी नेता भी भगतसिंह के आत्मोत्सर्ग से प्रभावित थे, नेहरूजी ने भगतसिंह के बलिदान को प्रेरक और प्रेरणा देनेवाला माना था। गांधीजी, यद्यपि भगतसिंह के हिंसक-शस्त्रवादी क्रान्ति के समर्थक नहीं थे, फिर भी भगतसिंह को उन्होंने साहसी और उत्साही का दर्जा दिया था। गांधीजी ने यह भी माना कि भगतसिंह और उनके साथियों की शहादत से स्वतन्त्रता प्राप्त करने की हमारी शक्ति में बहुत वृद्धि हो गई थी। कांग्रेस ने भी अपने करांची अधिवेशन में भगतसिंह की फांसी का विरोध करते हुये उनकी और उनके साथियों की बहादुरी व आत्मबलिदान की प्रशंसा की थी।[14] इन तथ्यों के आलोक में विचार करने पर यह बात सामने आती है कि तत्कालीन कांग्रेस के राष्ट्रीय अहिंसक आन्दोलन के नेतागण भी भगतसिंह और उनके साथियों को देशभक्त राष्ट्रवादी मानते थे। और उनका चल रहा राष्ट्रीय आन्दोलन भगतसिंह की शहादत से बल प्राप्त कर रहा था। भगतसिंह ने अपने समय के अनुभवों से जाना कि देश के कृषक-मजदूरों को साम्राज्यवादी अंग्रेजों और सत्ता के बिचौलियों दोनों के अमानुषिक कष्ट झेलने पड़ते हैं। ये कष्ट इतने दुखद थे कि निर्दयी व्यवहार सहने पर भी दो जून की रोटी सुरक्षित नहीं थी। साम्राज्यवादी और रजवाड़ी प्रवृति की यह व्यवस्था भगतसिंह को गहरे तक छेंदती थी। अतः उनके मन में विचार विकसित हुये कि अंग्रेजों के पलायन के बाद इस देश में शोषण मुक्त समाजवाद की स्थापना का अपना ध्येय प्रचारित किया जाय। निश्चित रूप से भगतसिंह के इस प्रकार के विचार बनने में दो बातें प्रधान थीं, एक तो देश की आंखों देखी परेशानी, दूसरे उनका मार्क्सवादी अध्ययन। पर इस बात से कुछ लेखकों ने भगतसिंह को कम्युनिस्ट विचारक प्रमाणित करने का प्रयास किया है। जो पूरी तरह क्रान्ति स्वतन्त्रता संघर्ष से मेल नहीं खाता। क्रान्तिकारियों का प्रथम स्पष्ट उद्देश्य देश को अंग्रेजों के चंगुल से आजाद कराना था। फिर उसके बाद समाजवाद स्थापना की बारी आती। इस प्रकार समाजवादी व्यवस्था उनका लक्ष्य जरूर थी, पर ध्येय नहीं थी। फिर उस समय राष्ट्रीय आन्दोलन कर्ताओं के मन में सत्ता के आज की तरह के न कोई विचार थे और न ही कोई योजना। सभी एकमत से देश को अंग्रेजों के शासन से मुक्त करा उन्हें देश से भगाना चाहते थे। सभी लोग

कृषक-मजदूरों, जनता की दुर्दशा से चिन्तित थे और सहानुभूति रखते थे। इस दृष्टि से देखने पर यह किसी प्रकार सिद्ध नहीं होता कि यशस्वी शहीद भगतसिंह एक कम्युनिस्ट विचारक थे। वे पूरी तरह राष्ट्रवादी देशभक्त थे और देश में शोषण मुक्त समाजवाद देखना चाहते थे। आज देश की कभी न कभी रहीं सरकारों का भी लगभग यही लक्ष्य रहा है। भगतसिंह प्रखर राष्ट्रवादी चिंतक थे, देश के युवाओं को अभी उनसे बहुत कुछ प्राप्त करना है।[15]

शहीद भगतसिंह ने देश के लिये शहादत देकर पूरे देश में राष्ट्रीय चेतना प्रवाहित की, राष्ट्रीय प्रवृत्तियों को जगाया। युवकों के आज वे श्रेष्ठ प्रेरणा स्रोत हैं। भगत सिंह के बलिदान ने देश में राष्ट्रीय आन्दोलनों की बाढ़ सी पैदा कर दी। भगतसिंह और उनके साथियों की आत्मबलिदानी कहानियां बाद में देश में राष्ट्रीय चेतना के संवाहन अर्थात् प्रेषण अथवा प्रचारित-प्रसारित करने में अग्रणी रहीं। और देश को सभी राष्ट्रीय आन्दोलनों के कारण स्वतन्त्रता प्राप्त हुई। भगतसिंह की जन्म शताब्दी के पुनीत दिन पर देश उन्हें कोटि-कोटि तरीकों से याद करे।

सन्दर्भ

1. डॉ0 शुभलक्ष्मी, *आधुनिक हिन्दी काव्य में राष्ट्रीय चेतना,* नचिकेता प्रकाशन, दिल्ली, 1986, पृ. 9-11, 37-55.
2. उदयनारायण सिंह, *अमर क्रान्तिकारी,* शब्दपीठ प्रकाशन, इलाहाबाद 1998, पृ. 68-73, 137-145; *सरदार भगतसिंह,* श्रीकृष्ण सरल, राष्ट्रीय प्रकाशन, उज्जैन, 1983, पृ. 18-23; *नयी ज्ञानोदय पत्रिका,* दिसम्बर 2006, भारतीय ज्ञानपीठ प्रकाशन, दिल्ली, पृ. 108-110; *पांजन्य,* शहीद भगतसिंह विशेषांक, 25 मार्च, 2007, भारत प्रकाशन झंडेवाला, दिल्ली, पृ. 12-14, 20-23.
3. संकलन गुरदेव सिंह सिद्धू, *फांसी लाहौर की,* नेशनल बुक ट्रस्ट दिल्ली 2007, पृ. 12; हरदान हर्ष, *नेताजी सुभाष चन्द्र बोस,* श्याम प्रकाशन जयपुर 1999, पृ. 49.
4. संकलन गुरदेव सिंह सिद्धू, *फांसी लाहौर की,* नेशनल बुक ट्रस्ट दिल्ली 2007, पृ. 15.
5. रामविलास शर्मा, *भारत में अंग्रेजी राज्य और मार्क्सवाद,* भाग एक, राजकमल प्रकाशन, दिल्ली, 1982, पृ. 102-111; श्रीकृष्ण सरल, *सरदार भगतसिंह,* पृ. 19; डॉ0 लालबहादुर सिंह चौहान, *क्रान्तिवीर चन्द्रशेखर आजाद,* स्वास्तिक प्रकाशन दिल्ली, 2007, पृ. 57; डॉ0 विजेन्द्रपाल सिंह, *भारतीय राष्ट्रीय आन्दोलन,* मोन प्रकाशन दिल्ली, 1999, पृ. 100; *पांजन्य शहीद भगतसिंह* विशेषांक 25 मार्च, 2007, भारत प्रकाशन झन्डेवाला, दिल्ली, पृ. 11-13.

6. श्वेताभ अश्क, *भारत के अमर शहीद*, संकेत प्रकाशन, इलाहाबाद, 2005, पृ. 18.

7. *हिन्दी साहित्य का वृहद इतिहास*, भाग-10, नागरी प्रचारिणी सभा, काशी, सं. 2028, पृ. 81.

8. संकलन गुरदेव सिंह सिद्धू, *फांसी लाहौर की*, नेशनल बुक ट्रस्ट दिल्ली, 2007, पृ. 17, भूमिका में।

9. सम्पा0 वचनेश त्रिपाठी, *क्रांति के वे दिन*, विक्रम प्रकाशन, दिल्ली 2002, पृ. 95-98; डॉ0 लालबहादुर सिंह, *चन्द्रशेखर आजाद*, पृ. 56; *सावरकर समग्र*, भाग-5, विनायक दामोदर सावरकर प्रभात प्रकाशन, दिल्ली 2002, पृ. 598.

10. बालमुकुन्द अग्रवाल, *आजादी के मुकदमे*, नेशनल बुक ट्रस्ट दिल्ली, 1995, पृ. 114-115; गुरदेव सिंह सिद्धू, *फांसी लाहौर की*, पृ. 14-15 भूमिका में।

11. गुरदेव सिंह सिद्धू, *फांसी लाहौर की*, पृ. 31.

12. शंकर बाम, *स्वाधीनता आन्दोलन का इतिहास*, संजीव प्रकाशन दिल्ली, 1988, पृ. 143.

13. रामजन्म शर्मा, *जप्तशुदा गीत आजादी और एकता के तराने*, सूचना एवं प्रसारण मंत्रालय, दिल्ली, 2006, पृ. 52.

14. पट्टाभि सीतारामैय्या, *कांग्रेस का इतिहास*, सस्ता साहित्य मंडल, दिल्ली, 1946, पृ. 351-352; उदय नारायणसिंह, *अमर क्रांतिकारी*, पृ. 144; बालमुकुन्द अग्रवाल, *आजादी के मुकदमे*, पृ. 114-116.

15. रामविलास शर्मा, *भारत में अंग्रेजी राज्य और मार्क्सवाद*, भाग-1, पृ. 102-112; डॉ0 विजेन्द्रपाल सिंह, *भारतीय राष्ट्रीय आन्दोलन*, पृ. 99-100; अजय कुमार घोष, *सरदार भगतसिंह व उनके साथी*, नवोदय सेल्स, दिल्ली, 2005, पृ. 22-41; वचनेश त्रिपाठी, *क्रान्ति के वे दिन, पृ. 87-98.*

20

युगद्रष्टा शहीद भगतसिंह के धर्म सम्बन्धी विचार एवं वर्तमान में उनकी प्रासंगिकता

डॉ. शिव कुमार भनोत

28 सितंबर, 1907 का दिन इतिहास में इसलिये अमर हो गया कि इस दिन भगतसिंह के रूप में एक साधारण से व्यक्ति ने जन्म लिया और अपने असाधारण कार्यों से हमारे देश की राजनीति को एक नई दिशा देकर आने वाली पीढ़ियों के लिये एक प्रकाश स्तम्भ बन कर चिर अमर हो गये।[1] अब पाकिस्तान का हिस्सा बन चुके जिला लॉयलपुर के गांव बंगा में अपने दादा अर्जुनसिंह तथा दादी जयकौर के यहाँ[2] एक राष्ट्राभिमानी सिक्ख जाट परिवार में जन्मे[3] भगतसिंह का समूचा परिवार वास्तविक अर्थों में राष्ट्रीयता की भावनाओं से ओतप्रोत एक क्रान्तिकारी परिवार रहा।[4] भगतसिंह के पूर्वज 18वीं सदी के पूर्वार्द्ध में लाहौर क्षेत्र के नर्ली गांव में रहा करते थे।[5] कालान्तर में उनका यह परिवार जालन्धर जिले के खटकड़ कलां गांव में जा बसा था।[6] आगे चल कर भगतसिंह के दादा 1900 ई. में लॉयलपुर जिले के बंगा गांव चले आए और वहीं बस गये।[7]

इस आशय के उल्लेख देखने को मिलते हैं कि जब सरदार अर्जुनसिंह ने अपने दो पड़ पोतों-जगतसिंह और भगतसिंह का यज्ञोपवीत किया था तो उन्होंने अपने इन दोनों वंशधरों को देश के लिए दान कर दिया था। सरदार भगतसिंह ने अपने एक पत्र में इस घटना का उल्लेख किया था।[8] भगतसिंह की फांसी ने उन्हें तोड़ कर रख दिया और उसके कुछ ही दिनों बाद पक्षाघात से जुलाई, 1932 में उनकी मृत्यु हो गई। भगतसिंह की दादी जयकौर एक सामाजिक क्रान्तिकारी की पत्नी, तीन क्रान्तिकारी पुत्रों (किशनसिंह, स्वर्णसिंह और अजीतसिंह) की जननी तथा क्रान्तिकारी पोतों की दादी थी। भगतसिंह के पिता किशनसिंह भी प्रारम्भ से ही क्रान्तिकारी

विभागाध्यक्ष (इतिहास) डूंगर कॉलेज बीकानेर (राजस्थान)

आंदोलन से जुड़े रहे[9] यद्यपि, यह बात सत्य है कि पुत्र मोह के वशीभूत होकर उन्होंने भगतसिंह की स्वीकृति के बिना ही उनके मुकदमें पर विचार के लिये सरकार को याचिका दे दी थी, जिस पर भगतसिंह ने उन्हें कड़ा पत्र लिखा था।[10] उनकी माता विद्यावती ने अपने पारिवारिक जीवन में अपने घर को सामाजिक-राजनीतिक गतिविधियों के केन्द्र के रूप में देखा था।[11] भगतसिंह के प्रति उनके मन में बहुत अनुराग था।[12] भगतसिंह भी अपनी माता से बहुत जुड़ाव अनुभव किया करते थे और प्रायः उन्हें हौंसला बँधाया करते थे। उल्लेखनीय है कि एक बार जेल में भगतसिंह से मिल कर जब वे रोने लगी थीं, तब भगतसिंह ने उन्हें चुप कराते हुए कहा था, "दुनिया क्या कहेगी कि भगतसिंह की माँ रो रही है।"[13]

भगतसिंह की इस राष्ट्रवादी, देशभक्त और क्रान्तिकारी विचारों की समर्थक पारिवारिक पृष्ठभूमि से यह ध्वनित होता है कि उनका समूचा जीवन राष्ट्रभक्ति और क्रान्तिकारी गतिविधियों में संलग्न परिवार के बीच बीता। वे क्रान्ति की सुसंस्कृति में विकसित हुए थे। उनके राजनीतिक कृतित्व ने इस पारिवारिक पृष्ठभूमि से पनपे उनके विचार-दर्शन को परिपक्वता प्रदान की थी। इस समग्र पृष्ठभूमि में उनके विचारों, चिन्तन तथा आदर्शों का शोधपरक अध्ययन तथा उनके विचारों की वर्तमान में प्रासंगिकता विषय पर विचार किया जाना उस महान पुरुष के व्यक्तित्व, कृतित्व और चरित्र के प्रति सच्ची श्रद्धांजली होगी। इस दृष्टि से उनके कतिपय प्रमुख विचारों, चिन्तन और आदर्शों एवं वर्तमान परिप्रेक्ष्य में उनकी प्रासंगिकता पर अपनी अध्ययन दृष्टि केन्द्रित करने पर हमारा ध्यान सर्वप्रथम भगतसिंह के धर्म सम्बन्धी विचारों पर जाता है जिनकी वर्तमान समय में सर्वाधिक प्रासंगिकता है।

भगतसिंह निश्चित तौर पर नास्तिक थे।[14] 'वह भगवान में अपना सम्पूर्ण विश्वास खो चुके थे और मानवता की सेवा को ही एकमात्र धर्म समझते थे तथा इसलिये वे किसी भी धार्मिक कर्मकाण्ड में विश्वास नहीं करते थे। अपने गहन अध्ययन द्वारा वे इस निष्कर्ष पर पहुँचे थे कि धार्मिक अंध विश्वास ही हमारी गुलामी का कारण है।'[15] उनका मानना था कि 'धर्म मानव जाति के लिये अफीम है'।[16] उनका मानना था कि, 'व्यक्ति धर्म का निर्माणकर्त्ता है, धर्म व्यक्ति का नहीं। धर्म के खिलाफ संघर्ष विश्व में उन लोगों के खिलाफ प्रत्यक्ष अभियान है, जिनके लिये धर्म आध्यात्मिक सुगंध है।'[17] उन्होंने मार्क्स के विचारों का हवाला देते हुए लिखा कि, "मैं इसे एक ऐसी बीमारी समझता हूँ, जो कि डर से पैदा हुई है जो मानव जाति के लिए भारी दुःखों और तकलीफों का कारण है।'[18]

भगतसिंह के धर्म सम्बन्धी इन विचारों की झलक हमें उनके बचपन में ही देखने को मिल जाती है। उनकी उम्र तब मुश्किल से 8-9 वर्ष की होगी। वे गांव के प्राइमरी

स्कूल में पढ़ते थे। एक दिन उनकी बहिन अमर कौर कहीं से एक कागज ले आई। यह किसी पुरानी धर्म पुस्तक का पन्ना था। बड़े चाव से अमर कौर ने यह पन्ना भगतसिंह को दिया। उन्होंने उसे देखा, पढ़ा और बोले–"अमरो, अंग्रेजों के साथ ही धर्म ने भी हमारे देश में बड़ी गड़बड़ कर रखी है। मैं अंग्रेजों के साथ ही इसे भी खत्म करूंगा।" बीबी अमर कौर के शब्दों में "उन्होंने कागज जमीन पर पटक दिया और दोनों पैर उसके ऊपर रख कर खड़े हो गये। उस समय उनका चेहरा तमतमा गया था। जैसे सचमुच वे अपने किसी दुश्मन को खत्म कर रहे हों।"[19] बचपन की यह छोटी सी घटना उनके धर्म विरोधी विचारों को स्पष्ट रूप से प्रदर्शित करती है। उनके इन धर्म विरोधी विचारों को परिपक्वता प्रदान की उनकी अध्ययन की ललक ने जिसने उन्हें कार्लमार्क्स, बर्टेन्ड रसेल, आसपेन, राबर्ट सी, बाकुनिन आदि को पढ़ने के लिये प्रेरित किया। उन्होंने लेनिन, ट्राटस्की व कतिपय अन्य लोगों को पढ़ा जो अपने देशों में सफलतापूर्वक क्रान्ति लाए थे, वे सभी नास्तिक थे। उन्होंने लिखा था कि, '1926 के अंत तक मुझे इस बात का विश्वास हो गया कि एक सर्वशक्तिमान परम-आत्मा की बात, जिसने ब्रह्माण्ड का सृजन किया, दिग्दर्शन का संचालन किया, एक कोरी बकवास है। मैंने इस विश्वास को प्रदर्शित किया। मैं एक उद्घोषित नास्तिक हो चुका था।[20] उनका मानना था कि सिर्फ विश्वास और अंधविश्वास खतरनाक हैं। यह मस्तिष्क को मूढ़ तथा मनुष्य को प्रतिक्रियावादी बना देते हैं।[21]

भगतसिंह धर्म को जन विरोधी भी मानते थे। उनकी धारणा थी कि धर्म शोषित-पीड़ित जनता के मार्ग में एक प्रमुख बाधा तथा समाज के तथाकथित ठेकेदारों के लिये उनके क्षुद्र स्वार्थों की पूर्ति हेतु हथियार का काम करता है। शिव वर्मा की पुस्तक संस्मृतियों में उल्लिखित भगतसिंह और केन्द्रीय समिति के सदस्य फनीदा (फणीन्द्रनाथ घोष) के मध्य, ईश्वर, धर्म, आदर्शवाद और उनकी बुराइयों पर हुई व्यापक चर्चा,[22] भगतसिंह की उक्त धारणा की पुष्टि करती है। उनका कहना था कि भगवान यदि सर्वशक्तिमान है तो वह अन्याय, अत्याचार, भूख, गरीबी, शोषण, असमानता, दासता, महामारी, हिंसा और युद्ध आदि का अंत क्यों नहीं करता?... मायावाद, भाग्यवाद, ईश्वरवाद आदि को मैं चंद सत्ताधारी शोषकों द्वारा जनसाधारण को भुलावे में डालने के लिये ईजाद की गई जहरीली घुट्टी से अधिक और कुछ नहीं मानता।[23]

फनीदा के साथ होने वाली चर्चाओं के दौरान भगतसिंह ने अपने धर्म को सर्वथा अलग अंदाज में परिभाषित किया। उन्होंने कहा कि मेरे अनुसार हर कदम जो इन्सान को सुखी बना सके, समता-समृद्धि और भाईचारे के मार्ग पर उसे एक कदम आगे ले जा सके, वही धर्म है। दो शब्दों में कहूँ तो धरती और उस धरती पर भी

भारत की यह पवित्र भूमि मेरा स्वर्ग है, उस पर विचरण करने वाला हर व्यक्ति, इन्सान मेरा देवता है, भगवान है और भगवान को भगवान से बड़ा कर मेरे स्वर्ग को नर्क बनाने वाली शक्तियाँ समाप्त कर, इन्सान को वर्गहीन समाज की ओर बढ़ाने वाला प्रयास, हर कदम, मेरा धर्म है।[24] भगतसिंह का यह विश्वास सर्वथा विपरीत परिस्थितियों में भी अकाट्य बना रहा। अपने अकाट्य तर्कों पर आधारित उनके कुछ प्रश्न विशेष रूप से आस्तिकों के लिए थे जिनका आस्तिकों के पास कोई जवाब नहीं हुआ करता था।[25]

वस्तुतः, जहाँ भगतसिंह के मार्क्सवादी अध्ययन ने उन्हें धर्म एवं ईश्वर सम्बन्धी समस्त विचारों को तार्किक ढंग से समझने तथा उनका निर्भयतापूर्वक खुलासा करने में मदद की, वहीं समाज में फैले अन्याय, अत्याचार, शोषण, दमन आदि कुचक्रों ने उन्हें नास्तिक बना दिया। उन्होंने स्वयं लिखा था कि, 'विश्व की व्याख्या धर्मशास्त्रीय और अधिभौतिक है जबकि मैं एक भौतिकवादी हूँ और हर घटना की मेरी व्याख्या सामयिक होगी।[26]

भगतसिंह के इन ईश्वर तथा धर्म सम्बन्धी विचारों ने उन्हें सच्चे अर्थों में एक मुकम्मल धर्म निरपेक्ष इन्सान बना दिया था। आज हम जिस समय से गुजर रहे हैं, उसमें भगतसिंह प्रवर्तित धर्मनिरपेक्षता के विचारों की महत्ता और प्रासंगिकता बहुत अधिक है। भारतीय समाज बहुधर्मी है। बहुधर्मी समाज विभिन्न धर्मों के बीच पारस्परिक सौहार्द के बिना नहीं रह सकता, लेकिन आज साम्प्रदायिकता की आँधी ने धार्मिक सौहार्द को संकटग्रस्त कर दिया है। आज के इस साम्प्रदायिक वैमनस्य के समय में भगतसिंह के धर्म, सम्प्रदाय सम्बन्धी विचारों की प्रासंगिकता पर विचार किया जाना निहायत ही जरूरी है। साम्प्रदायिकता भारतीय राजनीति की सबसे बड़ी समस्या रही है। इसी के चलते भारत विभाजन के समय लाखों लोगों की जानें गई और अतुल धन-सम्पत्ति तबाह हो गई। एक स्वतंत्रता सेनानी के रूप में भगतसिंह ने साम्प्रदायिकता की समस्या से गहरा साक्षात्कार किया था। वे धर्म को ही साम्प्रदोयिकता की भावना का बीज या आधार मानते थे जो आज भी सत्य है। भगतसिंह गांधीजी की तरह धर्म की उपस्थिति और राजनीति में उसके हस्तक्षेप को उचित नहीं मानते थे। वर्तमान भारतीय राजनीति की सबसे विकट समस्या यह है कि धर्म राजनीति पर हावी है। धर्म के नाम पर गंदी राजनीति का गोरखधन्धा जारी है तथा समाज को बांट कर टुकड़े-टुकड़े करने की राजनीति सक्रिय है। ऐसे समय में भगतसिंह के धर्म और साम्प्रदायिकता सम्बन्धी विचारों पर पुनर्विचार की नितान्त आवश्यकता है। वर्तमान भारतीय संदर्भ में राजनीति जब धार्मिक विद्वेष और कटुता का जहर घोलती जा रही है—ऐसे में व्यावहारिक स्तर पर भी भगतसिंह के धर्म सम्बन्धी विचार बहुत ही प्रासंगिक हो जाते हैं।

भगतसिंह द्वारा "सांप्रदायिक दंगे और उनका इलाज" शीर्षक से लिखे गये एक लेख में तत्कालीन साम्प्रदायिक विद्वेष की परिस्थितियों के संदर्भ में लिखा गया यह कथन वर्तमान भारतीय परिस्थितियों में भी काफी हद तक सही दृष्टिगोचर होता है—"भारतवर्ष की दशा इस समय बड़ी दयनीय है। एक धर्म के अनुयायी होना ही, दूसरे धर्म का कट्टर शत्रु होना है।" भगतसिंह ने भारत की धार्मिक संकीर्णताओं को उजागर करते हुए 'नौजवान भारत सभा' के घोषणा पत्र में लिखा था—"पीपल की एक डाल टूटते ही हिन्दुओं की धार्मिक भावनाएँ चोटिल हो उठती हैं। बुतों को तोड़ने वाले मुसलमानों के ताजिये नामक बुत का कौना फटते ही अल्लाह का प्रकोप जाग उठता है और फिर वह नापाक हिन्दुओं के खून से कम किसी अन्य वस्तु से संतुष्ट नहीं होता। मनुष्यों को पशुओं से अधिक महत्त्व दिया जाना चाहिये, लेकिन भारत में वे लोग पवित्र पशु के नाम पर एक दूसरे का सिर फोड़ते हैं।"[27]

अपने एक अन्य लेख में भगतसिंह यह लिखते हैं कि, "यह मार-काट इसलिये नहीं कि...फलाँ व्यक्ति दोषी है, वरन् इसलिये है कि फलाँ आदमी हिन्दू है, या सिख है या मुसलमान है। बस किसी व्यक्ति का सिख या हिन्दू होना मुसलमानों द्वारा मारे जाने के लिए काफी था और इसी तरह किसी व्यक्ति का मुसलमान होना ही उसकी जान लेने के लिए पर्याप्त तर्क था।"[28] भगतसिंह द्वारा चित्रित यह तस्वीर स्वतंत्र भारत में जो कुछ पंजाब में हुआ, जो कुछ गुजरात में हुआ तथा जो कुछ कश्मीर में हो रहा है या जो कुछ भी देश के किसी भी कोने में घटित होने वाले साम्प्रदायिक दंगों में घटित हुआ या होता रहा है—पर पूरी तरह सटीक सिद्ध होती है।

भगतसिंह इस साम्प्रदायिक विद्वेष की स्थिति के पीछे साम्प्रदायिक नेताओं और अखबारों का हाथ मानते हैं। वर्तमान भारत में भी धार्मिक व साम्प्रदायिक विद्वेष के पीछे साम्प्रदायिक नेताओं तथा काफी हद तक संचार साधनों की नकारात्मक भूमिका दोषी नजर आती है। जहाँ साम्प्रदायिक नेताओं ने भारतीय नागरिकों की धार्मिक भावनाओं को उद्वेलित करके वैमनस्य को बढ़ाया है वहीं संचार साधनों ने उत्तेजनापूर्ण समाचारों के माध्यम से आग में घी डालने का कार्य किया है, जिसका प्रत्यक्ष परिणाम है—गुजरात के दंगे।

भगतसिंह, राजनीति को धर्म से पृथक किये जाने के हिमायती रहे थे। उनका मानना था कि "झगड़ा मिटाने का यह भी एक सुन्दर इलाज है। यदि धर्म को अलग कर दिया जाये तो राजनीति पर हम सभी इकट्ठे हो सकते हैं। धर्मों में हम चाहे अलग-अलग ही रहें।"[29] उनके द्वारा सुझाया गया यह उपाय वर्तमान समय में भी बड़ा उपयोगी दिखाई देता है। आज देश की एक तिहाई जनता जो गरीबी रेखा के नीचे जीवन व्यतीत कर रही है, देश का किसान-मजदूर जो अपनी मूलभूत

आवश्यकताओं के लिये संघर्ष कर रहा है, वह किसी भी धर्म के क्यों न हों—सभी की तकलीफें और संघर्ष समान हैं। उनकी तकलीफें और संघर्ष, किसी धर्म या जाति विशेष के होने पर कम या ज्यादा नहीं हो पाते। अतः हमारी प्राथमिकता इस वर्ग की मूलभूत आवश्यकताओं को पूरा करना एवं उनके स्तर को उठाने की होनी चाहिये। इसी तरह धर्म का राजनीति में हस्तक्षेप पूर्णतः बंद होना चाहिये। धर्म के नाम पर वोट मांगने वालों, राजनीतिक संगठन बनाने वालों, धार्मिक तुष्टीकरण करने वालों आदि पर कानूनी रोक लगनी चाहिये। तभी हम अपने युगद्रष्टा शहीद भगतसिंह के सपनों के भारत निर्माण की ओर कदम बढ़ा पायेंगे जिसमें धर्म कोई समस्या नहीं वरन् निजी विचार होगा। निष्कर्षतः यह कहा जा सकता है कि शहीद भगतसिंह के धर्म सम्बन्धी विचार जहाँ एक ओर उनके अपने युग की राजनीतिक परिस्थितियों की अनिवार्य आवश्यकता थे, वहीं वह आज के युग में भी अक्षरशः प्रासंगिक और उपयोगी हैं।

सन्दर्भ

1. सिंधु वीरेन्द्र : *युगद्रष्टा भगतसिंह और उनके मृत्युंजय पुरखे,* राजपाल एण्ड संस, दिल्ली, 1997, पृ. 130.
2. एल.पी. माथुर : *भगतसिंह : द प्रिंस ऑफ मार्टयर्स,* पृ. 3.
3. परदमन सिंह तथा जे.सी. ढ़की (सं.) : *बरीड़ अलाइव : ऑटोबायोग्राफी ऑफ सरदार अजीतसिंह,* पृ. 21.
4. इनकी पारिवारिक पृष्ठभूमि के सम्बन्ध में प्रामाणिक जानकारी प्राप्त करने के लिए हमारे पास दो प्रामाणिक साधन हैं। एक सर्वश्री परदमनसिंह तथा जे.सी. ढ़की द्वारा सम्पादित भगतसिंह के चाचा सरदार अजीतसिंह की आत्मकथा *"बरीड़ अलाइव : ऑटोबायोग्राफी ऑफ सरदार अजीतसिंह"* है तथा दूसरी भगतसिंह के परिवार में ही जन्मी श्रीमती वीरेन्द्र सिन्धु द्वारा लिखित पुस्तक *"युगद्रष्टा भगतसिंह और उनके मृत्युंजय पुरखे।"*

   द्रष्टव्य—

   परदमन सिंह तथा जे.सी. ढ़की (सं.) : *बरीड़ अलाइव : ऑटोबायोग्राफी ऑफ सरदार अजीतसिंह,* पूर्वोक्त; वीरेन्द्र सिन्धु : *युगद्रष्टा भगतसिंह और उनके मृत्युंजय पुरखे,* पूर्वोक्त.
5. परदमन सिंह तथा जे.सी. ढ़की (सं.) : *बरीड़ अलाइव : ऑटोबायोग्राफी ऑफ सरदार अजीतसिंह,* पूर्वोक्त, पृ. 21.

6. वीरेन्द्र सिन्धु : *युगद्रष्टा भगतसिंह और उनके मृत्युंजय पुरखे*, पूर्वोक्त, पृ. 1-11.
7. एल.पी. माथुर : *भगतसिंह : द प्रिंस ऑफ मार्टयर्स*, पूर्वोक्त, पृ. 3.
8. भगतसिंह ने पहली बार घर से फरार होते समय यह पत्र अपने पिता किशनसिंह के लिए छोड़ा था। द्रष्टव्य–जगमोहन सिंह-चमनलाल (सं.) : *भगतसिंह और उनके साथियों के दस्तावेज*, द्वितीय संस्करण, राजकमल प्रकाशन, नई दिल्ली, 1997, पृ. 56.
9. वीरेन्द्र सिन्धु : *युगद्रष्टा भगतसिंह और उनके मृत्युंजय पुरखे*, पूर्वोक्त, पृ. 32.
10. जगमोहन सिंह -चमनलाल : *भगतसिंह और उनके साथियों के दस्तावेज*, पूर्वोक्त, पृ. 325.
11. गुप्त मन्मथनाथ : *भगतसिंह और उनका युग*, लिपि प्रकाशन, नई दिल्ली 1972, पृ. 86-87.
12. जगमोहन सिंह-चमनलाल : *भगतसिंह और उनके साथियों के दस्तावेज*, पूर्वोक्त, पृ. 335.
13. वीरेन्द्र सिन्धु : *सरदार भगतसिंह : पत्र और दस्तावेज*, प्रथम संस्करण, राजपाल एण्ड संस, दिल्ली, 1977, पृ. 52.
14. शिव वर्मा : डॉ. हरिदेव शर्मा व मनचंदा द्वारा 1 फरवरी, 1972 को लिया गया साक्षात्कार, मौखिक इतिहास विभाग, तीन मूर्ति भवन लाइब्रेरी, नई दिल्ली, पृ. 37.
15. जयदेव गुप्ता : मनचंदा द्वारा 10 मई 1970, को लिया गया साक्षात्कार, मौखिक इतिहास विभाग, तीन मूर्ति भवन लाइब्रेरी, नई दिल्ली, पृ. 9.
16. भगतसिंह की डायरी, पृ. 127.
17. वही, पृ. 37.
18. वही, पृ. 9.
19. वीरेन्द्र सिन्धु : *युगद्रष्टा भगतसिंह और उनके मृत्युंजय पुरखे*, पूर्वोक्त, पृ. 280.
20. भगतसिंह : *मैं नास्तिक क्यों* हूँ? कानपुर समाजवादी साहित्य सदन, कानपुर, 1981, पृ. 9-10; शिव वर्मा : *शहीद भगतसिंह की चुनी हुई कृतियाँ*, प्रथम संस्करण, नेशनल बुक सेन्टर, 23 मार्च, 1986, पृ. 206.
21. भगतसिंह : *मैं नास्तिक क्यों हूँ?* पूर्वोक्त, पृ. 5; शिव वर्मा : *शहीद भगतसिंह की चुनी हुई कृतियाँ*, पूर्वोक्त, पृ. 203.

22. सन् 1920 में शिव वर्मा के कमरे में यह विचार-विमर्श हुआ।
23. शिव वर्मा : *संस्मृतियाँ*, तृतीय संस्करण, विधि प्रकाशन, दिल्ली, 1983, पृ. 38-39.
24. वही, पृ. 39-40.
25. यथा–

    –सर्वशक्तिमान होकर भी ईश्वर ने ऐसी सृष्टि की रचना क्यों की जो दुखों और संतापों से त्रस्त है?;

    –हिन्दुओं, तुम जिन 84 लाख दण्डों को गिनाते हो, मनुष्य पर सुधारक के रूप में इनका क्या असर है?;

    –तुम्हारा सर्वशक्तिमान ईश्वर हर व्यक्ति को उस समय क्यों नहीं रोकता है जब वह कोई पाप या अपराध कर रहा होता है?

    द्रष्टव्य–शिव वर्मा : *शहीद भगतसिंह की चुनी हुई कृतियाँ*, पूर्वोक्त, पृ. 213, 14, 15, 16, 17.
26. ए.बी. वर्धन : *भगतसिंह की राह पर*, न्यू राज प्रिंटिंग प्रेस, नई दिल्ली, 1984, पृ. 19.
27. जगमोहन सिंह-चमनलाल : *भगतसिंह और उनके साथियों के दस्तावेज*, पूर्वोक्त, पृ. 262.
28. वही, पृ. 218.
29. वही, पृ. 221.

21

सार्थक क्रान्ति के प्रतीक–शहीद भगतसिंह

डॉ. अनिल कुमार वर्मा

1857 के प्रथम स्वतन्त्रता संग्रम ने भारतीयों के मन में जिस क्रान्ति की भावना को जगाया था कांग्रेस के उदारवादी चरण में उसका प्रभाव कुछ कम हुआ क्योंकि अपने प्रारम्भिक दौर में क्रांग्रेस का उद्देश्य संवैधानिक, आर्थिक, प्रशासनिक सुधार एवं नागरिक अधिकारों की मांग करना था। अतः शिक्षित वर्ग तक ही इसका प्रभाव रहा। किन्तु ब्रिटिश आर्थिक नीतियों की आलोचना करके इन्होंने विभिन्न वर्गों में विभाजित भारतीयों को एकता के सूत्र में बाँध दिया था।[1] कांग्रेस की उदार नीतियों के विरोध में कुछ राष्ट्रवादी उग्र विचारों के व्यक्ति आगे आए जिन्होंने बहिष्कार, स्वदेशी, स्वशासन एवं राष्ट्रीय शिक्षा के विचारों को आगे बढ़ाया। ब्रिटिश सरकार द्वारा भारतीयों का राजनीतिक एवं आर्थिक शोषण किए जाने के कारण ही कुछ लोग सशस्त्र क्रांति की आवश्यकता अनुभव करने लगे थे। यह सशस्त्र क्रान्तिकारी आन्दोलन दो चरणों में हुआ। पूना के प्लेग कमिश्नर मि. रैण्ड एवं ब्रिटेन में इंडिया हाउस में कर्जन वाइली की हत्या और 1912 में तत्कालीन वायसराय लार्ड हार्डिंग पर बम फेंका जाना तथा 1913 में सेनफ्रांसिस्को में गदर पार्टी का गठन तथा 1915 में अफगानिस्तान में राजा महेन्द्र प्रताप द्वारा भारत की प्रथम अस्थायी सरकार का गठन क्रान्ति के प्रथम चरण का परिणाम था।[2]

दूसरे चरण में शचीन्द्रनाथ सान्याल, रामप्रसाद बिस्मिल, अशफाक उल्ला खाँ, रोशन सिंह, राजेन्द्र लाहिडी, चन्द्रशेखर आजाद एवं भगतसिंह जैसे क्रान्तिकारियों ने राष्ट्र के लिए आत्म बलिदान की भावना को साकार ही नहीं कर दिखाया अपितु उन्होंने स्वतन्त्र भारत को धर्मनिरपेक्ष समाजवादी एवं समतावादी समाज में बदलने का एक क्रान्तिकारी दृष्टिकोण भी दिया।[3]

एसोसिएट प्रोफेसर–इतिहास विभाग, डॉ. बी. आर. अम्बेडकर विश्वविद्यालय - आगरा

भगतसिंह एवं उनके देशभक्त साथियों की फाँसी से एक ऐसी दूरदृष्टि का दमन हो गया जिस पर स्वतन्त्र भारत का वैकल्पिक प्रशासनिक ढाँचा आधारित था। भगतसिंह और बी.के. दत्त को असेम्बली बम केस में उम्र कैद की सजा सुनाने वाले न्यायाधीश मैडिल्टन ने अपने निर्णय में स्पष्ट किया कि इन युवकों द्वारा कोर्ट में लगाये गए नारों 'लाँग लिव रिवोल्यूशन', 'लाँग लिव प्रोलेटेरियट से' संकेत मिलता है कि किस प्रकार की राजनीतिक विचारधारा से वे पोषित थे, इन विचारों के प्रचार को रोकने के लिए ही उन्हें उम्रकैद की सजा सुनायी गई है ।[4]

भगतसिंह और उनके साथियों के अनुसार क्रान्ति का अर्थ अन्याय और शोषण पर आधारित तत्कालीन व्यवस्था में आमूलचूल परिवर्तन करके एक ऐसी सामाजिक व्यवस्था की स्थापना करना था जिसमें राजनीतिक एवं आर्थिक शोषण असम्भव हो।[5]

उक्त सामाजिक व्यवस्था के लिए एक क्रान्ति अनिवार्य थी। भगतसिंह के अनुसार क्रान्ति का अर्थ संगठित एवं क्रमबद्ध कार्य द्वारा सामाजिक परिवर्तन है और यह तोड़-फोड़, असंगठित, एकदम या स्वतः परिवर्तन के विरूद्ध है। इसके लिए गम्भीरता से जनसाधारण को समझाना होगा कि क्रान्ति उनके हित में है।[6]

भगतसिंह ने अपने पत्र में लिखा था कि इस समय हम नौजवानों से यह नहीं कह सकते कि वे बम और पिस्तौल उठाएं। आज विद्यार्थियों के सामने इससे भी अधिक महत्वपूर्ण काम है। आने वाले लाहौर अधिवेशन में कांग्रेस देश की आजादी के लिए जबरदस्त लड़ाई की घोषणा करने वाली है। राष्ट्रीय इतिहास के इन कठिन क्षणों में नौजवानों के कन्धों पर बहुत बड़ी जिम्मेदारी आ पड़ेगी। यह सच है कि स्वतन्त्रता के इस युद्ध में अग्रिम मोर्चों पर विद्यार्थियों ने मौत से टक्कर ली है। क्या परीक्षा की इस घड़ी में वे उसी प्रकार की दृढ़ता और आत्मविश्वास का परिचय देने से हिचकिचाएंगे? नौजवानों को क्रान्ति का यह सन्देश देश के कोने कोने में पहुँचाना है, फैक्ट्री कारखानों के क्षेत्रों में, गन्दी बस्तियों और गाँवों की जर्जर झोपड़ियों में रहने वाले करोड़ों लोगों में इस क्रान्ति का अलख जगाना है, जिससे आजादी आएगी और तब एक मनुष्य द्वारा दूसरे मनुष्य का शोषण असम्भव हो जाएगा।[7]

अपने जीवन के प्रारम्भिक चरण में भगतसिंह गाँधी जी के असहयोग आन्दोलन से भी प्रेरित हुए थे। सभी क्रान्तिकारी नेताओं ने इस आन्दोलन को स्वीकार कर लिया था। आन्दोलन में भाग लेने के लिए गाँधी जी ने जो भी रोकथाम की शर्तें लगाई थीं उन सबको तोड़कर किसान भी पूरे उत्साह के साथ आन्दोलन में कूद पड़े। सरकार घबरा गई, उन्हें लगा कि सरकार की अवज्ञा की छूत शहरों से चलकर करोड़ों किसानों तक पहुँच जाती है तो ब्रिटिश शासन के पास बचने के लिए कोई रास्ता नहीं रह जाएगा।[8]

गाँधी जी द्वारा एक वर्ष में स्वराज्य प्राप्ति की घोषणा से सभी प्रभावित थे। दुर्भाग्य से 1922 की चौरी चौरा की घटना से गाँधी जी ने असहयोग आन्दोलन को वापस ले लिया। फलस्वरूप उन क्रान्तिकारियों ने फिर से हथियार उठा लिए जिन्होनें गाँध ी जी के आग्रह पर असहयोग आन्दोलन में हिस्सा लिया था। इस घटना से भगतसिंह भी बहुत क्षुब्ध थे।

भगतसिंह जब लाहौर के नेशनल कॉलिज में पढ़ रहे थे, उन्होनें मैजिनी, गैरीबाल्डी, आयरलैण्ड के विद्रोहियों एवं रूस की क्रान्ति के विषय में पढ़ा एवं क्रान्ति के विषय में अपने विचारों को परिपक्व बनाया।

जब उनके माता-पिता ने उनके विवाह की योजना बनाई तो उन्हानें इस प्रस्तााव को ठुकरा दिया तथा अपना घर और कालिज दोनों को छोड़ दिया। उन्होंने अपने पिता को एक पत्र लिखा – मेरी जिन्दगी मक्सदे आला यानि आजादी-ए-हिन्द के असूल के लिए वक्फ (दान) हो चुकी है। इसलिए मेरी जिन्दगी में आराम और दुनियावी ख्वाइशें (इच्छाएँ) बायशे कशिश नहीं हैं। आपको याद होगा कि जब मै छोटा था तो बापू जी ने मेरे यज्ञोपवीत के वक्त ऐलान किया था कि मुझे खिदमते वतन के लिए वक्फ कर दिया गया है। लिहाजा मैं उस वक्त की प्रतिज्ञा पूरी कर रहा हूँ।[10] भगतसिंह घर छोड़ कर कानपुर चले गए। वहीं पर अपने खाली समय में गणेश शंकर विधार्थी के साथ प्रताप प्रेस में नौकरी कर ली एवं क्रान्तिकारी साहित्य का अध्ययन किया। कानपुर में ही भगतसिंह, शचिन्द्रनाथ सान्याल द्वारा गठित हिन्दुस्तान प्रजातंत्र संघ की गतिविधियों से प्रभावित होकर इसमें शामिल हो गए।[11]

1925 में काकोरी में ट्रेन डकैती के पश्चात् जब रामप्रसाद बिस्मिल अशफाक उल्लाखाँ, रोशनसिंह, राजेन्द्र लाहिड़ी जैसे हिंदुस्तान प्रजातन्त्र सेना के क्रान्तिकारी पकड़े गए तो संगठन की सारी जिम्मेदारी भगतहसिंह एवं चन्द्रशेखर आजाद के ऊपर आ गयी। भगतहसिंह के व्यक्तित्व में एक परिवर्तन आया। उन्होंने अपने विचारों को परिपक्व करने के लिए गहन अध्ययन किया। *मैं नास्तिक क्यों* हूँ ? में उन्होंने लिखा-अध्ययन करने की तरंगे मेरे मन में उठती रहीं। अध्ययन करूँ ताकि अपने विरोधियों के तर्कों का उत्तर दे सकूँ।[12]

भारत में एक समाजवादी गणतंत्र की स्थापना करने के उद्देश्य से भगतसिंह और उनके साथियों ने 1926 में लाहौर में *नौजवान भारत सभा* नामक एक संगठन का गठन किया। भगतसिंह को विश्वास हो गया था कि भारत को गुलामी से मुक्त करने के लिए राजनीतिक स्वतन्त्रता के साथ-साथ आर्थिक स्वतन्त्रता भी अनिवार्य है।[13]

भगतसिंह और उनके साथियों पर 1917 की रूसी क्रान्ति ने निःसन्देह व्यापक विचारात्मक प्रभाव डाला था। यदि यूरोप के एक सापेक्ष रूप से पिछड़े देश के मजदूर

और किसान एक सफल क्रान्ति का गठन कर सकते हैं, तब उपनिवेशवादी देश साम्राज्यवादी शक्तियों को क्यों नहीं उखाड़ फेंकते और ऐच्छिक सामाजिक परिवर्तन को क्यों नहीं लागू कर सकते? भगतसिंह 1927 ई. के बाद विशेष तौर पर किसानों, मजदूरों, युवको एवं बुद्धिजीवियों के जन आन्दोलन के संगठनकर्ता के रूप में उभरे। भगतसिंह पूर्ण परिवर्तन चाहते थे।[14]

1927 में भगतसिंह ने फिर से लिखना शुरू कर दिया। काकोरी के शहीदों को दिसम्बर 1927 मे फाँसी होने के बाद भगतसिंह ने अपने साथियों – भगवतीचरण वोहरा, शिव वर्मा, जयदेव कपूर, आदि से विचार विमर्श करते हुए अपने देश के शहीदों और क्रान्तिकारी आन्दोलन सम्बन्धी जानकारी देने के लिए निरन्तर यत्न किए। वे स्वयं भी इन आन्दोलनों का गहराई से अध्ययन कर रहे थे और नौजवान भारत सभा के माध्यम से देशवासियों को जाग्रत कर रहे थे। नौजवान भारत सभा का एक निश्चित उद्देश्य और स्पष्ट विचारधारा थी। एक स्वतन्त्र समाजवादी गणतंत्र की स्थापना और अन्य देशों में साम्राज्यवादी अत्याचारों को रोकना।[15]

जलियाँवाला बाग हत्याकाण्ड के पश्चात् घटी किसी भी घटना ने लोगों को इतना आंदोलित नहीं किया था, जितना साइमन कमीशन भारत पर थोपे जाने ने किया। नौजवान भारतसभा ने साइमन कमीशन के बहिष्कार का निर्णय लिया।[16]

लाहौर में लाला लाजपतराय के नेतृत्व में साइमन कमीशन के विरोध में धरना दिया गया। साइमन वापस जाओ के नारे लगाए गए। एस.एस.पी. स्काट के आदेश पर पुलिस ने लाठीचार्ज किया जिसमें लाला लाजपतराय गंभीर रूप से घायल हो गए। चोट के कारण कुछ ही दिनों में उनकी मृत्यु हो गई। भगतसिंह के नेतृत्व में हिन्दुस्तान समाजवादी प्रजातंत्र संघ के क्रान्तिकारियों ने सांडर्स को मारकर लाला जी के अपमान का बदला लिया।[17]

सांडर्स की हत्या पर भगतसिंह ने कहा कि हमें एक आदमी की हत्या करने का खेद है। परन्तु यह आदमी उस निर्दयी, नीच और अन्यायपूर्ण व्यवस्था का अंग था जिसे समाप्त कर देना आवश्यश्क था। इस आदमी की हत्या हिन्दुस्तान में ब्रिटिश शासन के कारिन्दे के रूप में की गयी है। यह सरकार संसार की सबसे अत्याचारी सरकार है। मनुष्य का रक्त बहाने का हमें खेद है। परन्तु क्रान्ति की वेदी पर कभी-कभी रक्त बहाना अनिवार्य हो जाता है। हमारा उददेश्य एक ऐसी क्रान्ति से है जो मनुष्य द्वारा मनुष्य के शोषण का अंत कर देगी।[18]

भगतसिंह अपनी आतंकवादी कारवाई के लिए प्रसिद्ध नहीं हुए। वे लाला लाजपतराय के सम्मान के माध्यम से राष्ट्र के सम्मान की रक्षा के लिए प्रसिद्ध हुए। वे एक प्रतीक बन गए। कार्य भुला दिया गया। प्रतीक बना रहा। कुछ ही महीनों

में पंजाब के प्रत्येक गांव एवं कस्बे में और कुछ हद तक सम्पूर्ण उत्तरी भारत में लोग उनके नाम से परिचित हो गए। उनके विषय में असंख्य गीत लिखे गए और उस व्यक्ति ने जो लोकप्रियता अर्जित की, वह बहुत आश्चर्यजनक थी।[19] भारतीय क्रान्तिकारी आन्दोलन के अध्ययन के साथ-साथ भगतसिंह ने अन्तर्राष्ट्रीय क्रान्तिकारी आन्दोलन का भी पर्याप्त अध्ययन किया और उस पर मनन किया। इसी सिलसिले मे '*किरती*' में 'अराजकतावाद क्या है'? आदि लेख व कुछ अनुवाद छपे थे। डेनब्रिन की आत्मकथा का भी उन्होंने अनुवाद किया था और यह अलग से पुस्तक के रूप में छपा था।[20]

भगतसिंह ने लिखा जब कोई व्यक्ति अपनी स्वतन्त्रता के लिए कहीं से पिस्तौल या बम लेकर निकलता है तो सभी नौकरशाह उसे अनार्किस्ट कहकर पुकारते हैं। इस शब्द को बहुत बदनाम किया गया है। भारत में राजपरिवर्तनकारियों को भी जनता में घृणा पैदा करने के लिए अनार्किस्ट कहा जाता है। हालांकि अराजकतावादी सर्वाधिक संवेदनशील मन वाले, सारी दुनिया का भला चाहने वाले होते हैं। उनके विचारों के साथ भिन्नता रखते हुए भी उनकी गम्भीरता, जनता से स्नेह, त्याग और उनकी सच्चाई आदि पर किसी प्रकार की शंका नहीं हो सकती। अराजकतावाद एक नया दर्शन है जिसके अनुसार एक नया समाज बनेगा। जनता का रहन-सहन या भ्रातृत्व ऐसा होगा जिसमें कि मनुष्य के बनाये नियम कोई अवरोध न पैदा कर सकेंगे। उनके अनुसार किसी भी शासन की जरूरत महसूस नहीं होती। क्योंकि प्रत्येक सरकार दमन पर टिकी होती है इसलिए यह अनावश्यक है।[21] भगतसिंह चाहते थे कि *हिन्दुस्तान समाजवादी प्रजातंत्र सेना* ऐसा कार्य करे जिसमें कि मजदूर एवं किसान आन्दोलनों से दल को जोड़ने की अभिव्यक्ति प्रकट हो सके।[22]

यद्यपि हिन्दुस्तान समाजवादी प्रजातांत्रिक सेना की केन्द्रीय समिति ने पहले जयदेव कपूर एवं बटुकेश्वरदत को बहरों के कान खोलने के लिए केन्द्रीय असेम्बली में बम फेंकने के लिए भेजने का निश्चय किया था, किन्तु अदालत को अपनी विचारधारा के प्रचार का केन्द्र बनाने के लिए सुखदेव की सलाह पर भगतसिंह को भेजा गया। भगतसिंह एवं बटुकेश्वरदत ने बिना किसी को हानि पहुँचाए एसेम्बली हाल में दो बम फेंके।[23] 8 अप्रैल सन 1929 को असेम्बली में बम फेंकने के बाद भगतसिंह एवं दत्त द्वारा बाँटे गये पर्चे का सार इस प्रकार है–

'हिन्दुस्तानी समाजवादी प्रजातान्त्रिक सेना'

सूचना

बहरों को सुनाने के लिए बहुत ऊँची आवाज की आवश्यकता होती है। प्रसिद्ध फ्रांसीसी अराजकतावादी शहीद वैलियां के यह अमर शब्द हमारे काम के औचित्य के साक्षी हैं।'

पिछले दस वर्षों में ब्रिटिश सरकार ने शासन - सुधार के नाम पर इस देश का जो अपमान किया है उसकी कहानी दोहराने की आवश्यकता नहीं और न ही हिन्दुस्तानी पार्लियामेंट पुकारी जाने वाली इस सभा ने भारतीय राष्ट्र के सिर पर पत्थर फेंककर उसका जो अपमान किया है, उसके उदाहरणों को याद दिलाने की आवश्यकता है। यह सब सर्वविदित और स्पष्ट है। आज फिर जब लोग 'साइमन कमीशन 'से कुछ सुधारों के टुकड़ों की आशा में आँख फैलाए हैं और इन टुकड़ों के लोभ में आपस में झगड़ रहे हैं, विदेशी सरकार 'सार्वजनिक सुरक्षा विधेयक' और 'औद्योगिक विवाद विधेयक' के रूप में अपने दमन को और भी कड़ा कर लेने का यत्न कर रही है। इसके साथ ही आने वाले अधिवेशन में अखबारों द्वारा राजद्रोह रोकने का कानून (प्रेस सेडिशन एक्ट) जनता पर कसने की भी धमकी दी जा रही है। सार्वजनिक काम करने वाले मजदूर नेताओं की अन्धाधुन्ध गिरफ्तारियाँ यह स्पष्ट कर देती है कि सरकार किस रवैये पर चल रही है।

राष्ट्रीय दमन और अपमान की इस उत्तेजनापूर्ण परिस्थिति में अपने उत्तरदायित्व की गम्भीरता को महसूस कर 'हिन्दुस्तान प्रजातन्त्र संघ' ने अपनी सेना को यह कदम उठाने की आज्ञा दी है। इस कार्य का प्रयोजन यह है कि कानून का यह अपमानजनक प्रहसन समाप्त कर दिया जाये। विदेशी शोषक नौकरशाही जो चाहे करे परन्तु उसकी वैधानिकता की नकाब फाड़ देना आवश्यक है।

जनता के प्रतिनिधियों से हमारा आग्रह है कि वे इस पार्लियामेंट के पाखण्ड को छोड़कर अपने-अपने निर्वाचन क्षेत्रों को लौट जाएं और 'जनता को विदेशी दमन और शोषण के विरुद्ध क्रांति के लिए' तैयार करें। हम विदेशी सरकार को यह बतला देना चाहते हैं कि हम 'सार्वजनिक सुरक्षा' और 'औद्योगिक विवाद' के दमनकारी कानूनों और लाला लाजपतराय की हत्या के विरोध में देश की जनता की ओर से यह कदम उठा रहे हैं।

हम मनुष्य के जीवन को पवित्र समझते हैं। हम ऐसे उज्ज्वल भविष्य में विश्वास रखते हैं जिसमें प्रत्येक व्यक्ति को पूर्ण शान्ति और स्वतन्त्रता का अवसर मिल सके। हम इन्सान का खून बहाने की अपनी विवशता पर दुखी हैं। परन्तु क्रांति द्वारा सबको समान स्वतन्त्रता देने और मनुष्य द्वारा मनुष्य के शोषण को समाप्त करने के लिए क्रान्ति में कुछ रक्त पात अनिवार्य है।[24]

इन्कलाब जिनदाबाद। ह. बलराज कमान्डर इन चीफ

भगतसिंह एवं बटुकेश्वरदत्त ने बम फेंकने के पश्चात् नारे भी लगाये। 'इन्कलाब जिन्दाबाद' और 'ब्रिटिश साम्राज्य का नाश हो'। दोनों को गिरफ्तार कर लिया गया।

असेम्बली में बम फेंकने के बाद, 6 जून, सन् 1929 को दिल्ली के सेशन जज मि. लियो नाड़ मिडिल्टन की अदालत में भगतसिंह एवं बटुकेश्वर दत्त ने वायसराय लार्ड इर्विन के इस कथन का समर्थन किया कि यह विद्रोह किसी व्यक्ति विशेष के खिलाफ नहीं सम्पूर्ण शासन-व्यवस्था के विरुद्ध था।[25]

भगतसिंह ने क्रान्ति के वास्तविक अर्थ को स्पष्ट किया। क्रान्ति क्या है? भारत के राष्ट्रीय हलकों में उसके बारे में एक बड़ी गलत धारणा बनी हुई है। आमतौर पर क्रान्ति को बम, रिवाल्वर और गुप्त संस्थाओं से जोड़ दिया जाता है। भारतीय राजनीतिक शब्दकोष में बहुप्रचलित वाक्य. 'क्रान्तिकारी अपराध' क्रान्ति की इसी गलत अवधारणा की उपज है। बहरहाल, क्रान्ति इस सबसे कहीं अधिक गम्भीर समस्या है। क्रान्ति एक महत्वपूर्ण ऐतिहासिक घटना है, जो प्रस्तुत ऐतिहासिक युग का अंत करती है। चूँकि जाने वाले समाज के प्रतिनिधि या दलाल, आर्थिक वर्ग और राजनीतिक संस्थायें, जो उस समाज में प्रचलित हालातों से लाभान्वित होते रहे हैं एक भयानक प्रतिरोध के बगैर ऐसा कोई परिवर्तन नहीं होने देंगे जिससे उनके प्रभुत्व का अन्त हो जाए, और जैसा कि आमतौर पर होता है। इसलिए आमतौर पर राजनीतिक हिंसा और सामाजिक उथल-पुथल 'क्रान्ति' कहलाने वाली ऐतहासिक घटना के अंग बन जाते हैं।[26]

भगतसिंह ने क्रान्ति के अपने उद्‌देश्य को स्पष्ट करते हुए कहा—यदि उद्‌देश्य को पूरी तरह भुला दिया जाए, तो किसी के साथ न्याय नहीं हो सकता, क्योंकि उद्‌देश्य को नजरों में न रखने पर संसार के बड़े-बड़े सेनापति भी साधारण हत्यारे नजर आयेंगे। सरकारी कर वसूल करने वाले अधिकारी चोर, जालसाज दिखाई देंगे और न्यायाधीशों पर भी कत्ल करने का अभियोग लगेगा। इस तरह सामाजिक व्यवस्था और सभ्यता खून खराबा, चोरी और जालसाजी बनकर रह जाएगी। यदि उद्‌देश्य की उपेक्षा की जाए, तो हर धर्म प्रचारक झूठ का प्रचारक दिखायी देगा और प्रत्येक पैगम्बर पर अभियोग लगेगा कि उसने करोड़ों भोले और अनजान लोगों को गुमराह किया।

हत्या, तोड़-फोड़, आगजनी और लूटमार जैसी सिर्फ आतंक फैलाने की गतिविधियों को भगतसिंह निरुद्‌देश्य गतिविधियाँ कहकर खारिज करते हैं। इन गतिविधियों से क्रान्ति का लक्ष्य जो पवित्र होता है, नष्ट भ्रष्ट हो जाता है। साथ ही जनता की सहानुभूति और समर्थन मिलना भी बंद हो जाता है। उनका विचार था कि जब तक किसी देश की जनता स्वयं अपनी माँगों के लिए लड़ने के लिए तैयार नहीं हो जाती, तब तक किसी ठोस लाभ की आशा नहीं की जा सकती।[27]

हिंसा और अहिंसा के प्रश्न पर भगतसिंह ने कहा- *'किसी विशेष हालत में हिंसा जायज हो सकती है, लेकिन जन-आन्दोलन का मुख्य हथियार अहिंसा होगी।'*[28]

अपने क्रान्तिकारी कार्यक्रम के मसौदे में भगतसिंह ने लिखा कि *साम्राज्य वादियों को गद्दी से उतारने का भारत के पास एक मात्र हथियार श्रमिक क्रान्ति है। कोई और चीज इस उद्देश्य की पूर्ति नहीं कर सकती।*[29]

गाँधी जी के आन्दोलन पर टिप्पणी करते हुए भगतसिंह ने कहा- *गाँधीवाद असहयोग आन्दोलन से दबाव बनाकर समझौता तो करा सकता है। वह गोरों की सत्ता में भूरों की हिस्सेदारी चाहता है और वर्तमान दाँचे में ही थोड़ी सी सुविधाएँ माँगने की फिराक में है। जबकि आजादी के बाद शासन-व्यवस्था में आमूलचूल परिवर्तन की आवश्यकता है। एक ऐसे सामाजिक ढाँचे का निर्माण करना होगा, जिसमें श्रमिकों के शोषण के लिए कोई स्थान न हो।*[30]

भगतसिंह ने कहा- *हम अपने देश के नौजवानों, मजदूरों, किसानों और बुद्धिमानों से अनुरोध करते हैं कि वे अपने देश की आजादी के झण्डे के नीचे एकत्रित होकर हमारा साथ दें। देश में ऐसी व्यवस्था लाने का प्रयत्न करें जिसमें राजनीतिक और सामाजिक दासता और आर्थिक शोषण असम्भव हो जाए। अहिंसा के नाम पर समझौतावादी नीति को ठोकर मार दीजिए। हमारी संस्कृति और गौरव का कोई अर्थ उस समय तक नहीं होगा, जब तक अहिंसा के नाम पर विदेशी दासता के सम्मुख सिर झुकाए रहेंगे।*[31]

भगतसिंह के अनुसार धर्म मानव जाति के लिए अफीम के समान है। उनका मानना था कि व्यक्ति धर्म का निर्माणकर्ता है, धर्म व्यक्ति का नहीं। भगतसिंह ने कार्लमार्क्स, बर्टेन्ड रसेल, राबर्ट.सी. बाकुनिन, लेनिन, ट्राट्स्की इत्यादि का अध्ययन किया था, ये सभी नास्तिक थे। उन्होंने लिखा था कि 1926 के अंत तक मुझे इस बात का विश्वास हो गया था कि एक सर्वशक्तिमान परम-आत्मा की बात जिसने ब्राह्माण्ड का सृजन किया है, सही नहीं है।[32]

भगतसिंह का मानना था- *भगवान यदि सर्वशक्तिमान है तो वह अन्याय, अत्याचार, भूख, गरीबी, शोषण, असमानता, दासता, महामारी, हिंसा और युद्ध आदि का अंत क्यों नहीं करता? मायावाद, भाग्यवाद, ईश्वरवाद आदि को मैं चंद सत्ताधारी शोषकों द्वारा जनसाधारण को भुलावे में डालने के लिए ईजाद की गई जहरीली घुट्टी से अधिक और कुछ नहीं मानता।*[33]

जेल में भगतसिंह की बुद्धिमत्ता में तेजी से वृद्धि हुई और उन्होंने अनेक किताबें लिखी जिनमें से चार प्रसिद्ध हैं—आत्मकथा, मौत का दरवाजा, समाजवाद का आदर्श और भारत में क्रांतिकारी आन्दोलन। दुर्भाग्य से सभी की पांडुलिपियाँ खो गई हैं।[34]

इसी दौरान पुलिस ने सांडर्स हत्याकाण्ड की फाईल भी खोल दी। ब्रिटिश सरकार किसी भी कीमत पर भगतसिंह को जीवित रखना नहीं चाहती थी। भगतसिंह, राजगुरु और सुखदेव तथा अन्य पर लाहौर षड्यंत्र केस चलाया गया जो 10 जुलाई 1929 से 7 अक्टूबर 1930 तक चला।[35]

स्वतंत्रता के लिए और अपने चरम उद्देश्य की प्राप्ति के लिए मृत्यु को गौरवान्वित करने का भगतसिंह का एक स्पष्ट दृष्टिकोण था। उन्होंने कहा- *ब्रिटिश हूकूमत के लिए मरा हुआ भगतसिंह जीवित भगतसिंह से ज्यादा खतरनाक होगा। मुझे फाँसी हो जाने के बाद मेरे क्रांतिकारी विचारों की सुगन्ध हमारे इस मनोहर देश के वातावरण में व्याप्त हो जाएगी। वह नौजवानों को मदहोश करेगी और वे आजादी और क्रान्ति के लिए पागल हो उठेंगे। नौजवानों का यह पागलपन ही ब्रिटिश साम्राज्यवादियों को विनाश के कगार पर पहुँचा देगा। मैं बेसब्री के साथ उस दिन का इन्तजार कर रहा हूँ जब मुझे देश के लिए मेरी सेवाओं और जनता के लिए मेरे प्रेम का सर्वोच्च पुरस्कार मिलेगा।*[36]

इसीलिए भगतसिंह ने अपने बलिदान के पहले अपने साथियों को अंतिम पत्र लिखा-

22 मार्च 1931

साथियो,

स्वाभाविक है कि जीने की इच्छा मुझमें भी होनी चाहिए, मैं इसे छिपाना नहीं चाहता। लेकिन मैं एक शर्त पर जिंदा रह सकता हूँ कि मैं कैद होकर या पाबंद होकर जीना नहीं चाहता।

मेरा नाम हिंदुस्तानी क्रांति का प्रतीक बन चुका है और क्रान्तिकारी दल के आदर्शों और कुर्बानियों ने मुझे बहुत ऊंचा उठा दिया है। इतना ऊंचा कि जीवित रहने की स्थिति में इससे ऊंचा मैं हर्गिज नहीं हो सकता।

आज मेरी कमजोरियाँ जनता के सामने नहीं हैं। अगर मैं फाँसी से बच गया तो वे जाहिर हो जाएँगी और क्रान्ति का प्रतीक-चिह्न मद्धिम पड़ जाएगा या सम्भवतः मिट ही जाए। लेकिन दिलेराना ढंग से हँसते-हँसते मेरे फाँसी चढ़ने की सूरत में हिंदुस्तानी माताएँ अपने बच्चों के भगतसिंह बनने की आरजू किया करेंगी। और देश की आजादी के लिए कुर्बानी देने वालों की तादाद इतनी बढ़ जाएगी कि क्रान्ति को रोकना साम्राज्यवाद या तमाम शैतानी ताकतों के बूते की बात नहीं रहेगी।

हाँ एक विचार आज भी मेरे मन में आता है कि देश और मानवता के लिए जो कुछ करने की हसरतें मेरे मन में थीं, उनका हजारवाँ भाग भी पूरा नहीं कर सका।

अगर स्वतंत्र, जिन्दा रह सकता तब शायद इन्हें पूरा करने का अवसर मिलता और मैं अपनी हसरतें पूरी कर सकता।

इसके सिवाय मेरे मन में कभी कोई लालच फाँसी से बचे रहने का नहीं आया। मुझसे अधिक सौभाग्यशाली कौन होगा? आजकल मुझे स्वयं पर बहुत गर्व है। अब तो बड़ी बेताबी से अन्तिम परीक्षा का इन्तजार है। कामना है कि यह और नजदीक हो जाए।[87]

आपका साथी
भगतसिंह

भगतसिंह ने अपनी फाँसी से पहले जेल में ऊँची आवाज में एक छोटा सा भाषण दिया था, जिसे अपनी कोठरियों में कैदी सुन सकें–

असली क्रान्तिकारी सेनाएँ गाँव और कारखानों में काम करने वाले किसान और मजदूर हैं, मगर हमारे उच्चवर्गीय नेता न तो उन्हें साथ ले सकते हैं और न ही लेने का साहस करेंगे, सोया हुआ शेर नींद से जागने के पश्चात् हमारे नेताओं के उनके लक्ष्य की प्राप्ति के बाद भी उनके नियंत्रण में नहीं आएगा। मौजूदा सामाजिक व्यवस्था को समाप्त कर उसकी जगह समाजवादी व्यवस्था की स्थापना, के लक्ष्य को प्राप्त करने के लिए जनता को शिक्षित करना तथा अपने सामाजिक उद्द्देश्यों के लिए अनुकूल वातावरण का निर्माण करना होगा। संघर्षों में हमें उन्हें बेहतरीन शिक्षा व प्रशिक्षण देना होगा। सर्वप्रथम अपने निजीपन को खत्म करें, व्यक्तिगत आराम के सपनों को छोड़ दें, फिर काम शुरु करें, इंचइंच आगे बढ़ना होगा। इसके लिए साहस, दृढ़ता और मजबूत संकल्प चाहिए। कोई भी मुश्किल या कठिनाई आपको रास्ते से डिगाए नहीं, कोई विफलता या विश्वासघात दिल ना तोड़े, पीड़ा और बलिदान से गुजरकर आपको विजय प्राप्त होगी। ये व्यक्तिगत जीतें क्रान्ति की बहुमूल्य संपदा बनेंगी।[88]

सरदार किशन सिंह द्वारा अपने पुत्र भगतसिंह के बचाव के लिए ट्रिब्यूनल को लिखे पत्र के उत्तर में भगतसिंह ने अपनी अप्रसन्नता प्रकट करते हुए लिखा- *इस पूरे मुकदमें में मेरे सामने एक ही विचार था और वह यह कि हमारे विरुद्ध जो संगीन आरोप लगाये गये हैं, बावजूद उनके हम पूर्णतया इस संबंध में अवहेलना का व्यवहार करें। मेरा नजरिया यह रहा है कि सभी राजनैतिक कार्यकर्ताओं को ऐसी स्थितियों में उपेक्षा दिखानी चाहिए और उनको जो भी कठोरतम सजा दी जाये, वह उन्हें हँसते-हँसते बर्दाश्त करनी चाहिए। इस पूरे मुकदमें के दौरान हमारी योजना इसी सिद्धान्त के अनुरूप रही है। हम ऐसा करने में सफल हुए या नहीं, यह फैसला करना*

मेरा काम नहीं। हम खुदगर्जी को त्यागकर अपना काम कर रहे हैं, मेरी जिन्दगी इतनी कीमती नहीं कि इसे सिद्धातों को कुर्बान करके बचाया जाये।[39]

जेल में भगतसिंह ने विभिन्न पुस्तकों का अध्ययन किया एवं उनसे कुछ पंक्तियाँ अपनी जेल डायरी में उतारी। ये पंक्तियाँ भगतसिंह की व्यक्तिगत भावनाओं को भी प्रतिबिम्बित करती हैं। उन्होंने बायरन, व्हिटमैन और वर्ड्सवर्थ की स्वतंत्रता के विषय पर पंक्तियाँ अपनी कापी में उतारी। उन्होंने इब्सन के नाटक, दोस्तोयेवस्की का *'अपराध और दंड'* और ह्यूगो का *पददलित* उपन्यास पढ़े। रूसी क्रांतिकारी वेरा फिग्नर तथा रूसी विद्वान और क्रांतिकारी मोरो जोव की रचनाओं से जेल जीवन की कठिनाइयों के जो उद्धरण लिए, वे उनकी मनोभावनाओं के अनुरूप थे।

भगतसिंह ने अपनी जेल डायरी के पृष्ठ 22 पर युजीन डेब्स के कथन को उद्धृत किया–*जब तक निम्नवर्ग है, मैं उसमें ही हूँ। जब तक कोई अपराधी तत्त्व है, मैं उसमें ही हूँ। जब तक कोई जेल में कैद है, मैं आजाद नहीं हूँ।* इससे भगतसिंह की मनोभावना पर प्रकाश पड़ता है। उनकी इसी मनोभावना का प्रकटीकरण उनकी जेल डायरी के पृ. 21 पर हेनरी इब्सन की उद्धृत पंक्तियों–में भी होता है–*राज्य दफा हो जाय। मैं ऐसी क्रांति में भाग लूगा। राज्य की समूची अवधारणा का मूलोच्छेदन कर दो, मुक्त चयन और आत्मिक बंधुता को ही किसी एकता की एकमात्र सर्वाधिक महत्त्वपूर्ण शर्त होने की घोषणा करो, तभी तुम एक ऐसी आजादी की शुरुआत करोगे जिसकी कोई सार्थकता होगी।*[40]

इस प्रकार भगतसिंह के क्रांतिकारी विचारों का विश्लेषण करने पर उनकी क्रान्ति की अवधारणा स्पष्ट हो जाती है। शहीद भगतसिंह अपने देश के लिए अपने जीवन को बलिदान करने वाले केवल साहसिक देशभक्त ही नहीं थे अपितु इनकी तत्कालीन उत्पीड़क व्यवस्था में आमूल चूल परिवर्तन करके एक ऐसी वैकल्पिक व्यवस्था देने की परिपक्व दूर दृष्टि थी जो स्वतंत्र भारत को धर्मनिरपेक्ष, समाजवादी और समतावादी समाज में रूपान्तरित करना चाहती थी।

अतः उनकी क्रान्ति वर्तमान व्यवस्था के परिवर्तन तक ही सीमित नहीं थी, अपितु स्वातंत्रयोत्तर भारत को नई दिशा देने वाली सार्थक क्रान्ति थी।

सन्दर्भ

1. बिपन चन्द्र, *भारत का स्वतंत्रता संघर्ष, 'औपनिवेशिक अर्थ तंत्र की मीमांसा,* पृ. 55; also see R.C. Majumdar, *Three Phases of India's struggle for freedom,* Bombay, 1961.

2. जगमोहन सिंह, चमन लाल (स.) *भगतसिंह और साथियों के दस्तावेज,* पृ. 24; *The Life & Times of Raja Mahendra Pratap*, (ed.) Dr. Vir Singh, P. 16
3. उपरोक्त दस्तावेज, पृ. 30
4. S. Irfan Habib, *To Make the Deaf Hear : Ideology and programme of Bhagat Singh and His Comrades,* P. XI
5. Shiv Verma (ed.), *Selected writings of Shaheed Bhagat Singh*, New Delhi, 1986, P.P. 190, 198-9
6. जगमोहन सिंह, चमनलाल (सं.) *भगतसिंह और साथियों के दस्तावेज,* पृ. 394.
7. भगतसिंह एवं बटुकेश्वर दत्त द्वारा जेल से भेजा गया पत्र जो 19 अक्टूबर 1929 को पंजाब छात्र संघ लाहौर के दूसरे अधिवेशन में पढ़कर सुनाया गया। 22 अक्टूबर 1929 के *ट्रिब्यून* (लाहौर) में प्रकाशित
8. Presidential Address to special (calcutta) session of the Indian National Congress, Sep. 1920. Quoted by R.P. Dutta, '*India Today*' P. 280
9. From, Niraja Rao, *Bhagat Singh and the Revolutionary Movement*' *Revolutionary Democracy,* vol III, No. 1 April 1997
10. मिश्र विनोद, *शहीदों के खत,* पृ.2
11. D.N. Gupta., (ed.) *Bhagat Singh Selected Speeches & Writings, Introduction,* XIII
12. जगमोहन सिंह, चमन लाल (सं.) *'भगत सिंह और साथियों के दस्तावेज'*, पृ. 100
13. NAI, Home Pol. File No. 27/5/1931; J.N. Sanyal, op. cit p.46.
14. Shiv Verma, *Selected Writings of Shaheed Bhagat Singh*, New Delhi, 1986, P. 74-75
15. NAI, Home Pol. File No. 27/5/1931
16. NAI, Home Pol. File No. 130 & kw/1930, P.41
17. जगमोहन, चमनलाल (सं.), *'भगतसिंह और साथियों के दस्तावेज'*, पृ. 284.
18. Gopal Thakur, *Bhagat Singh, The Man and his ideas*, New Delhi, 1961, P. 12.

19. Jawaharlal Nehru, *An Autobiography*, Delhi, 1962. P.P 175-76
20. जगमोहन चमन लाल (सं.), *भगतसिंह और साथियों के दस्तावेज,* पृ. 168.
21. उपरोक्त पृ. 171-72.
22. J.N. Sanyal, op. cit. P.72.
23. NAI, Home Pol. File. No. 192/1929.
24. जगमोहन चमन लाल (सं.), *भगतसिंह और साथियों के दस्तावेज,* पृ. 286-87
25. उपरोक्त, पृ. 288.
26. Suresh, *Krantikari Bhagat Singh*, Delhi 1971, P. 91-92.
27. जितेन्द्रनाथ सान्याल, *अमर शहीद भगतसिंह,* दिल्ली 2006, पृ. 69.
28. जगमोहन सिंह, चमन लाल (सं.), *भगतसिंह और साथियों के दस्तावेज,* पृ. 10
29. जितेन्द्र नाथ सान्याल, *अमर शहीद भगत सिंह,* दिल्ली 2006, पृ. 69.
30. जगमोहनसिंह, चमन लाल (सं.), *भगतसिंह और साथियों के दस्तावेज,* पृ. 399.
31. निगम एन के, *बलिदान,* पृ. 54.
32. भगतसिंह, *'मैं नास्तिक क्यों हूँ?'* कानपुर समाजवादी साहित्य सदन, कानपुर 1981, पृ. 9-10
33. शिव वर्मा, *स्मृतियाँ,* तृतीयसंस्करण, निधि प्रकाशन, दिल्ली 1983, पृ. 38-39.
34. Virendra Sandhu., op. cit. P.P. 237 and 306.
35. जगमोहन सिंह, चमनलाल (सं.), *भगतसिंह और साथियों के दस्तावेज,* पृ. 325.
36. Bhagat Singh quoted by ShivVerma, Introduction to the *Selected Writings of Bhagat Singh.*
37. जगमोहन, चमनलाल (सं.), *भगतसिंह और साथियों के दस्तावेज,* पृ. 338
38. D.N. Gupta (ed.), *Bhagat Singh Selected Speeches &* Writings, P. 92-93
39. D.N. Gupta. (ed.), *Bhagat Singh Selected Speeches &* Writings, P. 107-8.
40. *भगतसिंह की डायरी,* पृ. 22.23; *'शहीदे आजम की जेल नोट बुक',* (सं) सत्यम वर्मा, पृ. 54.